USING ENGLISH
GRAMMAR AND WRITING SKILLS

FIFTH COURSE

ADRIAN B. SANFORD

CENTER FOR THE STUDY OF INSTRUCTION
San Francisco

HARCOURT BRACE JOVANOVICH
New York Chicago San Francisco Atlanta Dallas *and* London

THE AUTHOR
ADRIAN B. SANFORD has taught English for more than a quarter of a century. He has also written materials for English instruction and conducted workshops for educators.

CONSULTING EDUCATORS AND TEACHERS

ENNO KLAMMER
Eastern Oregon State College
La Grande, Oregon

MARIAN O. JENKINS
Coral Springs High School
Coral Springs, Florida

JO ANN STEWART
Lowell High School
San Francisco, California

ROBERT LEON
Palo Alto High School
Palo Alto, California

KEITH CALDWELL
Kennedy High School
Fremont, California

KEITH WILL
San Juan Unified School District
Carmichael, California

CYNTHIA BAKER
Starr King Intermediate
Carmichael, California

JACK STRANGE
Arcade Intermediate
Carmichael, California

BARBARA S. DEAN
Will Rogers School
Fair Oaks, California

SYBILLE IRWIN
Winston Churchill Intermediate
Carmichael, California

JUDY A. KANTER
Howe Avenue Intermediate
Sacramento, California

BARBARA COULTER
Louis Pasteur School
Orangeville, California

ACKNOWLEDGMENTS
The publisher gratefully acknowledges the contributions of Charlotte Herbert to the preparation of the Review Exercises for the series.

For permission to reprint copyrighted material, grateful acknowledgment is made to the following:

Harcourt Brace Jovanovich, Inc.: Excerpts from *The HBJ School Dictionary*. Copyright © 1977 by Harcourt Brace Jovanovich, Inc.

The H. W. Wilson Company: Excerpt from *Readers' Guide to Periodical Literature*. Copyright © 1977 by The H. W. Wilson Company.

DIANA WHITELEY
Project Editor

PATRICIA HOSLEY
Editor

SALLY THOMPSON
Text Designer

Printed in the United States of America.

ISBN 0-15-311704-4

TO THE STUDENT

As you begin using this book, take time to become familiar with its special features. Notice the organization of sections and chapters of the book as shown in the Contents. Look within a chapter to see how the rules and definitions are printed. Note the use of color and special type to highlight important points.

An alphabetized index in the back of the book lists all the important topics in the textbook, with their page numbers. The colored tabs at the corners of the pages allow you to find any topic by its chapter number. The glossary in the back of the book gives an alphabetical listing of special terms in English. Each is followed by a definition. Many of the terms have examples to illustrate their meaning or use.

On certain pages you can see cross references printed in the margins. These refer you to other parts of the text where you can find additional information.

These features—and more—have been built into the book to aid you.

From this textbook you can learn a great deal about how to improve your use of English. Improvement, however, requires that you apply yourself to studying the book and to using what you can learn from it. As either a textbook assigned by your teacher or a reference tool in which you find what you need, this book offers you the opportunity to grow stronger in using English.

A.B.S.

CONTENTS

UNIT THREE: USAGE

UNIT FOUR: MECHANICS

UNIT FIVE: AIDS AND ENRICHMENT

UNIT ONE

GRAMMAR AND STRUCTURE

Parts of Speech
Phrases
Clauses
Sentences
Sentence Problems

CHAPTER

1

PARTS OF SPEECH

Nouns, Pronouns, Adjectives

Words in the English language serve eight different purposes in sentences. As you construct sentences, you use words for these eight purposes. The different kinds of words are called the eight *parts of speech*.

Nouns, pronouns, and *adjectives* are three of the eight parts of speech. All things, living or not, are named with nouns. Pronouns are used to take the place of nouns. Adjectives are used to help describe nouns or pronouns.

NOUNS

1a A noun is a word or group of words used to name someone or something.

Any persons, objects, or ideas you can see, hear, or think about have words that name them. These words are *nouns*. For example, you are a person.

The word *person* is a noun because it tells who you are. Your own name is also a noun, as is *sunlight*. The word *thought* is a noun when it refers to an idea in a person's mind.

Any word used to name a person or thing is a noun.

EXERCISE 1 Number a sheet of paper 1–8. After each number write the nouns from each of the following sentences.

EXAMPLE The young soldier could see no people on the walls of the castle.

soldier, people, walls, castle

1. The towers of the castle were deserted, and the windows seemed empty, too.
2. A red banner flew from the roof of the highest tower.
3. Was this bright flag a signal to the castle's missing troops?
4. Had the soldiers left the castle to fight a battle?
5. Was some enemy now waiting inside the walls for the soldiers?
6. The young girl wondered quietly about these questions as she surveyed the beautiful brown castle.
7. Then a powerful wave of water crashed down onto the castle.
8. The mighty walls of the sandcastle dissolved, melting away into salty puddles and lumps of soggy sand.

Common Nouns and Proper Nouns

(1) A common noun names any person, place, or thing. A proper noun names a particular person, place, or thing.

Here are some examples:

COMMON NOUNS	PROPER NOUNS
president	Abraham Lincoln
nation	Chile
food	McWhirtle's Oats

Hint: A proper noun always begins with a capital letter. If a proper noun has more than one word, each important word begins with a capital letter.

See Capitalization, pp. 295–300

EXAMPLE **S**ociety for the **P**reservation of **B**arbershop **S**inging

---

EXERCISE 2 The following list of words contains common nouns and proper nouns without capital letters. On a sheet of paper write the common nouns in one column, headed *Common Nouns*. Write the proper nouns in another column, headed *Proper Nouns*. Capitalize the proper nouns.

river, map, abigail adams, subway, asia, peanut butter, jimmy toshima, soap, hawaii, jet, halloween, box, montana, electricity, chicago, aretha franklin, ping pong, houston, rattlesnake, england

Singular Nouns and Plural Nouns

1b A noun may be singular or plural.

A singular noun names one person or thing. A plural noun names more than one person or thing.

EXAMPLES

SINGULAR NOUNS	PLURAL NOUNS
ape	apes
horse	horses
pipe	pipes
limb	limbs

See Spelling, p. 384

Most nouns that are singular add **s** to form the plural. Singular nouns ending in **s, x, ch, sh,** or **z** usually add **es** to form the plural.

EXAMPLES jinx, jinx**es**
witch, witch**es**
eyelash, eyelash**es**

Nouns ending in a consonant followed by **y** change the **y** to **i** and add **es.**

EXAMPLES sky, sk**ies**
ferry, ferr**ies**

Irregular Nouns

Irregular nouns do not form the plural in the usual way. Sometimes their plurals are different words. Sometimes irregular nouns do not change form at all. Nouns made up of more than one word, called *compound nouns,* also form the plural in special ways.

EXAMPLES

SINGULAR	PLURAL
man	men
ox	oxen
deer	deer
child	children
sister-in-law	sisters-in-law

You can find the plural of most irregular or compound nouns in a dictionary.

EXERCISE 3 Number a sheet of paper 1–8. Next to each number write the missing singular or plural form of the following nouns.

EXAMPLE country ______
countries

	SINGULAR	PLURAL
1.	charge	______
2.	wedge	______
3.	______	keys
4.	lorry	______
5.	mother-in-law	______
6.	box	______
7.	woman	______
8.	try	______

Possessive Nouns

1c A noun can show possession or ownership.

The special ending on a noun shows that it owns something. This form of the noun is in the *possessive case.* Most singular nouns form the possessive case by adding an apostrophe (') and **s**.

See Case, p. 440

EXAMPLES dog'**s** nose
house'**s** shingles
Carrie'**s** book

Any plural noun that already ends in **s** does not need another **s**. It needs only the apostrophe (').

EXAMPLES dogs' noses
houses' shingles
girls' books

Some irregular nouns, such as *women,* do not have an **s** ending in the plural. Since there is no **s**, the possessive for the plural adds both an apostrophe and **s** (**'s**).

EXAMPLES oxen'**s** yokes
women'**s** fashions

When you want to show that two or more people own something, add the possessive ending to the last person's name.

EXAMPLE Ev and Charlie'**s** car

EXERCISE 4 Number a sheet of paper 1–10. Next to each number write the correct form of the words in parentheses that belong in the blank.

EXAMPLE One of the insect ______ largest members is the tropical stick insect. (family)
family's

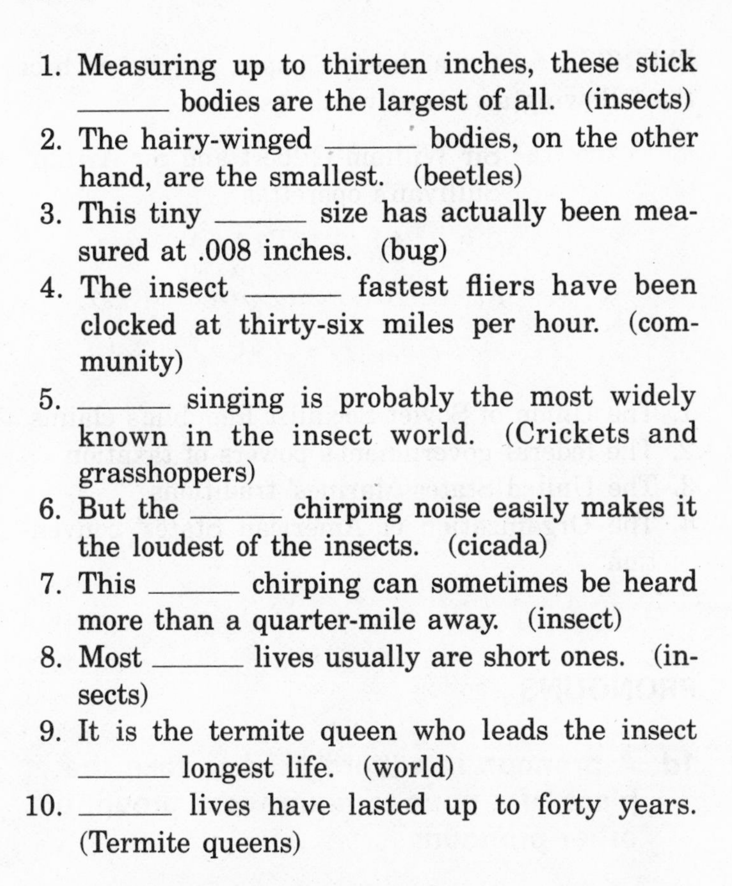

1. Measuring up to thirteen inches, these stick ______ bodies are the largest of all. (insects)
2. The hairy-winged ______ bodies, on the other hand, are the smallest. (beetles)
3. This tiny ______ size has actually been measured at .008 inches. (bug)
4. The insect ______ fastest fliers have been clocked at thirty-six miles per hour. (community)
5. ______ singing is probably the most widely known in the insect world. (Crickets and grasshoppers)
6. But the ______ chirping noise easily makes it the loudest of the insects. (cicada)
7. This ______ chirping can sometimes be heard more than a quarter-mile away. (insect)
8. Most ______ lives usually are short ones. (insects)
9. It is the termite queen who leads the insect ______ longest life. (world)
10. ______ lives have lasted up to forty years. (Termite queens)

Sometimes the possessive form of a noun sounds awkward. This may be the case with nouns of more than one word, for example, *The United Biscuit Company.* When a possessive form sounds awkward in your speech or writing, you can change its form without changing the meaning.

EXAMPLE

AWKWARD The United Biscuit Company's new product is Crumblies.

SMOOTHER Crumblies is the new product of the United Biscuit Company.

EXERCISE 5 On a sheet of paper, rewrite each of the following awkward wordings.

EXAMPLE Sir William Gilbert and Sir Arthur Sullivan's operettas

The operettas of Sir William Gilbert and Sir Arthur Sullivan

1. The Union of Soviet Socialist Republic's claims
2. The federal government's powers of taxation
3. The United States Marines' traditions
4. The Organization of American States' convention

PRONOUNS

1d A pronoun is a word used to take the place of a noun, a noun word group, or other pronouns.

Pronouns are especially useful parts of speech. They make it possible to avoid repeating nouns or noun word groups.

EXAMPLES *Houses* should not sit empty. *They* should be lived in.
[The word *they* is a pronoun. It takes the place of the noun *houses.*]

A good screen door would help keep out *flies. It* would protect the house from *them.*

[The word *it* is a pronoun. It takes the place of the noun word group *a good screen door.* The word *them* is a pronoun. It takes the place of the word *flies.*]

You and *she* can join *me* on Saturday morning. *We* can go downtown together.
[The word *we* is a pronoun. It takes the place of the pronouns *you, she,* and *me.*]

Personal Pronouns

1e A personal pronoun stands for a noun or noun word group that names a particular person, place, or thing.

People often use personal pronouns when they write or speak.

EXAMPLE Mrs. Adamich likes to jog. *She* jogs daily.

1f Some personal pronouns change form depending upon their use in a sentence.

Personal pronouns may be used in different ways in a sentence. The way a pronoun is used is called its *case.* In most sentences a pronoun that is the actor in a sentence is in the *subjective case.*

EXAMPLE *She* thawed the windshield. [*She* is the actor.]

A pronoun that receives the action in a sentence is in the *objective case.*

EXAMPLE The raindrops hit *her* in the face. [The pronoun *her* receives the action.]

A pronoun that shows possession or ownership is in the *possessive case.*

EXAMPLE She told him to put on *his* cap. [The pronoun *his* shows who owns the cap.]

FORMS OF PERSONAL PRONOUNS

SUBJECTIVE CASE	OBJECTIVE CASE	POSSESSIVE CASE
	Singular	
I	me	my, mine
you	you	your, yours
he	him	his
she	her	her, hers
it	it	its
	Plural	
we	us	our, ours
you	you	your, yours
they	them	their, theirs

EXERCISE 6 The second sentence in each pair of sentences repeats words from the first sentence. Number a sheet of paper 1–6. Rewrite the second sentence in each pair. Replace the repeated words with a pronoun. Underline the pronoun you use.

EXAMPLE a. Metal coat hangers often bend.
b. Metal coat hangers are not strong enough for heavy clothes.

They are not strong enough for heavy clothes.

1. a. The points of sharpened pencils break under pressure.
   b. The points of sharpened pencils are often too thin.
2. a. Forty years ago a ball-point pen was not known.
   b. When the ball-point pen was first invented, people did not trust the pen to work.
3. a. Bankers and other business people would not allow the use of a ball-point pen.
   b. Bankers and other business people required signatures written with a fountain pen.
4. a. One maker of ball-point pens advertised that his pen was better than a fountain pen.
   b. One maker of ball-point pens proved that a ball-point pen could write underwater.
5. a. Business people began to accept the new pen.
   b. But none of the business people really required a signature written underwater.
6. a. Wherever you and I go, we see ball-point pens.
   b. Perhaps you and I may never own a fountain pen.

EXERCISE 7 The following sentences have pronoun forms as the choices in parentheses. Number a sheet of paper 1–12. After each number write the correct form or forms of the pronouns in parentheses.

EXAMPLE The wolf needed food for ______ family. (it/its)

its

1. The farmers were talking about a wolf named Old Two Toes who was killing ______ cattle. (they/their)
2. "We must find a way," ______ said, "to get rid of that wolf and ______ mate." (they/them) (it/its)
3. A Black American cowboy named Peoples raised ______ voice above the others. (he/his)
4. "______ good work is known by all of ______," he said. (I/My) (you/your)
5. "Give me one month and ______ will take care of ______ problem with the wolves." (I/my) (you/your)
6. Peoples said ______ plan was to "walk the wolves down." (he/his)
7. For two weeks ______ did just that, following very closely on ______ trail. (he/him) (they/their)
8. By this time the female wolf had given up and left ______ mate. (it/its)
9. A few days later, ______ finished ______ job in a canyon. (he/him) (he/his)
10. There, ______ found the exhausted male wolf and quickly ended ______ struggle. (he/him) (it/its)
11. "Now ______ cattle will be safe," the thankful farmers said. "And all because of ______." (we/our) (you/yours)

12. "______ work has helped ______," they said. (You/Your) (us/our)

Other kinds of pronouns that are used in the English language are *relative pronouns, demonstrative pronouns, interrogative pronouns, indefinite pronouns,* and *reflexive pronouns.*

Relative Pronouns

Relative pronouns are used to begin groups of words that tell about someone or something mentioned earlier. A relative pronoun *relates* the word group to what it tells about. Some common relative pronouns are *that, which, who, whom,* and *whose.*

EXAMPLES Doug Tremaine, *who* writes a column now and then, has a piece in the paper *that* came this morning.

Demonstrative Pronouns

Demonstrative pronouns are used to point out particular persons or things. Some common demonstrative pronouns are *that, these, this,* and *those.*

EXAMPLE *This* comes before *those.*

Interrogative Pronouns

Interrogative pronouns are used to ask questions. Some common interrogative pronouns are *what, which, who, whom,* and *whose.*

EXAMPLES *Who* wants to stay?
Whom do you choose?

Indefinite Pronouns

Indefinite pronouns are used to refer to persons or things not definitely known. Some common indefinite pronouns are listed here.

all	each	more	one
another	either	most	others
any	everybody	much	several
anybody	everyone	neither	some
anyone	everything	nobody	somebody
anything	few	none	someone
both	many	no one	something

EXAMPLES *All* of the boards were warped.
One was even broken.

Reflexive Pronouns

Reflexive pronouns are used to refer back to nouns or other pronouns. Reflexive pronouns are *myself, yourself, yourselves,* and other forms of personal pronouns with *-self* or *-selves* added.

EXAMPLES Birds soon learn to feed *themselves.*
A weak bird cannot feed *itself.*

EXERCISE 8 Number a sheet of paper 1–6. Next to each number write all the pronouns appearing in the sentence.

EXAMPLE We know some of our cities are having a difficult time.

we, some, our

1. This is the information we hear most about.
2. Much of the news seems unhappy for someone.
3. Only a few of the mayors claim they have no troubles.
4. Others try to claim their cities are improving.
5. A refreshing report is one which tells of success.
6. Does the city you live in or near have something of value for everyone?

ADJECTIVES

1g An adjective is a word used to modify or describe a noun or pronoun.

Adjectives are used to tell *what kind, which one, how much,* or *how many.*

EXAMPLES

WHAT KIND a *fast* car, a *dry* well

WHICH ONE the *twentieth* century,

the *oldest* tree

HOW MUCH OR HOW MANY a *full* load

a *million* dollars

A single adjective in a sentence may modify more than one noun or pronoun.

EXAMPLE The *cold* wind and snow battered the city.

A noun or pronoun also may have more than one adjective modifying it.

EXAMPLE The horses raced on a *fast, dry* track.

The words *a, an,* and *the* are special adjectives called *articles.*

EXERCISE 9 The following sentences contain adjectives. Number a sheet of paper 1–10. After each number write the adjective or adjectives in the sentence. Do not write the articles.

EXAMPLE "Help! I am trapped behind a solid wall."

solid

1. "A mean man named Sandor put me here."
2. "Sandor is known for his terrible temper."
3. "I told Sandor a clever riddle I had heard from a wise man."
4. "When Sandor's sharp mind failed to answer the riddle, I laughed a loud laugh."
5. "He tied me to the wall with strong ropes."
6. "Then he built a thick wall of bricks in front of me."
7. "As my frightened eyes watched, he closed me away from the outside world."
8. "After several hours, I broke free from the rough ropes."
9. "But my tired arms cannot break through the thick wall."
10. "This is a tiny room with stuffy air and I fear that soon. . . ."

EXERCISE 10 The following sentences contain adjectives. Number a sheet of paper 1–10. After each number write the adjective or adjectives in the sentences. Do not write the articles.

EXAMPLE It was a close game.
close

1. The winning team would be champions of the county.
2. The Wildcats had a slim lead over the Knights with ten seconds to play.
3. Only two points separated the teams.
4. The best shooter for the Knights, Rosa Estrada, had the ball.
5. She leaped in a high jump and sent a long shot toward the basket.
6. As Rosa shot, a stray hand from a Wildcat hit her shooting arm.
7. With a crash, Rosa landed on the hard floor.
8. It was a wobbly shot, but somehow the ball made it through the basket.
9. Now both teams had the same score, and because of the foul Rosa had a free shot.
10. It was an easy basket for Rosa, and the happy Knights won the county championship.

The Position of Adjectives

Adjectives usually come in front of the nouns they modify. Occasionally, adjectives may be placed right after the nouns they modify.

EXAMPLE A pot, *empty* and *stained,* sat on the stove.
[The adjectives *empty* and *stained* describe the word *pot.* They come after the noun they modify. Note that commas are used to set off these adjectives from the rest of the sentence. You can read the sentence more clearly because of the commas.]

See Punctuation, p. 310

Hint: When placing adjectives after the nouns they modify, use commas to set off the adjectives.

See Linking Verbs, p. 34; Sentences, pp. 120, 128–129

In some sentences the adjective follows the verb. An adjective after the verb can modify the noun or pronoun in front of the verb. The adjective in this position is called a *subject completer.*

EXAMPLES Her coat was *grey* and *brown.*

It looked *clean.*
[The adjectives *grey* and *brown* describe the noun *coat.* The adjective *clean* modifies the pronoun *it.*]

EXERCISE 11 The following sentences are missing adjectives. Write each sentence on a sheet of paper. Fill in each blank with one or two adjectives. You may use ones from this list or provide your own.

POSSIBLE ADJECTIVES

old, weary, sad, quiet, small, cold, hard, cool, warm, beautiful, wonderful, soft, magical, alive, happy, glad, blind, blue, pale, young, exciting, dazzling

EXAMPLE The ______ monkey felt alone.

The sad, quiet monkey felt alone.

1. It sat on the ______ branch.
2. It felt the ______ night air.
3. Then it heard the ______ sounds.
4. ______ sounds came from a nearby tree.
5. It was ______.
6. Suddenly the night seemed ______.
7. The monkey felt ______.
8. Its ______ eyes could not see well.
9. But ______ noises filled the night.
10. The world seemed ______.

Comparison of Adjectives

1h An adjective may change form to show how one thing compares with another.

The adjectives in Exercise 11 are in the *positive form*. To compare two things, most adjectives in the positive form add **er**. Adding **er** shows that two things are compared. This makes the *comparative form* of an adjective.

EXAMPLES

POSITIVE FORM The ocean is *deep* near some Pacific islands.

COMPARATIVE FORM The ocean is *deeper* just east of the Philippines.

Most short adjectives add **er** to form the comparative.

EXAMPLES tall tall**er**
fair fair**er**

See Spelling, p. 390

When the positive form ends in **e**, only the **r** is added.

EXAMPLE rude rude**r**

When the positive form ends in a consonant after a vowel, the consonant is doubled before the **er** is added.

EXAMPLE thin thin**ner**

When the positive form ends in **y** with a consonant before it, the **y** changes to **i**.

EXAMPLE sloppy slopp**ier**

Most short adjectives add **est** to the positive form to show comparison of more than two things. This is called the *superlative form* of the adjective.

EXAMPLES

POSITIVE Bruno likes to write with a *stubby* pencil.

COMPARATIVE Andrea has some *stubbier* pencils.

SUPERLATIVE Ines boasts she has the *stubbiest* pencil of all.

Here are examples of the three forms of adjectives.

POSITIVE	COMPARATIVE	SUPERLATIVE
high	higher	highest
hot	hotter	hottest
ugly	uglier	ugliest

Long adjectives do not add **er** and **est** to form the comparative and superlative forms. Instead, long adjectives use the words *more* and *most* in front of the positive form.

EXAMPLES

POSITIVE	COMPARATIVE	SUPERLATIVE
restful	more restful	most restful
changeable	more changeable	most changeable
unsteady	more unsteady	most unsteady

Hint: If you are not sure how to form the comparative or superlative form of an adjective, say it to yourself in a sentence. A long adjective will usually sound too long and awkward. Do not use a word like *beautifulest,* for example, because it sounds too awkward. Use *most beautiful* instead.

Irregular Adjectives

A few adjectives, such as *much,* form their comparative and superlative forms in special ways.

These adjectives are called *irregular adjectives*. Here are some examples of irregular adjectives.

POSITIVE	COMPARATIVE	SUPERLATIVE
many, much, some	more	most
little	less	least
bad	worse	worst
good, well	better	best

EXERCISE 12 The blank in each sentence needs a form of the adjective in parentheses. Number a sheet of paper 1–10. Next to each number write the correct form of the adjective in parentheses.

EXAMPLE The winter of 1977 had the ______ weather we have had in fifty years. (bad)

worst

1. It was ______ than ever for small animals to survive. (difficult)
2. Temperatures dropped ______ than most of us could have imagined. (low)
3. Temperatures stayed low for ______ weeks than in our usual winters. (many)
4. High winds made that winter ______ than any in memory. (uncomfortable)
5. They created a chill that drove the mercury even ______ down the thermometer. (far)
6. It was about the ______ winter ever recorded. (cold)

7. Heating became the ______ problem of all. (serious)
8. With a fuel shortage, there was ______ fuel than ever to heat our houses and buildings. (little)
9. The ______ of all our scientists are still searching for more fuel. (concerned)
10. Until they find it, we should use the ______ amount of fuel we can. (little)

Adjectival Pronouns

1i Some pronouns may be used as adjectives.

Some pronouns are used to describe nouns. These pronouns are called *adjectival pronouns.* For example, *one, some, these,* and *those* are pronouns used as adjectives. The following sentences show their use:

One ride is not enough.

Some people take several rides.

These roller coasters scare me.

Those idiots can go on them, but I won't.

REVIEW EXERCISE A Nouns

Number a sheet of paper 1–10. Next to each number, write all the nouns from each of the following sentences.

EXAMPLE Over a million people starved in a famine in Ireland during the last century.

people, famine, Ireland, century

1. Many of those who survived left the country.
2. A great wave of Irish immigrants came to America.
3. Newcomers looking for work often saw signs saying, "No Irish Need Apply."
4. Life was hard for the new Irish Americans.
5. They were crowded into airless tenements full of rats and disease.
6. Thomas Fitzpatrick was one of the first Irish Americans to move out of the cities.
7. He was the guide for the first group of wagons that crossed the plains and went to California.
8. He helped to blaze the Oregon Trail.
9. He became an agent to the Native Americans.
10. People like Fitzpatrick have helped make our land a better nation.

REVIEW EXERCISE B Personal Pronouns

Each of the following sentences contains a blank where a personal pronoun should be. Number a sheet of paper 1–10. Next to each number write the personal pronoun that belongs in the blank.

EXAMPLE Many singing groups have made up ______ names in odd ways.

their

1. One example is the group Gladys Knight and the Pips, who took ______ name from a family member.
2. Their cousin, James Woods, had "Pip" as ______ nickname.
3. They decided to name the group after ______.
4. Pip became their manager and got engagements for ______.
5. Besides Gladys Knight, the group consisted of ______ brother, Merald, and two cousins.
6. Their first record, "Every Beat of My Heart," was heard by talent scouts for Fury Records, who sent it to ______ boss.
7. ______ became the group's first major hit.
8. I like all their songs, but ______ favorite is "I Heard It Through the Grapevine."
9. Gladys Knight knew that ______ and her group had a big hit; "I Heard It Through the Grapevine" was their first gold record.
10. "I Wish It Would Rain" was another big hit for ______.

REVIEW EXERCISE C Other Kinds of Pronouns

Following is a matching exercise. Number a sheet of paper 1–10. Next to each number write the letter of the pronoun that belongs in each blank. Use each pronoun from the list only once.

LIST OF PRONOUNS

a. most	e. those	i. one
b. themselves	f. everyone	j. which
c. whose	g. what	k. itself
d. others	h. all	

EXAMPLE By the early half of the eighteenth century, ______ of the Native Americans of the Plains had horses.

1. The horses, ______ came from the Spanish herds in Mexico, changed the lives of the people who had them.
2. ______ of the people had stayed peacefully in the river valleys.
3. ______ industrious brave would stay home when he could follow the bison herd and hunt from his horse?
4. Many Native Americans living on the plains made their saddles ______.
5. Some were rigid frame saddles; ______ were just simple leather envelopes stuffed with grass or hair.
6. ______ who saw the Native American riders was impressed by their skill.
7. The U.S. Cavalry ______ called these horsemen the finest light cavalry the world had yet seen.
8. ______ were the days of the struggles between the Native Americans, who were fighting for their homeland, and the ambitious settlers from the East.
9. The Native Americans, ______ equipment was simple and crude, could still ride rings around their enemies.
10. ______ of the ways the Native Americans used to break a wild horse was to ride it in water so that it could not throw off its rider.

REVIEW EXERCISE D **Adjectives**

Number a sheet of paper 1–10. Next to each number, write all the adjectives used in each sentence. Remember that pronouns may sometimes be used as adjectives. Include the adjectival pronouns in your list. Do not write the articles.

EXAMPLE The night wind, cold and mournful, sang in the chimney.

night, cold, mournful

1. The young woman was alone in the neglected mansion.
2. She got up slowly from her worn chair and walked quietly across the empty room.
3. Looking around her, she drew the flowered drapes.
4. She walked over to the birdcage and covered it with a dark cloth.
5. Now the loudest sound besides the moaning of the wind was the ticking of the clock.
6. The woman walked to the English antique desk and opened its one drawer.
7. Her eyes appeared brighter as she picked up a small key.
8. Although her footsteps were slow and measured, she was eager to get to the kitchen.
9. In the kitchen she unlocked a cupboard and took down a sack of white flour, a sifter, and a bowl.
10. Gold, hard and yellow, gleamed in the sifter as she poured the flour through it.

CHAPTER

2

PARTS OF SPEECH

Verbs, Adverbs, Prepositions, Conjunctions, Interjections

The three parts of speech presented in Chapter 1 do only part of the work in sentences. The rest of the work is done by the five other parts of speech, which are treated in this chapter. These are *verbs, adverbs, prepositions, conjunctions,* and *interjections.*

VERBS

2a A verb is a word used to help tell what happens or what exists.

EXAMPLES Workers *climbed* across the beams.
They *painted* with red paint.
They *were* busy.

There are two kinds of verbs: *action verbs* and *linking verbs.*

Action Verbs

(1) An action verb tells what someone or something does.

EXAMPLES The workers *stepped* from beam to beam.
[*Stepped* tells what the workers did.]

A beam *swung* across the opening.
[*Swung* tells of the action of the beam.]

EXERCISE 1 Number a sheet of paper 1–10. Next to each number write the action verb in the sentence.

EXAMPLE A small elevator carried the workers up to the forty-fifth floor.

carried

1. Here they walked on thin metal beams.
2. They worked with noisy rivet guns.
3. Those guns drove rivets into the beams.
4. The workers attached new beams for the walls and floors.
5. The skeleton of the building reached higher in the sky.
6. Day by day, the building grew.
7. Soon walls and windows filled the spaces.
8. Workers no longer balanced on dangerous beams.
9. Other workers finished the inside with tile, paint, and carpets.
10. Then the new building opened for the public.

Transitive and Intransitive Verbs

(2) An action verb is transitive if its action is received by someone or something.

Transitive means "crossing over." The transitive verb shows how the action crosses over from the doer of the action to the receiver of the action. The receiver is called the *object*.

See Sentences, pp. 123–124

EXAMPLES Laser guns *shot* the enemy.
[*Shot* is the transitive verb. *Enemy* receives the action and is the object.]

The general *ordered* the soldiers to retreat.
[*Ordered* is the transitive verb. *Soldiers* is the object because they receive the action expressed in the verb.]

See Sentences, p. 122

(3) An action verb is intransitive if there is no receiver of the action.

Intransitive means "not crossing over." No person or thing receives the action of the verb. There is no object of the verb.

EXAMPLES The soldiers *hid* in caves.
[*Hid* is the intransitive verb. The action has no receiver.]

They *stayed* there a long time.
[*Stayed* is the intransitive verb. It tells the action, but it has no receiver of that action.]

Many verbs can be either transitive or intransitive depending on the way they are used in sentences.

EXAMPLES
TRANSITIVE Justina Chavez *boiled* some water.
INTRANSITIVE The water *boiled.*

EXERCISE 2 On a sheet of paper write a sentence for each verb listed here. If the verb is followed by *T,* use it as a transitive verb. If it is followed by *I,* use it as an intransitive verb.

EXAMPLE freeze T

Strong, cold winds freeze exposed skin quickly.

1. play I
2. bake T
3. practice T
4. lost T
5. laugh I
6. fall I
7. lift T
8. rise I
9. sing I
10. throw T

Linking Verbs

(4) A linking verb joins words that name someone or something with words that describe or rename that person or thing.

There are fewer linking verbs than action verbs. The most common linking verbs are forms of the verb *be.* Of these, the verb forms *am, are, is, was,* and *were* are used most often.

EXAMPLES She *was* happy at the party.
Her smile *is* pleasant.

Other linking verbs are *appear, become, look,* and *seem*. They often can be used in place of a form of the verb *be*.

EXAMPLES He *is* fat.
He *seems* fat.
He *looks* fat.

Usually a linking verb cannot complete the thought of a sentence by itself. It needs another word or words called a *subject completer.* Completers may be nouns, pronouns, adjectives, or adverbs.

See Sentences, pp. 120, 128–129

EXAMPLES The horses are *restless*.
[*Are* is the linking verb. *Restless* is an adjective that describes the horses. *Restless* is the subject completer.]

The white horse is the *leader.*
[*Is* is the linking verb. *Leader* is a noun that tells what the white horse is. *Leader* is the subject completer.]

Certain linking verbs can be used as action verbs in some sentences. The verbs *look* and *appear* are two examples.

EXAMPLES
ACTION VERB She *looked* in the window.
LINKING VERB She *looked* thin.

ACTION VERB We *appeared* in the talent show.
LINKING VERB We *appeared* busy.

EXERCISE 3 Number a sheet of paper 1–8. Next to each number write the linking verb in each sentence.

EXAMPLE Suddenly I was unable to sleep.

was

1. I am not usually a worrier.
2. But something seemed wrong.
3. Upstairs everything looked all right.
4. But I became aware of strange noises downstairs.
5. They sounded almost musical, like a soft clinkety-clinking.
6. The kitchen was the source of the noise.
7. At the table, Dad seemed lost in a huge bowl of ice cream.
8. His latest diet appeared over once again.

Hint: Remember that a linking verb joins with another word or words to describe or rename a person, place, or thing. An action verb helps tell of something that happens or has happened.

Auxiliary Verbs

(5) An auxiliary verb helps the main verb tell what happens or what exists.

EXAMPLES Cheese *is* made from milk.
[The auxiliary verb *is* works with the main verb *made.*]

I *could* eat cheese all day.
[The auxiliary verb *could* works with the main verb *eat.*]

Here are some of the most common auxiliary verbs in the English language.

am	have	can	might
are	has	may	must
is	had	should	do
was	shall	would	does
were	will	could	did

When used together, the auxiliary verb and the main verb make up the *complete verb.* The complete verb is sometimes called the *verb phrase.*

See Phrases, pp. 68–69

EXAMPLES Tae *has been eating* bean curd all her life.
It *has made* her healthy.

In some sentences words come between the auxiliary verb and the main verb. The complete verb is still made up of the auxiliary verb and the main verb, despite the extra words.

EXAMPLES We *should* not *gobble* so much.
We *will* very likely *become* fat.

EXERCISE 4 Number a sheet of paper 1–10. Next to each number write the complete verb. Underline the auxiliary verb.

EXAMPLE I could hear the Kitchen Wizard laughing at me.
could hear

1. I was sinking in a thick pool of butter.
2. But the Kitchen Wizard would not win today.
3. This buttery whirlpool might lead to my escape.
4. It was tugging me down toward something.
5. But what was waiting for me at the bottom of the pool?
6. I would find the answer no matter what the cost.
7. I was pulled quickly down into the butter.
8. Almost as quickly, I was spurting forth from a spout.
9. My risk had landed me outside, but where?
10. I had found freedom again—on the Oatmeal River.

Tense

2b Most verbs change form to show a change in tense.

Verbs can show *tense,* or the time of the action or condition they describe, through a change in form.

EXAMPLES

PRESENT Cranberry juice *tastes* good in punch.

SIMPLE PAST Cranberry juice *tasted* good in that punch we had yesterday.

FUTURE Cranberry juice *will taste* good tomorrow if we do not drink too much today.

The form of the *present tense* is usually the same as the *infinitive,* or base form, of the verb.

See Infinitive, p. 452

This form adds **s** or **es** to make the third person singular in the present tense. The third person singular is the form used when *he, she,* or *it* is the subject of the verb.

EXAMPLES

INFINITIVE	PRESENT TENSE	
	Singular	Plural
smile	I smile	we smile
	you smile	you smile
	he / she / it } smiles	they smile

Another form of the present tense is made by adding **ing** to the infinitive form of the main verb and combining it with a form of the verb *be* as an auxiliary. The **ing** form of a main verb is called the *present participle.*

See Participle, p. 456

EXAMPLES

INFINITIVE	PRESENT PARTICIPLE	PRESENT TENSE
walk	walking	is walking
nail	nailing	am nailing
fly	flying	are flying

Future tense in its regular form is shown by adding an auxiliary verb such as *will* to the infinitive form of the verb. There are several other ways of showing the future tense in addition to this one.

EXAMPLES

REGULAR FORM OF FUTURE TENSE	She *will eat* the apples.
ADDITIONAL FORMS	She *is going to eat* the apples.

She *may eat* the apples tomorrow.

Most verbs show *simple past tense* by adding **d** or **ed** to the infinitive. These are *regular verbs.* Some verbs, however, do not show simple past tense in this way. Instead, they have special forms for the past tense. These are *irregular verbs.*

Another form of the past tense is called the *present perfect.* This form uses the *past participle* form of the main verb and the present tense of the auxiliary verb *have* to show that an action has been completed in the past.

See Participle, p. 456

EXAMPLES

INFINITIVE	PAST PARTICIPLE	PRESENT PERFECT
speak	spoken	have spoken
paint	painted	have painted

Regular Verbs

2c Regular verbs add *ed* or *d* to the infinitive form to show the past tense.

EXAMPLES

INFINITIVE	SIMPLE PAST	PRESENT PERFECT
walk	walked	have walked
tape	taped	have taped

Irregular Verbs

2d Irregular verbs may change form to show past tense, but they do not add *ed* or *d* to the infinitive form.

EXAMPLES

INFINITIVE	SIMPLE PAST	PRESENT PERFECT
begin	began	have begun
drive	drove	have driven
rise	rose	have risen
see	saw	have seen

PRESENT Nan *eats* the avocado in its skin.
SIMPLE PAST Nan *ate* the avocado in its skin.
PRESENT PERFECT Nan *has eaten* the avocado in its skin.

EXERCISE 5 In the following list the simple past or the present perfect tense is missing for each verb. Number a sheet of paper 1–10. Skip a line between numbers. Next to each number write the correct missing form. Next to it write a sentence that uses the form correctly. If you have questions, check a dictionary.

EXAMPLE

INFINITIVE	SIMPLE PAST	PRESENT PERFECT
run	ran	______

have run – The players have run around the field.

	INFINITIVE	SIMPLE PAST	PRESENT PERFECT
1.	hold	held	______
2.	swim	swam	______
3.	blow	______	have blown
4.	sit	______	have sat
5.	see	saw	______
6.	sing	______	have sung
7.	steal	______	have stolen

8. drink	______	have drunk
9. break	broke	______
10. go	went	______

VERBALS

A verb form used as another part of speech is called a *verbal*. The three kinds of verbals are *gerunds, participles,* and *infinitives.*

Gerunds

2e A gerund is a verb form usually ending in *d, ed,* or *ing* that is used as a noun.

EXAMPLES *Skating* is fun.
[The act of *skating* is the name of something. It is a noun.]

The *hunted* never sleep calmly.
[The *hunted* are persons or animals.]

Participles

2f A participle is a verb form usually ending in *d, ed,* or *ing* that is used as an adjective.

EXAMPLES The *flickering* star is below the moon.
[*Flickering* describes *star.*]

A *rolling* stone gathers no moss.
[*Rolling* describes *stone.*]

The *hunted* animal could get no rest.
[*Hunted* modifies *animal.*]

Infinitives

2g An infinitive is the base form of the verb used as a noun, an adjective, or an adverb.

The infinitive is often preceded by *to.*

EXAMPLES

INFINITIVE USED AS A NOUN
To skate is fun.

INFINITIVE USED AS AN ADJECTIVE
She had no more energy *to give.*
[*To give* modifies the noun *energy.*]

INFINITIVE USED AS AN ADVERB
Uranium is dangerous *to handle.*
[*To handle* modifies the adjective *dangerous.*]

EXERCISE 6 Number a sheet of paper 1–6. Write the verbal you find in each sentence. Put *G* after each gerund, *P* after each participle, and *I* after each infinitive.

EXAMPLE Jogging keeps Carmen's body healthy.

1. Looking for healthful activities is her hobby.
2. Dancing is also good exercise for her.

3. She thinks it is more fun to dance.
4. Carmen's jogging days will soon be over.
5. However, she hopes she is never too old to dance.
6. The ageing process is part of life.

ADVERBS

2h An adverb is a word used to modify an action verb, an adjective, another adverb, or a complete statement.

Whenever an adverb modifies an action verb, it tells something about the action. It can tell *when, where, how, how much,* or *how often* the action happens.

Example of an adverb that tells *when* an action happens:
The storm came *early.*

Example of an adverb that tells *where* an action happens:
The frightened kitten remained *inside.*

Examples of adverbs that tell *how, how much,* or *how often* actions happen:
Frances Bumpers smashed the clamshell *expertly.* She struck *again* and *again.*

EXERCISE 7 Write the following sentences on a sheet of paper. Skip a line between each sentence. Underline each adverb. Draw an arrow from the adverb to the verb it modifies.

EXAMPLE Anne Royall traveled widely in the United States.

Anne Royall traveled widely in the United States.

1. In books about her travels, she described many kinds of things well.
2. She wrote sharply about people she disliked.
3. She often wrote about bad actions in business and government.
4. People in all walks of life soon feared Anne Royall's pen.
5. Politicians quickly turned against her.
6. The government treated Anne Royall badly.
7. People sometimes called Anne Royall a common scold.
8. She obviously enjoyed finding fault.
9. But most of the time she described accurately the evils she saw.
10. The best people of her time grudgingly respected Anne Royall.

EXERCISE 8 Write the following sentences on a sheet of paper. Skip a line between each sentence. Underline the adverb in each sentence. Draw an arrow from the adverb to the verb it modifies.

EXAMPLE The Chicago fire of 1871 burned first on the west side of the city.

The Chicago fire of 1871 burned first on the west side of the city.

1. People hurried anxiously across bridges to the other side of town.
2. The fire quickly jumped the river to the north side.
3. Some houses exploded violently in the heat.
4. Glass and burning planks fell dangerously on all sides.
5. People escaped hastily with just the clothes on their backs.
6. The fire roared constantly like a giant waterfall.
7. A wall of red and yellow flame swept savagely through the streets.
8. People huddled fearfully in parks all night.
9. The fire completely destroyed three square miles of city.
10. About 100,000 people lost their homes then.

Some adverbs modify adjectives.

EXAMPLE Renick Brock runs with *ridiculously* high steps.
[*Ridiculously* modifies the adjective *high.*]

A few adverbs modify other adverbs.

EXAMPLE Melva Cannon sings *quite* badly.
[*Quite* modifies the adverb *badly.*]

Sometimes an adverb modifies an entire statement.

EXAMPLE *Now* I am happy.
[The adverb *now* modifies the rest of the sentence *I am happy.*]

Certain adverbs can be used in different places in the same sentence.

EXAMPLE *Often* he snores while asleep.
He *often* snores while asleep.
He snores *often* while asleep.

The words *not* and *never* are special adverbs which can modify verbs, adjectives, or other adverbs. *Not* and *never* make the words they modify the opposite of their original meanings.

EXAMPLES These buses do run on Saturday.
These buses do *not* run on Sunday.
Try to catch one on Saturday.
Never try to catch one on Sunday.

EXERCISE 9 The following sentences contain adverbs that modify adjectives or other adverbs. Number a sheet of paper 1–12. Skip a line between numbers. Next to each number write the sentence. Underline each adverb that modifies an adjective or another adverb. Draw an arrow from the adverb to the adjective or other adverb it modifies.

EXAMPLE Mountain men in frontier days were often friendly with wild animals.

Mountain men in frontier days were <u>often</u> friendly with wild animals.

1. Grizzly Adams was especially fond of grizzly bears.
2. Grizzly Adams lived quite happily in the Sierra Nevada of California.
3. A grizzly bear is an amazingly fierce animal.
4. Only a very unusual man could make friends with a grizzly bear.
5. Grizzly Adams had some frighteningly close escapes from death.
6. A bear named Ben Franklin was his most delightful pet.
7. Ben Franklin was very young when Adams caught him.
8. Adams got surprisingly good results from training his bears.
9. Some bears carried packs for him quite willingly.
10. Mountain lions and other animals also responded extremely well to the attention of Grizzly Adams.
11. Adams put on a show with his unusually tame animals.
12. Other men were not too eager to repeat his tricks.

EXERCISE 10 Each of the following sentences contains one or more adverbs. Number a sheet of paper 1–10. Next to each number write the adverb or adverbs from the sentence.

EXAMPLE In warm weather our pets wander freely and sleep outdoors.

freely, outdoors

1. When winter comes early, all the pets appear suddenly.
2. Even Laura's cat sleeps inside.
3. She always sleeps upstairs.
4. Even though Laura's cat sleeps nearby, Molly's turtle sleeps soundly.
5. Laura's cat watches curiously but the turtle snores loudly.
6. "Turtles never snore!" you object knowingly.
7. Molly's turtle, however, does snore occasionally.
8. Frankly, I prefer a cat that purrs softly to a turtle that snores noisily.
9. I understand that snakes sleep quietly.
10. I'll look in the field tomorrow to see if I can find a snake somewhere.

EXERCISE 11 Use the following adverbs in sentences of your own. Include a sentence in which an adverb modifies a verb, another in which an adverb modifies an adjective, and another in which an adverb modifies another adverb. You should have ten sentences when finished.

1. fully
2. miserably
3. happily
4. quite
5. usually
6. cleverly
7. hardly
8. dully
9. gruesomely
10. lightly

2i Adverbs help compare the action of verbs.

Most short adverbs show comparison by adding **er** to form the *comparative* and **est** to form the *superlative*.

EXAMPLES

POSITIVE Paulo Cruz rises *early* on weekdays.

COMPARATIVE On Saturday he gets up *earlier.*

SUPERLATIVE However, on Sunday he gets up *earliest.*

Adverbs ending in **ly** use the words *more* and *most* in front of them to show comparison. They do not add **er** and **est.**

EXAMPLES

POSITIVE	COMPARATIVE	SUPERLATIVE
gracefully	more gracefully	most gracefully
proudly	more proudly	most proudly

EXERCISE 12 Number a sheet of paper 1–10. Next to each number write the correct form, either positive, comparative, or superlative, of the adverb in parentheses in each sentence.

EXAMPLE Bush pilots in Alaska had to fly (carefully) than most pilots.

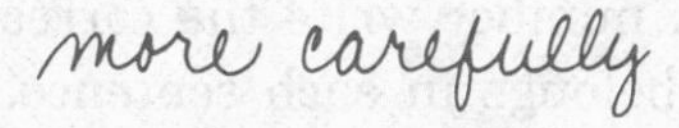

1. Bush pilots (courageously) helped people travel across Alaska in the 1920's and 1930's.
2. The earliest pilots had to take more risks than those who flew (late).
3. Bush pilots flew (skillfully) over snow and ice than most pilots could fly over corn fields.
4. In their tiny planes they worked (hard) than pilots of big jets.
5. Their passengers looked forward to the trip (nervously) than passengers in big jets.
6. But afterward, they said bush pilots flew the (carefully) of all.

7. Some bush pilots flew (daringly) than others.
8. Landing on ice is a (difficult) bush pilot skill.
9. Even today, many people wish to travel (widely) in Alaska than big airlines will let them.
10. Those who want to see Alaska (completely) than weekend visitors still depend on bush pilots.

Irregular Adverbs

Some adverbs change form in irregular ways to show the comparative and superlative forms.

EXAMPLES

POSITIVE	COMPARATIVE	SUPERLATIVE
well	better	best
badly	worse	worst

EXERCISE 13 Number a sheet of paper 1–10. Next to each number write the correct form of the adverb that belongs in each sentence.

EXAMPLE The ghost scared Helen and Horace (terribly) than they had ever been scared before.

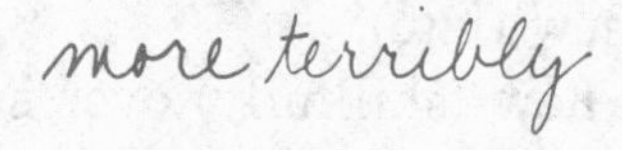

1. It scared Hilary (badly) of all.
2. It seemed (likely) to be Great-Uncle Toby.
3. Great-Uncle Toby had treated the children (unpleasantly) than any other relative.
4. He made them do arithmetic homework (thoroughly) than they had before.

5. Hilary did arithmetic even (unwillingly) than Horace or Helen.
6. The ghost visited Hilary (long) than it visited Horace or Helen.
7. It made her do arithmetic (steadily) than she cared to.
8. Horace and Helen thought hard about ways to get rid of the ghost, but Hilary thought (hard) of all.
9. Hilary finally found a way to make the ghost treat her (fairly) than it had.
10. She showed it her report card, which said that she did arithmetic (well) of all her class.

PREPOSITIONS

2j A preposition is a word used to relate the noun or pronoun that usually follows it to other words in a sentence.

EXAMPLES The soup is *in* the can.
[The preposition *in* relates the noun *can* to the verb *is*.]

Dessert comes *after* the main course.
[The preposition *after* relates the noun *course* to the verb *comes*.]

We can have cake *with* dessert.
[The preposition *with* relates the noun *dessert* to the noun *cake*.]

Prepositions show special relationships of *time, place, manner,* or *kind*. Here is a list of common prepositions.

TIME	PLACE			MANNER OR KIND
after	about	beside	on	by
before	above	between	over	except
during	across	down	through	for
since	against	in	to	like
till	around	into	toward	of
to	at	inside	under	with
until	behind	near	up	without
	below			

Some prepositions are made up of more than one word. These prepositional word groups work just like prepositions.

EXAMPLES

because of	by means of	in addition to
in back of	instead of	on account of

EXERCISE 14 Number a sheet of paper 1–15. Next to each number write the preposition in the sentence.

EXAMPLE A good place to sleep is in bed.

1. Humans usually sleep at night.
2. We still know very little about sleep.
3. Scientists study sleep through observation.
4. They examine what happens when we sleep and when we go without sleep.
5. Imagine that when falling asleep you are going down an escalator.
6. You get more and more sleepy with every step.
7. When you reach the bottom, you have fallen into a deep sleep.

8. Imagine that when awakening you are coming up the escalator again.
9. When you are at the top, you awaken.
10. Instead of a dreamless sleep, we all have dreams.
11. We usually remember the last dream we had before waking.
12. When you are dreaming, there is a quick, jerky movement under your eyelids.
13. Scientists call this movement REM, which means "rapid eye movement" in sleep.
14. Have you ever noticed a dog's eyelids twitching in its sleep?
15. It may be dreaming that it is running through the woods.

Object of the Preposition

The *object* of a preposition is the noun or pronoun that follows it. The preposition shows the relationship of its object to some other word in the sentence.

EXAMPLES

He threw a stone *across* the stream.

It landed *on* a green stick.

The stick slithered *into* the bushes.

It was a snake that looked *like* a stick.

EXERCISE 15 The following sentences contain prepositions with their objects. On a sheet of paper write each sentence. Skip a line between every sentence. Underline each preposition and draw an arrow from it to its object.

EXAMPLE Hummingbirds can be compared to helicopters in their flight.

Hummingbirds can be compared to helicopters in their flight.

1. Both of them can hover at a standstill.
2. Both of them can fly vertically into the sky.
3. The hummingbird's tiny wings beat rapidly through the air eighty times in a second.
4. The helicopter's blades spin in a circle above its body.
5. Like a flashing jewel, the hummingbird darts toward a flower.
6. Hovering near the blossom, it sips nectar with its tongue.
7. Hovering over the sea or near a cliff, the helicopter rescues people.
8. Hummingbirds can fly in any direction.
9. Helicopters can fly backwards and even turn in a tight circle.
10. The name *hummingbird* comes from the sound of the birds' wings, which hum.
11. The name helicopter comes from two Greek words: *helix* meaning "spiral," and *pter* meaning "wing."
12. Helicopters are also known as whirlybirds.

2k A preposition may have more than one object.

EXAMPLE

You can see *across* the river and the marsh.

It stands *between* the fence and the road.

EXERCISE 16 Write the following sentences on a sheet of paper. Underline each preposition. Draw arrows to one or both objects of each preposition.

EXAMPLE It was July 1876, and our country's hundredth birthday was being celebrated in cities and towns.

It was July 1876, and our country's hundreth birthday was being celebrated in cities and towns.

1. Centennial celebrations were marked by parades and fireworks.
2. Dozens of gaily dressed horses and riders passed cheering adults and children.
3. Blasts from trumpets and tubas filled the air.
4. Many centennial celebrations ended with big dinners or dances.
5. Then the blazes of pinwheels and skyrockets lit the night sky.
6. Philadelphia's Centennial International Exhibition had displays from the U.S. and foreign countries.
7. The displays were brightened by folk arts and crafts.

8. There was room for new inventions and industrial machinery, too.
9. The exhibition showed the best work of every state and country.
10. No exhibition visitor from the U.S. or abroad could doubt that America was a wonderful land.

CONJUNCTIONS

2l A conjunction is a word used to join other words or groups of words.

Two kinds of conjunctions are used in English: *coordinating* and *subordinating.*

Coordinating Conjunctions

See Phrase, p. 457; Clause, p. 441

Coordinating conjunctions join ideas of equal value. These ideas may be in single words, in phrases, or in whole clauses. The common coordinating conjunctions are *and, but, for, nor,* and *or.*

EXAMPLES Dairy products *and* cold drinks are kept in the cooler section *or* in the back room.

Cereals are in front, *but* fresh fruits are in the rear.

A few pairs of conjunctions are used in English. These are a kind of *coordinating conjunction* called *correlative conjunctions.* Examples are *either . . . or, neither . . . nor, not only . . . but also.*

EXAMPLE *Either* the pet food *or* the fertilizer is stacked by the window.

EXERCISE 17 Number a sheet of paper 1–6. Next to each number write each sentence. Draw a circle around the coordinating conjunction or the correlative conjunction that you find in the sentence. Underline the words or word groups joined by each conjunction.

EXAMPLE Either porpoises are getting smarter, or the ocean is running out of porpoises.

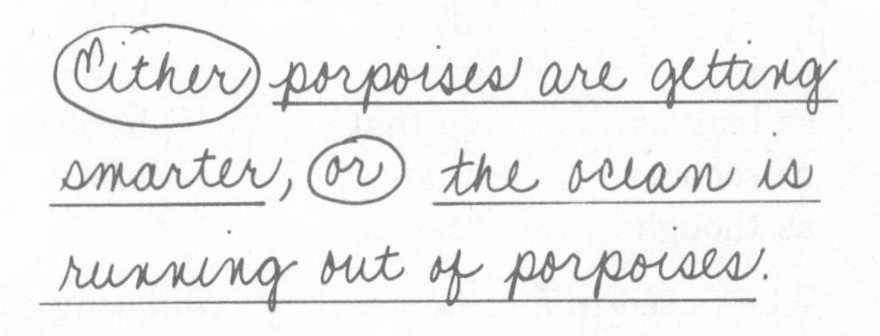

1. Tuna fish swim with porpoises, and the porpoises often get caught in tuna fishing nets.
2. Porpoises will drown if the nets keep them underwater too long, for they are air-breathing mammals.
3. The porpoises are learning how to recognize tuna nets and how to avoid them.
4. They let a net surround them, but they swim out before it closes.
5. Neither all the porpoises nor all the tuna are caught.
6. The porpoises and the tuna seem to be learning new tricks all the time.

Subordinating Conjunctions

See Clauses, pp. 86–94

Subordinating conjunctions join word groups that are of unequal value. The word *subordinate* means "less important." The job of these conjunctions is to join a word group that is less important with one that is more important. Some subordinating conjunctions are made up of more than one word.

A list of subordinating conjunctions follows:

after	because	unless
although	before	until
as	if	when
as if	since	whenever
as long as	so that	wherever
as soon as	than	while
as though	though	

When used in a sentence, a subordinating conjunction shows the relation between the main idea and a subordinate—or less important—idea.

EXAMPLES European countries built supermarkets *after* American business developed them.

European markets were little corner stores *before* the idea for supermarkets grew in this country.

Word groups introduced by subordinating conjunctions usually modify the idea in the main word group to which they are joined. The subordinate word groups tell *when, where, how,* and *why* about the main idea.

EXAMPLES

WHEN Let's leave *after this cartoon is over.*

WHERE I'll sit *where you want me to sit.*

HOW She closed her eyes *as if she were asleep.*

WHY We chose that color *because it reminds us of our school colors.*

The subordinate word group can be either in the first or the last position in a sentence.

Example of a last position:
Small markets are disappearing *because the competition of large markets is so strong.*

Example of a first position:
Because the competition of large markets is so strong, small markets are disappearing.

EXERCISE 18 Each of the following sentences contains a subordinating conjunction. Number a sheet of paper 1–10. Next to each number write the subordinating conjunction.

EXAMPLE Before Valerie Pope came along, the old neighborhood was run down.
Before

1. She fixed up the houses so that people would have good places to live.
2. After Valerie worked on the houses, they doubled in value.
3. Valerie wanted to try new ways of heating because regular heat costs so much money.
4. While Valerie repaired the houses, Nate Rekosh designed a solar heating system for them.

5. Sixty-five-year-old Nate enjoys useful work more than he enjoys living in retirement.
6. After installing Nate's solar heating system, people in the houses got half their heat for free.
7. Since other people helped to build the solar heating systems, Valerie's project gave people both jobs and houses.
8. Although Nate's design is a new one, it may soon be tried in many cities.
9. More neighborhoods will be wasted unless people like Valerie and Nate go to work on them.
10. Whenever people work hard, amazing things can be done.

INTERJECTIONS

2m An interjection is a word or group of words used to express strong feeling.

EXAMPLES *Oh, heck!*
Rats, how can they do that to us?
Whew! What a lucky accident.

An interjection has no grammatical connection with other words in a sentence. It should be set off with commas or an exclamation mark.

See Punctuation, pp. 307, 310

EXERCISE 19 Number a sheet of paper 1–5. List the interjections from the following sentences.

EXAMPLE Hurrah! The last one is finished.
Hurrah

1. The cowboys shouted "Yippee! Ride that bronco!"
2. My beloved Esmerelda, alas, has left this earth.
3. "Zounds!" cried Professor Zutt. "I have been undone."
4. The child's nurse stamped her foot and exclaimed, "Heavens to Betsy!"
5. "Give me that pot of gold or, blast you, I'll make you sorry," the intruder snarled.

REVIEW EXERCISE A **Identifying Verbs**

Number a sheet of paper 1–10. Next to each number write the complete verb from each of the following sentences. Underline the auxiliary verbs.

EXAMPLE The plastics industry was begun because of billiard balls.

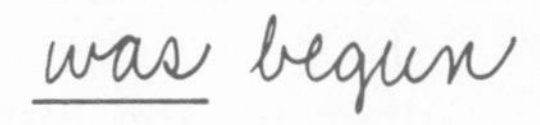

1. Hunters would ruthlessly slaughter elephants for their ivory tusks.
2. Soon ivory had become very scarce.
3. A billiard ball manufacturer, Phalen and Collander, offered $10,000 in 1863 for an ivory substitute.
4. The plastics industry grew.
5. Soon plastic was being used for other purposes besides billiard balls.
6. It wore well.
7. Stiff celluloid collars became fashionable in the 1920's.
8. Dentists used plastic in dental plates.

9. Today the uses of plastic have spread widely.
10. Manufacturers mold plastics in a variety of shapes.

REVIEW EXERCISE B **Verbals**

Each of the following sentences contains an underlined word or words used as a verbal. Number a sheet of paper 1–10. Next to each number, write *G* if the underlined verbal is a gerund, *P* if it is a participle, or *I* if it is an infinitive.

EXAMPLE To find the source of the White Nile was the goal of two English explorers, Richard Burton and John Speke.

I

1. In 1857 they set out toward the rolling hills of East Africa.
2. Exploring was dangerous and difficult.
3. In February of 1858, the two reached the sparkling water of Lake Tanganyika.
4. But both men soon became too sick to continue.
5. Needing a rest, they headed toward Ujiji.
6. Soon Speke went off by himself to explore a lake described to him by an Arab trader.
7. Speke was eager to see if this lake was the source of the Nile.
8. In twenty-five days Speke came to a gradually inclined hill.
9. At the top was a glittering expanse of water that Speke named Lake Victoria.
10. Investigating had brought Speke to what was essentially the source of the Nile.

REVIEW EXERCISE C **Adverbs**

Each of the following sentences contains an adverb. Number a sheet of paper 1–10, skipping a line between the numbers. Copy each sentence. Then underline the adverb and draw an arrow from the adverb to the word it modifies.

EXAMPLE Surprisingly little is known about the early life of Ira Aldridge.

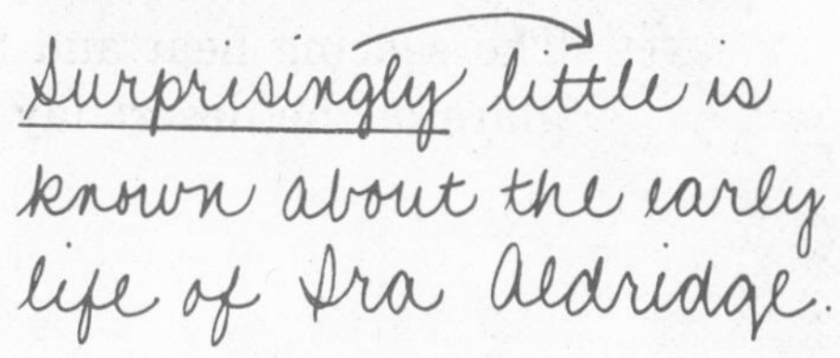
Surprisingly little is
known about the early
life of Ira Aldridge.

1. The great Black American actor was probably born in 1805.
2. He somehow became the personal valet of a famous English actor, Edmund Kean.
3. Aldridge worked very hard at becoming an actor himself.
4. In 1833 he played Shakespeare's Othello and was wildly applauded.
5. Then he came to the United States.
6. His reception was exceedingly bad.
7. Americans were unwilling to accept the well acclaimed Black actor.
8. Quite heartbroken, Aldridge returned to Europe.
9. Widely honored in England and on the Continent, he remained a star.
10. Although he was considered a great success, Aldridge always longed for acceptance in his homeland.

REVIEW EXERCISE D **Prepositions and Conjunctions**

Each of the following sentences contains one or more underlined words. Number a sheet of paper 1–10. Next to each number write *CC* if the underlined word or words is a coordinating conjunction, *SC* if it is a subordinating conjunction, *CRC* if it is a correlative conjunction, or *P* if it is a preposition.

EXAMPLE The searing heat and the white glare of the desert lay before him.

1. Before he could cross it, he had to wait until sundown.
2. He crawled under the wagon and lay down.
3. The hours passed in the silent, terrible heat.
4. Not only the heat of the sun, but also the flies and mosquitoes tormented him.
5. If he had not thought constantly of the freedom that awaited him, he would have turned back.
6. But the group of men who rode after him would catch up with him.
7. They would never believe he was not the cattle rustler and horse thief they sought.
8. As soon as he got to Mexico, he would try to clear his name.
9. Time would show that he was not the criminal because the stealing would continue.
10. The sun finally began to go down behind the distant mountains.

CHAPTER

3

PHRASES

Noun Phrases, Verb Phrases, Prepositional Phrases, Participial Phrases

Parts of speech often are single words. However, certain groups of related words may also work together as parts of speech. These groups of related words presented in this chapter are called *phrases.*

Four kinds of phrases are discussed in this chapter: *noun phrases, verb phrases, prepositional phrases,* and *participial phrases.*

KINDS OF PHRASES

3a A phrase is a group of related words used as a single part of speech.

EXAMPLES *Donald's red and brown beard* needed shaving.
[*Donald's red and brown beard* names something. These related words make a noun phrase.]

His lips *were twitching.*
[*Were twitching* tells of the action of his lips. These words make a verb phrase.]

He had dirty smears *on his chin.*
[*On his chin* tells where the smears were. These words make a prepositional phrase used as an adjective.]

Twinkling with pleasure, his eyes flashed in an otherwise tired face.
[*Twinkling with pleasure* describes his eyes. These words make a participial phrase that acts as an adjective to modify *eyes.*]

Hint: All the words in a phrase work together as a single part of speech.

Noun Phrases

See Noun, p. 454

3b A noun phrase is made up of a noun and its modifiers.

EXAMPLE *The silver balloon* was *a strange sight.*
[*Balloon* is the noun. Its modifiers are *the* and *silver. Sight* is another noun. Its modifiers are *a* and *strange.* These words make up the two noun phrases in this example.]

You can understand noun phrases more easily if you remember that a noun phrase can usually be replaced with a pronoun.

See Pronoun, p. 458

EXAMPLES *The silver balloon* floated in the air.
It floated in the air.
[The pronoun *it* replaces the noun phrase *the silver balloon.*]

The silver balloon bumped against *a little boy.*
It bumped against *him.*
[The pronoun *it* replaces the noun phrase *the silver balloon,* and the pronoun *him* replaces the noun phrase *a little boy.*]

Hint: The words in a noun phrase work together like a noun.

EXERCISE 1 Copy the following sentences on a sheet of paper. Underline each noun phrase. Some sentences have more than one noun phrase. Be sure to underline all the related words that belong in each noun phrase.

EXAMPLE Fourteen California residents saw some strange sights.

Fourteen California residents saw some strange sights.

1. An odd green cloud contained a human outline.
2. It could have been an other-worldly visitor.

3. Another watcher saw a bright orange cloud.
4. The cloud had a square shape.
5. An airborne vehicle chased one couple.
6. Another craft drained a farmer's pond.
7. Intelligent and truthful people saw these things.
8. The most respectable people were the least willing talkers.
9. Their various stories could have been imaginative lies.
10. What is your opinion?

Verb Phrases

See Verbs, pp. 35–36

3c A verb phrase is made up of the main verb and its auxiliaries.

The main verb and its auxiliaries make up the verb phrase. Together they work like a single verb in a sentence. The verb phrase is sometimes called the *complete verb*.

EXAMPLES Dogs and cats *can live* together.
Some people *have considered* them enemies.
However, most dogs *have become accustomed* to the ways of cats.

Verb phrases tell about the action or condition of the person or thing being talked about in the sentence.

In some sentences the verb phrase is split by another word. Even when this happens, the parts of the verb phrase still work as a verb.

EXAMPLE Merrie *had* hardly *reached* the front door when the phone began to ring. [The verb phrase *had reached* is split by the adverb *hardly*.]

Hint: The words in a verb phrase work together like a verb.

EXERCISE 2 Number a sheet of paper 1–10. Next to each number write the verb phrase from each of the following sentences.

EXAMPLE Abigail Adams is now considered by many as one of the first American feminists.

is considered

1. From the beginning of her marriage, Abigail had been an equal partner with her husband, John Adams.
2. She had run his large farm during his absence.
3. Without her work, John Adams might easily have lost much land and money.
4. Although not with her husband in Philadelphia in 1776, she did have an influence on the birth of the United States.
5. Abigail had once written to Adams to "remember the ladies" in the Constitution.
6. If not, the women might take matters into their own hands.
7. Abigail had hinted at a second American Revolution.

8. She had also argued for the abolition of slavery.
9. Later, both Abigail's husband and her son would become presidents of the United States.
10. American history would have been poorer without the influence of Abigail Adams.

Prepositional Phrases

3d A prepositional phrase begins with a preposition and usually ends with a noun or pronoun.

See Preposition, p. 458

A prepositional phrase is made up of a preposition, the noun or pronoun that is its object, and any words that modify its object.

EXAMPLES under the bath mat
after the dance
about you
of the school marching band

Note that in these examples a noun phrase may be part of the prepositional phrase. For example, *the bath mat* is a noun phrase contained in the prepositional phrase *under the bath mat.*

Some prepositions are made up of more than one word.

EXAMPLES		
	according to	next to
	because of	on account of
	in spite of	out of
	instead of	up to

EXERCISE 3 Number a sheet of paper 1–12. Next to each number write the prepositional phrase or phrases in the sentence. Underline the preposition. Draw an arrow from it to its object.

EXAMPLE Alligators are a common sight in the city of Miami.

1. The huge animals live in swamps near this city in Florida.
2. Canals run near the streets throughout Miami.
3. In the mating season, lonesome alligators swim into the canals.
4. They have been found on golf courses and in people's backyards.
5. One even crawled onto a runway at the airport.
6. No plane could land on that runway while the alligator was there.
7. For many years people hunted alligators for their skins.
8. The alligators' skins were used for handbags and shoes.
9. Soon there were few alligators in any part of Florida.
10. Hunting alligators was made illegal in most places.
11. Now the alligator population is on the rise in the swamps.
12. Some people treat the city alligators like pets and feed them with tidbits.

(1) A prepositional phrase may be used as an adjective.

See Adjective, p. 438

EXAMPLES The bread *in the hot oven* will be ready soon.
[The prepositional phrase *in the hot oven* modifies *bread.*]

The top *of the brown loaf* is breaking open.
[The prepositional phrase *of the brown loaf* modifies *top.*]

Hint: The noun or pronoun modified by the prepositional phrase comes *before* the phrase. The prepositional phrase follows the noun or pronoun it modifies.

EXERCISE 4 Each of the following sentences has a prepositional phrase used as an adjective. Copy each prepositional phrase. Then list the noun or pronoun it modifies.

EXAMPLE Harvard University once presented a symphony of sleep called Dreamstage.

of sleep, symphony

1. A young man from a nearby college slept there each night.
2. A special bed for the experiment was designed.
3. Electrical impulses from his brain activated a laser and a synthesizer.
4. The laser made patterns of colored light, and the synthesizer produced a weird symphony.
5. Then people could watch and hear the designs of the young man's dreams.
6. Other demonstrations at the exhibit described human sleep.
7. The four stages of sleep were described.
8. The complex activities during sleep are not yet fully understood.

(2) A prepositional phrase may be used as an adverb.

See Adverb, p. 438

Almost all prepositional phrases used as adverbs modify verbs. They work the same way an adverb works. That is, prepositional phrases tell *when, where, how long,* or *how much.*

EXAMPLES The robbers entered the bank *at noon.*
[This prepositional phrase tells *when* the robbers entered the bank.]

They walked *across the entryway.*
[This prepositional phrase tells *where* they walked.]

They inspected the bank *for ten minutes.*
[This prepositional phrase tells *how long* the robbers inspected the bank.]

A prepositional phrase used as an adverb may also modify an adjective or another adverb.

Example of a prepositional phrase used as an adverb to modify an adjective:

It always seems cold *in the morning.*
[This phrase modifies the adjective *cold.*]

Example of a prepositional phrase used as an adverb to modify another adverb:

The car runs faster *on the radial tires.*
[This phrase modifies the adverb *faster.*]

Most prepositional phrases end with a noun or pronoun. However, some end with an adverb.

EXAMPLE The money is stacked *in here*. [This prepositional phrase, which ends with an adverb, tells *where* the money is stacked.]

Hint: The words in a prepositional phrase work together either like an adjective or an adverb. They do not work like a preposition.

EXERCISE 5 Each of the following sentences has one or two prepositional phrases used as adverbs. Copy each sentence on a sheet of paper. Underline each prepositional phrase. Draw an arrow from it to the word it modifies.

EXAMPLE Some Native Americans lived in the central United States.

Some Native Americans lived in the central United States.

1. In the nineteenth century, these hunters rode on horses.
2. They hunted bison with guns.
3. Some people think all Native Americans lived like this.
4. But they got guns and horses from the Spanish explorers.

5. Before those days, the Native Americans lived in a different way.
6. They got most food from their own farms.
7. Women farmed near the villages while the men hunted in the open lands.
8. Native Americans have lived on the Great Plains for 11,000 years.

EXERCISE 6 Following are ten prepositional phrases. Use each in a sentence of your own. Underline each phrase. Draw an arrow from the prepositional phrase to the word it modifies.

EXAMPLES of the can

The top of the can was split

1. in a heap
2. between the rows
3. from the start
4. except for a hole
5. under a large bundle
6. into the icy stream
7. around the deserted building
8. with a shotgun
9. until noon
10. by the fence

Participial Phrases

3e A participial phrase is made up of a participle and its related words working as an adjective.

See Participle, p. 456; Adjective, p. 438

EXAMPLES *Standing in neat rows,* the flowers looked almost unreal.

[*Standing* is the present participle. The other words in the participial phrase are *in neat rows*. This phrase modifies the noun *flowers*.]

Seen at a closer range, the flowers were indeed unreal.
[The past participle *seen* and its related words make up the participial phrase. The entire phrase modifies *flowers*.]

Fooled by plastic, I walked away in a hurry.
[*Fooled* is the past participle. It and the related words *by plastic* make up a participial phrase that modifies the pronoun *I*.]

EXERCISE 7 Each of these sentences contains a participial phrase. Number a sheet of paper 1–10. Next to each number write the participial phrase. Next to that write the noun or pronoun it modifies.

EXAMPLE In the summer many a beach has its band of body builders flexing their muscles in the sun.

flexing their muscles, body builders

1. Working with weights, many young people exercise regularly.
2. The young people, tasting the thrill of accomplishment, lift heavier and heavier weights.

3. Parading their agility and strength, they show off in front of their friends.
4. Others, trying an easier exercise, jog for miles.
5. Running up hill and down, joggers force their hearts to beat faster.
6. Wearing specially made shoes, joggers try to protect their feet and legs.
7. Straining the pocketbooks of even serious joggers, some shoes cost over $60.
8. Some old people, building their health, have joined the army of joggers.
9. Running several miles a day, they are as strong as the younger runners.
10. Staying in good condition, young and old alike are improving the health of America.

REVIEW EXERCISE A **Noun Phrases**

Each of the following sentences contains at least one noun phrase. Number a sheet of paper 1–10. Next to each number write the complete noun phrase or phrases from each sentence.

EXAMPLE You will enjoy the night sky better if you can recognize some of the well-known constellations.

the night sky, the well-known constellations

1. Bright groups of stars appear and disappear with the changing seasons.
2. Most people cannot tell if one star is brighter than another just by looking at it.

3. A very brilliant star might be very far away.
4. The very great distance would make it appear to shine with a faint light.
5. Astronomers call the brightness of a star its magnitude.
6. The sky is divided into eighty-eight constellations.
7. Some of the constellations were named by ancient stargazers.
8. The brightest star is known as the alpha of the constellation.
9. Lesser stars are named by using the other letters of the Greek alphabet.
10. A star map will help you find out where to look for each season's constellations.

REVIEW EXERCISE B **Verb Phrases**

Number a sheet of paper 1–10. Next to each number write the verb phrase from each of the following sentences.

EXAMPLE The alarm clock had been buzzing for a long time.

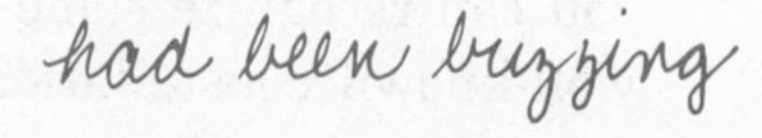

1. Lisa had hidden her head under the pillow.
2. If only she had not stayed up so late last night.
3. But the "Late Show" had certainly been good.
4. It had shown an old musical.
5. The hero had traveled north alone to the frozen Yukon.
6. She was looking for her long-lost brother.

7. But the law was also searching for him.
8. A Canadian Mountie had helped the hero.
9. Without his help, she would have vanished.
10. The movie did not seem very realistic.

REVIEW EXERCISE C Prepositional Phrases

Each of the following sentences contains a prepositional phrase. Number a sheet of paper 1–10. Next to each number write the prepositional phrase from each sentence. Underline each preposition and draw an arrow to its object in the prepositional phrase.

EXAMPLE Lightning is a rapid succession of big electrical sparks.

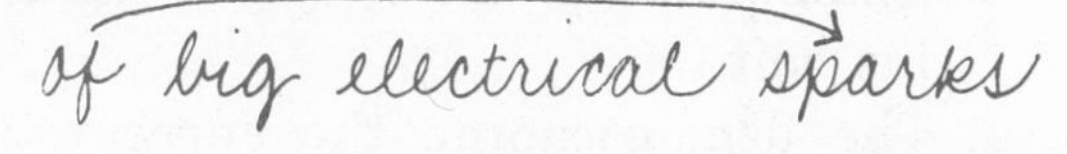

1. The roar of thunder usually follows lightning.
2. The air around a lightning flash is heated.
3. Expansion of the air results.
4. This pressure wave makes the sound of thunder.
5. Our knowledge of sound's speed enables us to tell how far away lightning is.
6. Start counting the seconds after a lightning flash.
7. Stop at the first thunder clap.
8. Divide the seconds by five.
9. You will now have the approximate mileage to the lightning stroke.
10. Heat lightning is light produced during distant storms.

REVIEW EXERCISE D **Participial Phrases**

Each of the following sentences contains a participial phrase. Number a sheet of paper 1–10. Next to each number write the participial phrase. Then write the noun or pronoun it modifies.

EXAMPLE Rafael, making his own trout flies, prepares for a fishing trip.

making his own trout flies, Rafael

1. Practicing his casting, Rafael swings his rod over and over.
2. His line, glistening in the sun, floats overhead.
3. Examining his line closely, he finds he still has his bait.
4. The fish, escaping the current, rest behind sunken logs and rocks.
5. Trying to catch a water skimmer, they flip out of the water.
6. Minnows, darting in shallow water, are a sign of bigger fish nearby.
7. A person looking for these signs caught a fish.
8. A shadow moving on the water scared the fish.
9. Carrying their lunches, many fishermen and women like to spend all day at the water.
10. Rafael, loving the sport, is one of these people.

CHAPTER

4

CLAUSES

Independent Clauses, Dependent Clauses

A clause is a group of words stating something about a person or thing. Some clauses need other words or statements to make their thought complete. Other clauses can stand alone. A clause that can stand alone is a complete sentence.

See Sentence, p. 459

THE PARTS OF A CLAUSE

4a A clause is a group of related words containing a subject and a predicate.

The *complete subject* of a clause contains all the words that describe the person or thing being talked about. The complete subject includes a noun or a pronoun or words that act as a noun or a pronoun. This noun or pronoun is called the *simple subject*. Other words may also belong to the complete subject.

See Noun, p. 454, Pronoun, p. 458

The *complete predicate* is made up of words that tell about an action or condition of the subject. The predicate includes a verb, called the *simple predicate*. Additional words may be part of the complete predicate as well.

See Verb, p. 462

EXAMPLES The sugar melted quickly.
[*The sugar* is the subject of the clause. *Melted quickly* tells what the sugar did. It is the predicate.]

When the sugar spilled into the sink
[*The sugar* is also the subject of this clause. *Spilled into the sink* tells what the sugar did. It is the predicate.]

Here are more examples of clauses. The complete subjects are underlined once and the complete predicates are underlined twice.

The freezer keeps food cold
If the electricity is shut off
Food melts

Hint: A clause cannot have a subject without a predicate or a predicate without a subject.

EXERCISE 1 Eight of the following word groups are clauses. The others are not. Write each clause on a sheet of paper. Underline the complete subject once and the complete predicate twice. If a word group is not a clause, write NC.

EXAMPLE People dream about fantastic voyages

People dream about fantastic voyages

1. A ship with gold sails
2. He pursued four finned monsters
3. With a magic sword strapped to his side and an invisible helmet on his head
4. Horses discussed politics in that land
5. He tried the princess's plan
6. The talking head bounced after him
7. Under the dragon's scaly wings
8. She struck swiftly
9. All the gold and silver as well
10. The king promised them half the treasure
11. Lands beyond the edge of the world
12. No one had ever come out alive
13. In the shining of her robes
14. When the excitement was over
15. The greatest adventure of all time

KINDS OF CLAUSES

The two kinds of clauses are *independent* and *dependent*.

Independent Clauses

4b An independent clause needs no other words to complete its thought.

EXAMPLES Spanish is spoken in many parts of the world.
Millions of Americans speak Spanish.

Independent clauses make complete statements. Each can stand by itself as a sentence, even if it is part of a larger sentence.

Two or more independent clauses may be joined into a single sentence.

EXAMPLE *Millions of Americans speak Spanish as their first language,* and *many others know it as a second language.* [In this example two independent clauses are joined by a comma and the conjunction *and.*]

See Punctuation, p. 318; Conjunction, p. 433

Dependent Clauses

4c A dependent clause needs other words to complete its thought.

A dependent clause *depends* on other words to complete it. Often these other words are an independent clause.

EXAMPLES When Thomas Jefferson built Monticello
[What was going on when Jefferson built Monticello? This dependent clause does not complete the thought. It needs an independent clause to go with it.]
When Thomas Jefferson built Monticello, he was still young.

After he had written the
Declaration of Independence
[What happened afterward? An
independent clause is needed to
answer the question.]
After he had written the
Declaration of Independence, he
returned home from Philadelphia.

Any dependent clause beginning with a subordinating conjunction and coming before an independent clause is separated from it with a comma.

See
Punctuation,
p. 317

Hint: Dependent clauses must be combined with independent clauses to make complete sentences.

EXERCISE 2 Six of the following clauses are independent. The others are dependent. Number a sheet of paper 1–12. Next to each number write *I* if the clause is independent. Write *D* if the clause is dependent.

EXAMPLE Before the Civil War's battles began
D

1. Bad feeling built up slowly on both sides
2. When shots were fired on Fort Sumter
3. Although people in the South did not want war
4. People should not own other people
5. Many were killed at Shiloh and Bull Run
6. Whenever the Union was threatened
7. After nurse Clara Barton established the Red Cross

8. Churches and barns were converted into hospitals
9. Lincoln spoke about the fallen men of Gettysburg
10. Although people tried to heal the wounds of the Civil War
11. If brother fights against brother
12. It was a tragic time in American history

EXERCISE 3 The following dependent clauses need more words to complete them. Write each clause on a sheet of paper. Add words to complete each dependent clause. Include the comma. Put a period at the end of each completed word group to show it is a sentence.

EXAMPLE If the office has an application form,

If the office has an application form, fill it out.

1. While you are in the office,
2. If you have time,
3. Whether or not you want to,
4. As soon as you complete the form,
5. Whenever you get the chance,
6. Even though others are ahead of you,

Kinds of Dependent Clauses

There are three kinds of dependent clauses: the *noun clause,* the *adjective clause,* and the *adverb clause.* Each of these dependent clauses works like a single part of speech in a sentence.

(1) A noun clause is a dependent clause used as a noun.

See Noun, p. 454

EXAMPLES What you find in the room
Whatever she wants

These dependent clauses serve as nouns in a sentence. To see how they work, look at the following sentence frame:

They should let her have ______.

A noun can fill the blank in this sentence.

EXAMPLE They should let her have *a flute.*

A noun clause can also fill the blank.

EXAMPLES They should let her have *what you find in the room.*
They should let her have *whatever she wants.*

In these examples the noun clause acts as the direct object of the verb. A noun clause may also serve as the subject of a sentence.

See Direct Object, p. 450; Subject, p. 460

EXAMPLE *Whoever comes* will be welcome.

Most noun clauses begin with one of the following words:

that
what
whatever
whichever
who
whoever
whom
whomever

Hint: Substitute the word *someone* or *something* for the clause. If either word completes the sentence, then the clause is a noun clause.

EXERCISE 4 Number a sheet of paper 1–10. Next to each number write the noun clause from each sentence.

EXAMPLE Whatever happens in the future should be planned now.

Whatever happens in the future

1. That a well-planned future will be better seems obvious.
2. Students in some high school courses imagine what the future will be like.
3. They begin with trends of today and try to predict what those trends might lead to.
4. They use whichever trends seem most likely to continue into the future.
5. They look at what effects population growth will have, for instance.
6. Some students decided that sports would be less violent in the future.
7. Which trends should continue is another question they discuss.
8. They learn that the process of change can be studied and sometimes guided.
9. Whoever takes a course like this becomes more thoughtful.
10. What happens to their world may be their responsibility, students realize.

(2) An adjective clause is a dependent clause used as an adjective.

See Adjective, p. 438

An adjective clause modifies a noun or pronoun, just as an adjective does. An adjective clause is also called a *relative clause* because it relates to a noun or pronoun.

EXAMPLES Jane Hickenlooper gave a shout *that scared the baby.*
[The adjective clause is *that scared the baby.* It modifies the noun *shout.* The clause tells what kind of shout it was.]

Teresa Ortiz had the ticket *that won the prize.*
[The adjective clause *that won the prize* tells which ticket she had.]

Anyone *who came after five o'clock* was forced to wait outside.
[The adjective clause *who came after five o'clock* modifies the word *anyone.*]

The show *that they came to see* was postponed.
[The adjective clause *that they came to see* modifies *show.*]

Notice that in each example the adjective clause follows the noun or pronoun it modifies.

Hint: The adjective clause always comes right after the word it modifies.

The most frequently used words that introduce adjective clauses are as follows:

that	whom
which	whose
who	

EXERCISE 5 Number a sheet of paper 1–6. Next to each number write the adjective clause in the sentence.

EXAMPLE Janet Guthrie is the first woman who has qualified to race at Indianapolis.

who has qualified to race at Indianapolis

1. The first Indianapolis race that Guthrie qualified for was in 1977.
2. Unfortunately, the car that she drove did not work right during the race.
3. She was stopped by mechanical problems that kept coming back.
4. She is a driver whose skill deserves better luck.
5. Guthrie has plans that include many more successful races.
6. She is a woman whom many male drivers are pleased to race against.

See Adverb, p. 438

(3) An adverb clause is a dependent clause used as an adverb.

An adverb clause works like an adverb in a sentence. This means it can modify a verb, an adjective, or another adverb. An adverb clause begins with a subordinating conjunction such as *after, before,* or *when.*

See Conjunctions, pp. 58–59

Example of an adverb clause that modifies a verb:

The water circulates *as it is heated.*
[The adverb clause modifies the verb *circulates.*]

Example of an adverb clause that modifies an adjective:

Luisa was proud *that she had hooked up the pipes.*
[The adverb clause modifies the adjective *proud.*]

Example of an adverb clause that modifies an adverb:

Antonia sang more quietly *than she had sung before.*
[This adverb clause modifies the adverb *more quietly.*]

Hint: An adverb clause works in a sentence the way an adverb does.

EXERCISE 6 Number your paper 1–12. Next to each number write the adverb clause from the sentence.

EXAMPLE When people rushed to the West in search of gold, they left family and friends behind.

When people rushed to the West in search of gold

1. Since both land and sea travel were very slow, mail took over a month to go from East to West.
2. Miners and other settlers were unhappy that news from home took so long to reach them.
3. Doing without letters from the East often seemed harder than doing without new clothes or fresh food supplies.
4. Before many years had passed, each mining camp had a mail delivery.
5. Whenever a shipment of mail arrived in a western city, a man and a mule carried letters to the distant mining camps.
6. If people would pay a lot to get letters more quickly, a faster mail service might be profitable.
7. Three men thought of a way to deliver mail by relay across the country faster than it had ever gone before.
8. After planning their idea, they named their service the Pony Express.
9. Because the service depended on riders and horses, the men obtained only the finest of both.
10. The last Pony Express rider, racing through deserts, arrived in California ten days after the first rider started.
11. When the Californians saw the rider coming, they threw their hats in the air and cheered.
12. Although the Pony Express lasted only eighteen months and lost money, its story was a glorious chapter in the history of the West.

Sometimes an adjective clause can be shortened. For example, the adjective clause in the following sentence need not be as long as it is.

EXAMPLES

FULL ADJECTIVE CLAUSE	The helmet *that a football player wears* is strong but light.
SHORTENED ADJECTIVE CLAUSE	The helmet *a football player wears* is strong but light.
SHORTENED ADJECTIVE CLAUSE MADE INTO A PARTICIPIAL PHRASE	The helmet *worn by a football player* is strong and light.

The different ways of writing an adjective clause make it possible for you to vary your writing style. You may wish to use one or another way to change the emphasis.

An adverb clause may also be shortened.

EXAMPLES

FULL ADVERB CLAUSE	*As he fell,* Vinnie grabbed at the rope.
SHORTENED TO A PARTICIPLE	*Falling*, Vinnie grabbed at the rope.
FULL ADVERB CLAUSE	*When they were finished,* the girls left the room.
SHORTENED ADVERB CLAUSE (SUBJECT UNDERSTOOD)	*When finished,* the girls left the room.

EXERCISE 7 On a sheet of paper rewrite each sentence by shortening the adjective or adverb clause. Each clause is in italics.

EXAMPLE Some of the animals *that live in and around a northern stream* seem to have a civilization of their own.

Some of the animals living in and around a northern stream seem to have a civilization of their own.

1. A pair of beavers *that work year-round* build a home on a stream.
2. *As they cut down trees and drag them across the stream,* the water backs up in a meadow above.
3. *When they have stacked trees and branches across the stream,* the beavers pack mud and twigs against the wood.
4. The dam *that the beavers build* serves as their home.
5. *After they have made a home in the dam,* they sometimes breed a family.
6. *Since they are completely safe from enemies,* beavers appear fearless.
7. *As it floods the meadow above the beaver dam,* the stream becomes a pond.
8. Many large and small animals *that a pond supports* make their home above a beaver dam.

REVIEW EXERCISE A **Dependent and Independent Clauses**

The following clauses are either dependent or independent. Number a sheet of paper 1–10. Next to each number write *I* if the clause is independent and *D* if it is dependent.

EXAMPLE When you walk into a room

D

1. If your shoulders are hunched and bent
2. Because you make no eye contact
3. You seem unfriendly
4. Although you may feel shy
5. Body language speaks to others
6. Normal eye contacts last about one second
7. If you want to show friendliness
8. Hold another person's gaze longer
9. Most listeners have more eye contact
10. Frequent blinking may be a sign of tension

REVIEW EXERCISE B Noun Clauses

Each of the following sentences contains a noun clause. Number a sheet of paper 1–10. Next to each number write the noun clause from the sentence.

EXAMPLE Who I am is not important.

Who I am

1. What is going on in your mind is known to me.
2. You believe that I am a stranger.
3. But the truth is that I know you very well.
4. I have been watching what you do.
5. How I have done it will surprise you.
6. Did you know that I live in your mirror?
7. I will demonstrate for you that I can walk into it now.
8. Whoever sees me will not believe it.

9. I can tell that you are frightened and astonished.
10. Smile; do not feel that you must be afraid of me.

REVIEW EXERCISE C Adjective Clauses

Number a sheet of paper 1–10. Next to each number, write the adjective clause from the sentence. Then write the noun or pronoun the clause modifies.

EXAMPLE Agatha Christie was a mystery writer who gave pleasure to millions of people.

who gave pleasure to millions of people, writer

1. The books that she has written have sold over three hundred million copies.
2. She also wrote a play, *The Mousetrap,* which holds the record for the longest continuous run in one theater.
3. It was her mother who encouraged her writing.
4. Singing was the talent that Agatha Christie wanted to develop.
5. Her voice, which was good, was not of star quality.
6. During World War I, she wrote the novel that was to become her first real success.
7. The detective who was featured in it was Hercule Poirot.

8. Many consider Hercule Poirot to be a fictional hero who ranks as one of the greatest detectives of all time.
9. Agatha Christie herself was once part of a mystery that was never quite solved.
10. She disappeared from home with amnesia and was later found through an anonymous letter that described her whereabouts.

REVIEW EXERCISE D Adverb Clauses

Following is a list of adverb clauses. Write a complete sentence using each adverb clause that is given.

EXAMPLE Unless you know how to refinish furniture

Unless you know how to refinish furniture, you had better read up on it before you begin work on that chair.

1. Although it is not a hard job to learn
2. If you have no furniture stripping solution
3. After you have applied it
4. Since you have to scrape off the old varnish
5. Because it takes a long time
6. As soon as you have done that
7. After you have finished sanding
8. If you are going to use a wood stain
9. Until it dries
10. When you have oiled and varnished your chair

CHAPTER

5

SENTENCES

When you want to share your thoughts with another person, you may choose to write them. If you do, you will put them across most effectively if you use *sentences.* A sentence expresses a complete thought about someone or something. By learning to write sentences well, you are practicing a basic skill of English.

THE SENTENCE

5a A sentence is a group of related words that expresses a complete thought.

See Sentence Problems, pp. 144–149

Be careful not to write *fragments* instead of sentences. A fragment expresses only part of a complete thought.

EXAMPLES

SENTENCES We saw apples growing on trees.
Cows like to eat old apples.

FRAGMENTS Apples growing on trees
Like to eat old apples

Don't be fooled by the words in fragments. Sometimes they seem to state a complete thought. Study them carefully. You will find that some information is missing.

EXERCISE 1 Number a sheet of paper 1–8. Some of the following word groups are sentences. Some are fragments. Write *S* next to the number of each sentence. Add words to each fragment to make it a sentence.

EXAMPLE Bad auto accident

There was a bad auto accident.

1. A terrible car crash
2. They rushed to save the man's life
3. Police cars rushed to the scene
4. Sirens screaming on the highway
5. It was almost too late
6. The ambulance lights flashing
7. Someone cried
8. Glass and metal all over the road

5b A simple sentence must contain a subject and a predicate.

The Subject

(1) The subject of a sentence is what the sentence tells about.

See Noun, p. 454; Pronoun, p. 458

Most sentences have a noun or pronoun as the subject.

EXAMPLES Painters with brushes worked across the billboard.
[Who or what is doing the action? Is it the painters or the brushes? Answer: *painters*. *Painters* is the subject.]

The letters on the sign were clearly visible.
[Who or what is being talked about? Answer: *letters*. *Letters* is the subject.]

Hint: To find the subject of a sentence, ask: *Who or what is doing the action?* If there is no action in the sentence, then ask: *Who or what is being talked about?*

The single noun or pronoun that serves as the subject of a sentence is called the *simple subject*. Words that modify the simple subject are grouped with it in the *complete subject*.

EXAMPLES

simple subject: letters

The bright red letters on the sign glistened in the sunlight.

complete subject: The bright red letters on the sign

simple subject: One

One of the letters was painted green.

complete subject: One of the letters

A prepositional phrase may be a part of the complete subject. In the first sentence, the prepositional phrase *on the sign* is part of the complete subject. In the second sentence, the prepositional phrase *of the letters* is part of that complete subject.

EXERCISE 2 Number a sheet of paper 1–10. Write the complete subject of each sentence that follows. Underline the simple subject.

EXAMPLE The document on the wall was almost lost.

The document on the wall

1. A copy of the Declaration of Independence hung in a courthouse in White Plains, New York.
2. The old, dirty copy did not seem very interesting.
3. None of the hundreds of visitors to the courthouse paid any attention to it.
4. Over the years, armies of janitors dusted it with their mops.
5. The ancient courthouse was finally going to be torn down.

6. One man took a new look at the old piece of paper.
7. The historical society studied it, too.
8. One of the oldest copies of the Declaration had been hanging in that courthouse.
9. This copy was written only a few days after Jefferson wrote the original Declaration itself.
10. A quarter of a million dollars was the price of the copy of the Declaration from that courthouse.

The Predicate

See Verb, p. 462

(2) The predicate of a sentence is the verb and related words that tell something about the subject.

The complete predicate in a sentence is made up of the verb and all the other words closely related to the verb. The *simple predicate* is made up of the complete verb, which includes the main verb and its auxiliaries. The main verb and its auxiliaries may also be called the *verb phrase.*

See Phrases, pp. 68–69

EXAMPLES Juanita Cortes lives in a magic castle.
[What does the subject do? Answer: *lives in a magic castle. Lives* is the verb or simple predicate. The complete predicate is *lives in a magic castle.*]

She is very happy.
[The verb or simple predicate is the one word *is.* The complete predicate includes the verb and its related words: *is very happy.*]

Hint: To find the predicate in a sentence, ask either of these questions: *What does (or did) the subject do?* or *What tells about the condition of the subject?*

EXERCISE 3 Number a sheet of paper 1–10. Next to each number write the complete predicate from each sentence. Underline the verb that is the simple predicate.

EXAMPLE An early toy for throwing and catching was a pie tin.

was a pie tin

1. Today, throwing a dish-like plastic toy is a popular sport.
2. The round object flies through the air for many feet.
3. Players invent new kinds of games.
4. Teams play football with it.
5. The players spin the toy back and forth.
6. The playing field is about twenty meters long.
7. Seven people are on each team.
8. Some teams compete for world championships.
9. At one college you can study the theory of the toy's flight.
10. Some of the longest throws are over 120 meters.

Hint: Every sentence must have at least one subject and one predicate.

Once you have a subject and a predicate in a sentence, you can add words to those parts to explain them more exactly or make them more interesting.

EXAMPLE The castle sparkles.
The magic castle with a dozen towers sparkles brilliantly in the morning sun.

Adding to the simple subject and the simple predicate to make longer sentences can enrich your writing. However, take care that you do not overdo the expansion. Sometimes two or three short sentences are better than a long sentence.

EXAMPLES

OVEREXPANDED SENTENCE Even though she sometimes wanted to leave, Juanita, who often grew tired of her magic castle, would not have known how to live a simple life outside her rich surroundings.

SHORTER SENTENCES Juanita often grew tired of her magic castle. She sometimes wanted to leave. However, she would not have known how to live a simple life outside her rich surroundings.

EXERCISE 4 Following is a list of five simple subjects and simple predicates. Use these words in sentences of your own. On a sheet of paper write sentences by adding modifiers to each subject and predicate.

EXAMPLE Students invent games.

Clever students invent various team games of skill.

1. Avalanches slide.
2. Waterfalls tumble.
3. Snakes slither.
4. Sharks eat fish.
5. Plumbers work.
6. Truckers drive.

Sentences may also be expanded by adding another subject or another predicate.

Compound Subject and Compound Predicate

(3) A compound subject is made up of two or more complete subjects in a sentence.

The compound subjects in a sentence are often connected by a coordinating conjunction such as *and, or,* or *but.*

See Conjunction, p. 443

EXAMPLES *Yvonne* and *Mattie* listen to their records together.
All of the children but *none of the adults* were there.

EXERCISE 5 Each of the following sentences has a compound subject. Write each sentence on a sheet of paper. Underline each part of the compound subject.

EXAMPLE The demons and evil spirits of the night terrify superstitious people.

The demons and evil spirits of the night terrify superstitious people.

1. Vampires and werewolves haunt the human imagination.
2. Garlic or a ray of sunlight will terrify a vampire.
3. Werewolves and vampires may take animal shapes on moonlit nights.
4. Many novels and stories have been written about these creatures.
5. Were-tigers in Malaya and were-leopards in Africa add to the list of "human animals."
6. Some unusual vampires and other evil spirits come from Bulgaria.
7. Count Dracula and Frankenstein have both become known from books and movies.
8. Both young readers and adult readers have been thrilled by these bloody accounts.

(4) A compound predicate is made up of two or more verbs and their related words.

EXAMPLES

verb

Both girls *like country music* but

complete predicate

verb

also play some classical music.

complete predicate

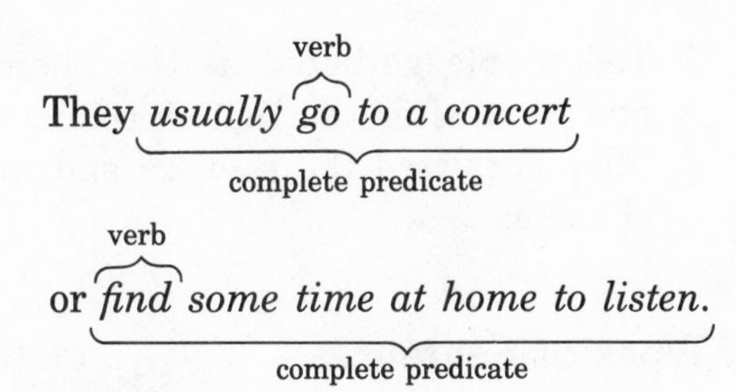
verb
They usually go to a concert
complete predicate
verb
or find some time at home to listen.
complete predicate

EXERCISE 6 Following are eight sentences with compound predicates. Write each sentence on a sheet of paper. Underline both parts of the compound predicate.

EXAMPLE A Revolutionary War hero rode through the night and warned people about the British.

A Revolutionary War hero <u>rode through the night</u> and <u>warned people about the British.</u>

1. One rainy night in April 1777, Sybil Ludington put her brothers and sisters to bed and helped them say their prayers.
2. A man rode up to the house and told her father terrible news.
3. British soldiers had burned and robbed the town of Danbury.
4. Sybil's father had to go right away but needed someone to alert other people.
5. Sybil rode through the night and warned all the people in the countryside.
6. She galloped three times as far as Paul Revere and was never stopped.

7. The people gathered at the Ludingtons' house and went after the British soldiers.
8. They surprised the soldiers and captured many of them.

Types of Sentences

The four types of sentences are *simple, compound, complex*, and *compound-complex*. What type a sentence is depends on the kind and number of clauses in it.

See Clauses, pp. 83–85

5c A simple sentence contains one independent clause.

EXAMPLES The lead guitar plays the melody.
The drums provide the basic rhythm.

Each of the examples is a simple sentence. Each one is made up of one independent clause. Remember that a dependent clause cannot stand alone as a sentence. Only an independent clause can do this.

5d A compound sentence contains two or more independent clauses.

EXAMPLES *The bass guitar usually plays harmony,* but *now and then it plays the melody.*

The melody may be in a different key, and *later it may come back to the original key.*

In each of these examples the two independent clauses are joined by a comma and a conjunction. This is the most common way that two independent clauses are joined.

See Punctuation, p. 318

However, a semicolon without a conjunction is sometimes used to join the clauses. If the two clauses are closely related, the semicolon works well.

See Punctuation, p. 323

EXAMPLES The entire band plays several bars; then one instrument picks up the melody.

The soloist varies the melody; the other players provide harmony.

Hint: Independent clauses in a compound sentence are joined as follows:
Independent clause, (**conjunction**) independent clause
or
Independent clause; independent clause

Whenever a compound sentence has more than two clauses, the clauses are joined together as items in a series. That is, a comma is used between each clause. Between the next-to-last and the last clause a comma and a coordinating conjunction are used.

See Punctuation, p. 308

EXAMPLE The entire band played the melody through once, the lead guitar played a long solo, *and* the band then repeated the melody at the finish.

EXERCISE 7 Some of the following sentences are simple sentences. Some are compound sentences. Number a sheet of paper 1–10. Next to each number write *S* if the sentence is simple. Write *C* if the sentence is compound.

EXAMPLE Little-known explorers have revealed important parts of North America.

1. Esteban, a Black man, helped to find a route across the American Southwest.
2. He and two other men crossed America from the Atlantic Ocean to the Pacific.
3. They were looking for wealth, for they had heard about the famous Seven Cities of Gold.
4. These Native American cities might hold wonderful treasures, but no explorer could find them.
5. Esteban had been a slave, but on this trip he was a leader.
6. Esteban asked many Native Americans about the fabulous Cities of Gold.
7. At last Esteban saw a city finer than those in his richest dreams.
8. Brightly colored cliffs shone like towers of gold, but the Native American village was really only a small one.
9. The inhabitants attacked the group, and Esteban was killed.
10. Esteban was wrong about the cities, but his sense of adventure pointed a way through the new land.

5e A complex sentence is made up of one or more dependent clauses combined with an independent clause.

The two clauses in a complex sentence are closely related. The dependent clause usually qualifies the idea stated in the independent clause.

EXAMPLE When you press this button, the bell rings.
[The independent clause is *the bell rings*. This clause could stand alone as a complete simple sentence. However, the dependent clause *when you press this button* is related to it. The dependent clause tells something about the idea in the independent clause.]

A dependent clause cannot stand alone as a sentence. Nonetheless, it plays an important part in the complex sentence. It often tells *when, why,* or *in what way* about the idea in the independent clause. Notice in the following examples how the dependent clauses and the independent clauses are closely tied.

EXAMPLES The audience will respond if the music is good.
[The independent clause is *the audience will respond. If the music is good* is the dependent clause. It cannot stand alone as a complete sentence. Yet it is important to the meaning of the whole complex sentence.]

When the music becomes really forceful, the audience claps and cheers.
[The independent clause, *the audience claps and cheers,* could be a sentence by itself. The dependent clause with it, *when the music becomes really forceful,* helps clarify the meaning of the whole sentence.]

EXERCISE 8 The following sentences are complex, compound, or simple. Number a sheet of paper 1–10. Next to the number of a complex sentence write *Cx*. Next to the number of a compound sentence write *C*. Next to the number of a simple sentence write *S*.

EXAMPLE Gold has been one of America's great attractions, but only a few have found it.
C

1. Old Doc Noss told people that he had found a cave full of gold bars.
2. After Noss had taken out some of the bars, a dynamite accident sealed off the cave.
3. Then Noss and another man had a fight, and Noss was killed.
4. After the story of Noss spread around, many people began to look for the lost cave with its gold.
5. They hunted all around Victoria Peak, but no one could find a cave.

6. To this day, people are still hunting for Doc Noss's gold.
7. Some have gone to the mountain with metal detectors and radar.
8. The mountain is on a missile range, so the Army does not like these visitors.
9. Some people finally found a cave, but there was no gold in it.
10. The legend of Doc Noss's fabulous gold probably will never die.

5f A compound-complex sentence contains two or more independent clauses and one or more dependent clauses.

EXAMPLE The band played across the country, and it repeated performances in several locations whenever there was a special demand for the music. [The dependent clause is *whenever there was a special demand for the music*. The two independent clauses are *the band played across the country* and *it repeated performances in several locations*.]

EXERCISE 9 The following sentences are of several kinds. Number a sheet of paper 1–12. Next to each number write one of the following symbols to show what kind of a sentence each is: *S* (simple), *C* (compound), *Cx* (complex), *CCx* (compound-complex).

EXAMPLE When they get cold, most warm-blooded animals automatically begin to shiver.

1. Many warm-blooded creatures, including human beings, shiver to keep warm.
2. The shivering of the body causes the body cells to give off more heat, and the heat acts against the cold.
3. Certain animals use another system to fight cold, however.
4. The system is an increase in the burning of body fat, but there is no shivering.
5. The baby harp seal is born into arctic temperatures well below freezing; since it has no layer of blubber fat, the baby should not be able to live.
6. The baby seal's body does have special muscle cells and fat cells that burn to produce heat.
7. Called "brown fat," the tissue is found in seals, bats, and other animals.
8. The heat from brown fat means that a newborn seal lying alone on the ice can stay alive even though the temperature is –30°C.
9. When a hibernating bat is asleep, its body temperature is naturally low; when it wakes up, its temperature quickly rises from the sudden burning of brown fat.
10. Nonshivering body warmth is a vital means some animals have for saving their lives.
11. We humans are not so lucky, but we have made warm clothes to put on in cold weather.

12. Of course, if you have forgotten a coat or sweater and get caught out in the cold, you will start shivering; you had better find a warm place, or you could catch a cold.

EXERCISE 10 Following are sets of independent clauses. Combine them into compound or complex sentences. Use the conjunctions in the list at the beginning of the exercise. You may change a few words to make clauses fit together. You should have six sentences when you are finished.

EXAMPLE Every age seems to have its popular music.
Not everyone likes the popular music.

Every age seems to have its popular music, even if the music is not always popular with everybody.

even	and
as	yet
when	before
but	

1. Ragtime became the rage.
   World War I was being fought.
2. Jazz was born in America.
   Ragtime was becoming popular.
3. We discover that jazz has roots in the rhythms and melodies of the Black people in America.
   We search for the beginnings of jazz.

4. Some say the origins of jazz go back to ancient African songs.
   No one has an accurate record.
5. Calypso music was born in the Caribbean.
   It has also become widely popular in this century.
6. Rock music first gained a following in the 1950's.
   Who knows how long it will remain on top?

The Purposes of Sentences

You have a purpose in writing a sentence. You may, for example, want to give some information or ask a question. You may also want to request something or just express some idea or feeling. Four kinds of sentences are useful for these purposes. The four kinds are called *declarative, interrogative, imperative,* and *exclamatory.*

Sometimes you can tell what kind a sentence is by how its words are put together.

5g A declarative sentence declares a fact, an opinion, or a feeling.

EXAMPLES The band played a familiar piece for the crowd.
The next piece was new to the audience.

Most declarative sentences begin with the subject. The predicate follows the subject. A declarative sentence always ends with a period (**.**).

5h An interrogative sentence asks a question.

EXAMPLES Do you know the name of that piece?
Where have we heard that before?

An interrogative sentence always ends with a question mark (?). In most interrogative sentences the positions of the subject and the verb are switched, and the main verb or the auxiliary verb comes before the subject.

See Punctuation, p. 306

EXAMPLES

DECLARATIVE SENTENCE	That song was an old tune.
INTERROGATIVE SENTENCE	Was that song an old tune?

When an auxiliary verb such as a form of the verb *do* is used, only the form of *do* comes before the subject.

EXAMPLES

DECLARATIVE SENTENCE	We know that song.
INTERROGATIVE SENTENCE	*Do* we know that song?

5i An imperative sentence requests or orders something.

EXAMPLES Turn off the music.
Find some news.

The purpose of an imperative sentence is to request something of someone. You may name the person you are requesting to do something.

EXAMPLE Barbie, stop playing that music.

Sometimes the person you are addressing does not need to be named.

EXAMPLE Stop playing that music.

Although the person is not named in some imperative sentences, it is understood that the sentence is addressed to someone. The subject is understood to be *you.* This is true even though the word *you* is not in the sentence.

See Punctuation, p. 305

An imperative sentence usually ends with a period (.).

5j An exclamatory sentence expresses shock or surprise.

EXAMPLES The crowd is going wild!
Who would have thought we'd be in such trouble!

See Punctuation, p. 307

An exclamatory sentence ends with an exclamation point (!).

EXERCISE 11 Number a sheet of paper 1–10. After each number tell what kind of sentence each of the following is. Mark *D* for declarative, *I* for interrogative, *Im* for imperative, and *E* for exclamatory. Then write the missing end punctuation.

EXAMPLE Did the boys go to the beach for their party

I, ?

1. Can you come to the beach party
2. Bring the hot dogs and the buns
3. Help, I've got sand in my pickle relish
4. The high tide is almost in
5. The waves are so beautiful
6. Is it safe to go surfing
7. I think it's all right
8. Wait for the biggest wave
9. Your grandfather must have been a fish
10. Was that a shark

Completers

Often the complete predicate of a sentence will contain a word called a *completer* because it completes or makes clear what the subject and verb are telling about. Completers may be either *objects* or *subject completers*.

5k The direct object receives the action of the verb.

EXAMPLE Consuela waved her scarf. [*Scarf* receives the action of the verb *waved*. It is the direct object in the sentence.]

Hint: Here are the steps to find the direct object of an action verb:
Find the verb. In the example the verb is *waved*.
Ask: *Who or what waved?*
Answer: *Consuela. Consuela* is the subject of the sentence.

Ask: *Who or what did Consuela wave?* Answer: *her scarf. Scarf* is the direct object of the action verb *waved.*

EXERCISE 12 Number a sheet of paper 1–5. Write the direct object of the action verb in each sentence.

EXAMPLE Ms. Passmore spaded the garden.

garden

1. She mixed fertilizer into the soil.
2. She picked up the hoe.
3. Carefully she turned the ground.
4. At last she planted the seeds.
5. A few months later she ate fresh green peas.

See Linking Verbs, pp. 33–34

5l The subject completer follows the linking verb and completes the meaning of the sentence.

A subject completer may be a noun, a pronoun, an adjective, or an adverb. A subject completer that is a noun or a pronoun names the person or thing the sentence is talking about.

EXAMPLES Mary Tsai was the *leader.*
The winner was *she.*

See Adjective, p. 438

A subject completer that is an adjective describes or modifies the person or thing the sentence is talking about.

EXAMPLE Mary seemed *sad.*

A subject completer that is an adverb is a word such as *here* or *there.*

EXAMPLE The answer is *there.*

Hint: Here are the steps to follow to find the subject completer:
Find the linking verb. In the first example, the verb is *was.*
Find the subject. Ask: *Who or what was?*
Answer: *Mary Tsai.*
Then ask: *Mary Tsai was who, what, or where?*
Answer: the *leader. Leader* is the subject completer.

EXERCISE 13 Number a sheet of paper 1–5. Next to each number write the subject completer in the sentence.

EXAMPLE School elections are exciting.

1. Jean seemed anxious yesterday.
2. She is a candidate in the school elections.
3. It was she who ran last year.
4. Jean looks more confident this year.
5. She will undoubtedly become calmer as the elections progress.

Sentence Patterns

The words and word groups in any English sentence are put together in a certain pattern. All but a few English sentences follow one of the following patterns.

Sentence Pattern 1: SUBJECT-VERB (S-V)

See Intransitive Verbs, pp. 32–33

Sentence Pattern 1 is made up of a subject and an intransitive verb.

EXAMPLES	SUBJECT	VERB
	The wind	stopped.
	The boat	drifted.

The basic S-V pattern can be expanded with modifiers of the simple subject and the verb.

EXAMPLE The boat (S) full of tired passengers drifted (V) without direction in a wide curve.

The subject and the verb may be compounded.

EXAMPLE The boat (S) and the low waves (S) rose (V) and fell (V) together.

However, even when modifiers are added, or the subject and predicate are compounded, a sentence is a Pattern 1 sentence as long as it contains only subjects and intransitive verbs.

Hint: As you study a sentence pattern, learn first how to find the simple subject and the verb. Take the following steps:
Find the verb. Ask: *What is the action or condition that the sentence tells about?* In the last example, the answer is *rose* and *fell*. *Rose* and *fell* are the verbs.
Find the subject. Ask: *Who or what does the action being described?*
Answer: *boat* and *waves*. *Boat* and *waves* are the compound subject.

EXERCISE 14 Copy the following sentences on a sheet of paper. Put *S* above each subject and *V* above each verb.

EXAMPLE The horses prepared for the race.

S V
The horses prepared for the race.

1. The bay mare paced swiftly.
2. The crowd in the stands cheered loudly.
3. The young men and women in the stable area stopped and listened.
4. Only one young woman did not pause.
5. She worked and waited for the bay mare.

Sentence Pattern 2: SUBJECT-VERB-OBJECT (S-V-O)

See Transitive Verbs, pp. 32–33

Sentence Pattern 2 is made up of a subject, a transitive verb, and an object. This pattern is probably used more than any other in English. Pattern 2 allows a sentence to tell of action being done by someone or something to another person or thing.

EXAMPLES

SUBJECT	VERB	DIRECT OBJECT
The waves	lifted	the boat.
The fresh wind	pushed	it.

Sentence Pattern 2 may be expanded with other words. These words are usually modifiers of the subject, the verb, or the object.

EXAMPLE The fresh wind (S), gusting strongly at times, pushed (V) the rudderless boat (O) in a southerly direction.

Hint: As you study S-V-O sentences, you can find the basic parts by taking the following steps:
Find the verb. Ask: *What is the action?*
Answer: *pushed.* The verb is *pushed.*
Find the subject. Ask: *Who or what does the action?*
Answer: *wind. Wind* is the subject.
Find the object. Ask: *Who or what receives the action?*
Answer: *boat.* The object is *boat.*

EXERCISE 15 Write the following sentences on a sheet of paper. Some are S-V pattern sentences (Pattern 1), and some are S-V-O pattern sentences (Pattern 2). Put *S* above each subject, *V* above each verb, and *O* above each object. Then identify each sentence as Pattern 1 or Pattern 2.

EXAMPLE The speaker called her name.

The speaker called her name. Pattern 2

1. Juanita raised her hand.
2. Nobody saw her.
3. Her friends and relatives stood patiently and waited for her.
4. Juanita rose from her seat and walked slowly forward.
5. Her curly head of hair appeared suddenly above the railing.

Sentence Pattern 2a: SUBJECT-VERB-INDIRECT OBJECT-DIRECT OBJECT (S-V-IO-DO)

Sentence Pattern 2a is made up of a subject, a transitive verb, an indirect object, and a direct object. The only difference between Pattern 2 and Pattern 2a is the addition of an indirect object in Pattern 2a. The indirect object tells to whom or for whom something is done.

PATTERN 2 The captain (S) gave (V) some water (O) to the passengers.

PATTERN 2a The captain (S) gave (V) the passengers (IO) some water (DO).

Hint: As you study S-V-IO-DO sentences, look for the basic parts. You can find them by taking the following steps:
Find the verb. Ask: *What is the action?* In the example above, the answer is *gave*. *Gave* is the verb.
Find the subject. Ask: *Who or what gave?* Answer: the *captain*. *Captain* is the subject.
Find the direct object. Ask: *Who or what was given?*
Answer: *water*. *Water* is the direct object.
Find the indirect object. Ask: *To whom did the captain give water?*
Answer: *passengers*. The indirect object is *passengers*.

EXERCISE 16 Write the numbers 1–8 on a sheet of paper. After each number write the subject in the sentence. Put *S* after it. Then write the complete verb, followed by *V*. Next, write the indirect object and *IO*. Finally, write the direct object and *DO*.

EXAMPLE A trial lawyer must offer the jury proof for arguments.

lawyer S, must offer V, jury IO, proof DO

1. A butcher must sell customers good meat to stay in business.
2. A roofer builds homeowners a sound roof to avoid leaks.

3. A doctor gives patients good medical treatment to maintain their health.
4. Citizens pay the government taxes in order for the country to keep running.
5. Textbooks offer readers lessons in a variety of subjects.
6. Rangers show visitors the sights of our national parks.
7. Posted signs tell tourists the background information about landmarks.
8. Tourists in the parks should not offer wildlife the food they eat.

A Pattern 2a sentence can be changed to become a Pattern 2 sentence by moving the indirect object so that it follows the direct object. Change the indirect object into a prepositional phrase beginning with *to* or *for*. The sentence then becomes a Pattern 2 sentence.

EXAMPLES

PATTERN 2a Rita Gogol (S) brought (V) Mrs. Allsop (IO) some fruit (DO).

PATTERN 2 Rita Gogol (S) brought (V) some fruit (DO) for Mrs. Allsop.

This change from a Pattern 2a sentence to a Pattern 2 sentence is one kind of variation you can use in writing. Variety in sentence patterns makes your writing more interesting while keeping its meaning clear.

EXERCISE 17 On a sheet of paper rewrite the following Pattern 2a sentences. Make each sentence a Pattern 2 sentence.

EXAMPLE Construction engineers give bridges some supports.

Construction engineers give some supports to bridges.

1. One kind of fan gives the air a push.
2. Another kind of fan gives a team loud applause.
3. One kind of coach gives passengers a ride.
4. Another kind of coach gives players some instruction.
5. One kind of spring gives tired people a soft rest.
6. Another kind of spring gives thirsty people refreshment.

Sentence Pattern 3: SUBJECT-LINKING VERB-SUBJECT COMPLETER (S-LV-SC)

See Completer, p. 442

Sentence Pattern 3 is made up of a subject, a linking verb, and a subject completer. A subject completer may be an adjective, a noun, a pronoun or an adverb. Sentence Pattern 3 usually says something about the subject.

EXAMPLE The woman was tall.

The subject of this Pattern 3 sentence is *woman*. The linking verb *was* ties together the subject with the subject completer *tall*. *Tall* is an adjective that describes the subject.

Here are more examples of Pattern 3 sentences.

ADJECTIVE COMPLETER The goat (S) seems (LV) thirsty (SC).

NOUN COMPLETER The girl (S) became (LV) a woman (SC).

Hint: You can find the parts of a Pattern 3 sentence by taking these steps:
Find the linking verb. In the first example, the verb is *seems*.
Find the subject. Ask: *Who or what seems?*
Answer: *goat. Goat* is the subject.
Find the subject completer. Ask: *What does the goat seem?*
Answer: *thirsty. Thirsty* is the subject completer.

EXERCISE 18 On a sheet of paper write the numbers 1–10. From each sentence write the subject of the sentence followed by *S*. Then write the linking verb and *LV*. Finally, write the subject completer and *SC*.

EXAMPLE Hunger is painful.
Hunger S, is LV, painful SC

1. A boy became hungry.
2. He felt ravenous.
3. His appetite was tremendous.
4. His pockets, however, were empty.
5. He looked desperate.
6. His hands were clenched.
7. He was undecided.

8. Then he became employed.
9. Soon his luck seemed good.
10. His pockets were full.

5m Some sentence patterns can be reversed.

Sentence Pattern 2 can be reversed to form Sentence Pattern 1. In that case, the original subject will no longer be the subject. Instead it follows the verb in a prepositional phrase beginning with *by.* The object becomes the subject and comes before the verb.

EXAMPLE

PATTERN 2 Mrs. Aramburu (S) met (V) Doug (O) at the airport.

PATTERN 1 Doug (S) was met (V) by Mrs. Aramburu at the airport.

Remember that the subject of the original Pattern 2 sentence is no longer the subject of the reversed sentence.

Note also that the form of the verb changes when the Pattern 2 sentence is reversed. The main verb takes an auxiliary. In the above example, the auxiliary verb is *was.* This makes the complete verb *was met.*

See Voice, p. 462

This form of the verb is called the *passive voice.* It changes from the *active voice,* which is the original form of the action verb. The following examples show more verbs in the passive voice.

Doug *has been sent* by the State Department.
He *was trained* in foreign affairs.
He *had been assigned* by the authorities to make this trip.

If you use the passive voice too often, you weaken the force of your writing. Therefore, use the passive voice and Pattern 1 sentences with care, mostly when the subject of a Pattern 2 sentence is not known or is of no importance.

EXAMPLES A telegram had been sent ahead of him.
His passport was approved in advance.

When you find sentences in your writing that seem weak, look to see whether they are reversed Pattern 2 sentences. The passive voice of the verb will give you a clue. Try to rewrite the weak sentences. Switch the pattern of the sentence to Pattern 2. Put the verb in the active voice.

EXAMPLES
PASSIVE VOICE (WEAK) The plane was brought to a stop by the pilot.
ACTIVE VOICE (STRONGER) The pilot brought the plane to a stop.
PASSIVE VOICE (WEAK) The plane was left by the passengers.
ACTIVE VOICE (STRONGER) The passengers left the plane.

EXERCISE 19 The following sentences use the passive voice of verbs. On a sheet of paper rewrite each sentence to make use of the active voice of the verb.

EXAMPLE Many energy experiments have been supported by the U.S. Energy Research and Development Administration (ERDA).

The U.S. Energy Research and Development Administration (ERDA) has supported many energy experiments.

1. New sources of energy are needed by our country.
2. Research for energy sources has been funded by ERDA.
3. The manufacture of gas from coal has been studied by scientists at ERDA.
4. Coal gas in gaslights was used by our great-grandparents.
5. Better ways to get gas are being sought by researchers.
6. Huge amounts of energy are generated by the sun.
7. Sunlight is being converted into electricity by a new machine in southern California.
8. This machine is considered by scientists as an important energy converter.
9. Energy from underground steam has been explored by ERDA scientists.
10. Many of our future energy needs will be met through the efforts of ERDA.

Sentence Pattern 2a (S-V-IO-DO) can also be reversed. In many cases, you can make either object the subject of the sentence. When you do, change the verb to the passive voice.

EXAMPLE

PATTERN 2a	The officials (S) gave (V) Doug (IO) his passport (DO).
PATTERN 2a REVERSED	A passport (S) was given (V) to Doug by the officials. [The direct object has become the subject.]
PATTERN 2a REVERSED	Doug (S) was given (V) his passport (O) by the officials. [The indirect object has become the subject. The direct object is unchanged.]

Most Pattern 2a sentences that have been reversed are weaker than the regular Pattern 2a sentences. Remember, use the reversed Pattern 2a mostly when the subject of the 2a sentence is unknown or is unimportant.

5n Any sentence pattern that is a statement can be made into a question.

Certain questions use a kind of reversed sentence pattern. For example, this Pattern 1 sentence is a declarative sentence.

The lion is sleeping.

In the form of a question, the words in this sentence are moved to become the following.

Is the lion sleeping?

The auxiliary verb *is* moves in front of the subject. This reverse of auxiliary verb and subject marks the difference between many declarative sentences and interrogative sentences.

EXAMPLES

DECLARATIVE The car was speeding.

INTERROGATIVE Was the car speeding?

DECLARATIVE The highway patrol had seen it.

INTERROGATIVE Had the highway patrol seen it?

Some questions add the word *do* or one of its forms in front of the subject as a signal that the sentence is a question. The form of *do* shows the time (the tense) of the action.

EXAMPLES

DECLARATIVE She got a ticket.

INTERROGATIVE *Did* she get a ticket?

EXERCISE 20 On a sheet of paper rewrite each of these sentences. If the sentence is a declarative sentence, write it as an interrogative sentence. If the sentence is an interrogative sentence, rewrite it as a declarative sentence.

EXAMPLE Is packaging a major industry?

Packaging is a major industry.

1. Some packages are made of cardboard.
2. Are these packages made of wood?

3. Do you know of other package material?
4. Plastic is a common package material.
5. Some plastic wrappers are transparent.
6. Do we use foam plastic for packages?
7. Thin aluminum works well for wrapping.
8. Is aluminum expensive?

SENTENCE COMBINING

5o Two or more sentences may sometimes be combined in a variety of ways.

The process of putting two or more related sentences together into one is called *sentence combining*. This process is useful when the ideas in several sentences are closely related.

(1) Combine one sentence with another by making one into a dependent clause.

See Clause, p. 441

EXAMPLE Julio took another step.
His foot slipped on the rock.

As Julio took another step, his foot slipped on the rock.
[The two sentences have become a single complex sentence by turning the first sentence into the dependent clause *as Julio took another step*.]

A dependent clause often qualifies the idea in the main independent clause. Or the dependent clause may show a time relationship with the action in the main clause. When you have two closely related sentences, they usually can be combined.

The dependent clause you write can be an adverb clause. It can tell *when, why, where,* or *how long.*

EXAMPLES Julio began to slide backwards. Maria held tightly to the rope connecting them.

As Julio began to slide backwards, Maria held tightly to the rope connecting them.
[The dependent clause shows *when* the action described in the independent clause took place.]

He stopped short of the rim of the canyon.
Maria held onto the rope to help him stop.

He stopped short of the rim of the canyon because Maria held the rope.
[The dependent clause shows *why* the action described in the independent clause took place.]

EXERCISE 21 Combine the following pairs of sentences. Make one sentence into a dependent clause.

EXAMPLE Mt. Everest stands as the world's highest mountain. Climbers can test themselves.

Mt. Everest, where climbers can test themselves, stands as the world's highest mountain.

1. Some people feel the challenge of high places. They get this feeling at the sight of Mt. Everest.
2. Mt. Everest had resisted all efforts by climbers. The peak was finally scaled in 1953.
3. Dozens of climbers had failed to climb it. The mountain offers no mercy to humans.
4. The top is especially cruel. Storms rage there much of the year.
5. Two climbers tried to reach the top in 1924. They vanished less than a thousand feet from it.

A dependent clause also can be either a noun clause or an adjective clause. It can name or modify someone or something.

EXAMPLE Some people wish to become expert climbers.
Expert climbers must train hard.

Whoever wishes to become an expert climber must train hard.
[The dependent clause *whoever wishes to become an expert climber* is the subject of the sentence.]

EXERCISE 22 Combine each of the following pairs of sentences. Make one sentence into a dependent clause. It may be a noun clause, an adjective clause, or an adverb clause.

EXAMPLE Edmund Hillary reached the top of Mt. Everest in 1953. He was an experienced climber.

Edmund Hillary, who was an experienced climber, reached the top of Mt. Everest in 1953.

1. Hillary came from New Zealand. He was a member of a British climbing team.
2. A Sherpa guide was with him. The guide knew the danger of the mountain.
3. They prepared carefully for the climb. They made the climb in the best weather.
4. A team of climbers went with them. The team helped them to the top.
5. The first Americans climbed Everest in 1963. The team was made up of five Americans and one Sherpa.

See Phrase, p. 457

(2) Combine one sentence with another by making one into a phrase.

Remember that phrases may be prepositional phrases or participial phrases.

EXAMPLES The rope caught fast around a rock. Maria held on with all her strength.

With the rope around a rock, Maria held on with all her strength. [The first sentence has become a prepositional phrase beginning with the preposition *with*.]

Julio was frightened but safe. He pulled himself up to a flat spot.

Frightened but safe, Julio pulled himself up to a flat spot. [The first sentence has become a participial phrase.]

Maria had a few shivers.
She finally settled down when she saw Julio was all right.

With only a few shivers, Maria finally settled down when she saw Julio was all right.
[The first sentence has been changed into a prepositional phrase.]

EXERCISE 23 Combine the following pairs of sentences. Make one of each pair into a phrase.

EXAMPLE Good climbers become experienced through practice. They conquer higher and higher mountains.

Experienced through practice, good climbers conquer higher and higher mountains.

1. Some climbers have specialized in rock climbing. These climbers learn to scale vertical faces of rocks.
2. They use strong ropes and spikes. They can actually climb a smooth rock face.
3. They drive spikes into the rock. They attach a long rope to the spikes.
4. They reach high above them with a spike. They hammer the spike in.
5. The rope goes through an eye in the spike. The climber pulls up with the rope.

REVIEW EXERCISE A Sentences

Some of the following word groups form sentences, and some do not. Number a sheet of paper 1–10. Next to each number write the word group if it is a complete sentence. Draw a circle around its simple subject and put a box around its complete verb. Then underline its complete subject once and its complete predicate twice. If the word group does not form a sentence, write *O* next to the number.

EXAMPLE Many deserts receive only about four inches of rainfall a year.

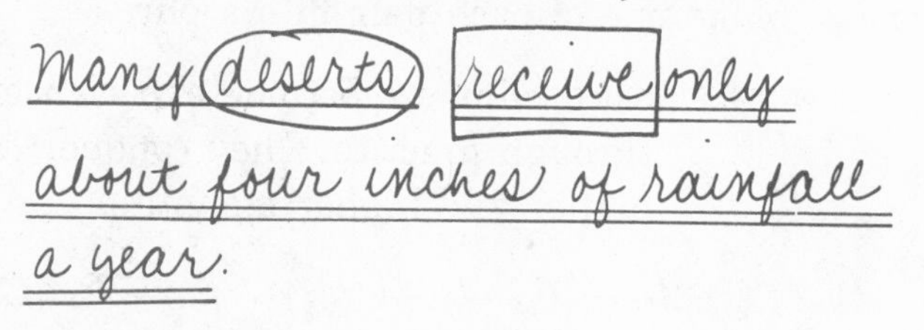

1. A great sea of rippling sand
2. The wind-blown sand polishes small stones on the desert floor
3. Daily expansion and contraction of the rocks because of temperature extremes
4. You can see old, sand-filled stream beds
5. Flash floods often follow desert rains
6. Eventually sinking into the sand
7. Some sand dunes move considerable distances in a hundred years
8. You can drive an automobile almost anywhere in a desert
9. Landing an aircraft on the flat desert floor
10. The location of desert trails is helpful information

REVIEW EXERCISE B Types of Sentences

Following is a list of simple sentences. Combine each simple sentence with words of your own to form a compound, complex, or compound-complex sentence. Number a sheet of paper 1–10. Next to each number write the sentence you have formed. Then write *C* if it is a compound sentence, *Cx* if it is a complex sentence, or *CCx* if it is a compound-complex sentence. Make sure that you have at least one of each kind in this exercise.

EXAMPLE I'll get on a plane.

Some day when I'm rich, I'll get on a plane; and I'll go to the most beautiful place I can think of. CCx

1. People will wait on me hand and foot.
2. I will lie in the sun.
3. I will have all the food I can eat.
4. Maybe I'll wear only old clothes.
5. At night I'll walk down to the sea.
6. The sound of the waves will put me to sleep.
7. All my cares will vanish.
8. Everyone will like me.
9. I'll have an endless supply of money.
10. It is a dream.

REVIEW EXERCISE C The Purposes of Sentences

Following is a list of sentences. Number a sheet of paper 1–10. Next to each number write *D* if the sentence is declarative, *I* if it is interrogative, *Im* if it is imperative, or *E* if it is exclamatory.

EXAMPLE Have you ever heard of Nellie Bly?
I

1. Her real name was Elizabeth Cochrane, and she was a reporter for the *New York World* newspaper.
2. On November 14, 1889, she set out on a trip around the world.
3. What an undertaking that was!
4. Her publisher wanted to send a man.
5. Don't stop reading; there's more.
6. Don't you want to find out if Nellie Bly beat Phineas Fogg's fictional record in *Around the World in Eighty Days?*
7. She set out from New York across the Atlantic.
8. She ended up in San Francisco and raced across the country.
9. What excitement there was when she got back in seventy-two days!
10. Her editor had even sponsored a lottery based on the time of her arrival.

CHAPTER

6

SENTENCE PROBLEMS

Fragments, Run-on Sentences, Dangling and Misplaced Modifiers, Nonparallel Structure

Many of the sentences you write now are longer and more complex than those you wrote several years ago. Long sentences have more room for errors than short sentences.

The kinds of problems may also increase as you continue to write longer sentences. *Run-on sentences* and sentences with *nonparallel structure* are two kinds of problems. Another kind of sentence problem is the *sentence fragment,* while yet another kind involves *dangling* or *misplaced modifiers.*

By studying this chapter you will learn how to identify these types of sentence problems. You will also learn ways to correct and avoid them in your writing.

SENTENCE FRAGMENTS

6a A sentence fragment is an incomplete sentence.

A fragment is only a part of a sentence. The part that is missing may be one important word or several words. Without the missing words, the fragment fails to state a complete thought, which a true sentence must do.

EXAMPLES

FRAGMENT *The energy required to launch one rocket*
[This group of words identifies *energy,* but it lacks a predicate that tells what the energy does. Nor does it say anything about the condition of the energy. The reader needs to know *what about* the energy.]

See Predicate, p. 457

COMPLETE SENTENCE *The energy required to launch one rocket* would drive a million cars.
[Now the sentence tells what the energy can do.]

FRAGMENT *Makes an impressive sight as it soars upward*
[This fragment lacks a subject. What makes an impressive sight? The words do not say.]

See Subject, p. 460

COMPLETE SENTENCE The gigantic rocket *makes an impressive sight as it soars upward.*
[Now this sentence tells what makes an impressive sight.]

EXERCISE 1 Each of the following word groups is a sentence fragment. On a sheet of paper numbered 1–10 write each word group as a complete sentence. Add whatever words are needed.

EXAMPLE Partly hidden in a fiery explosion

The giant rocket was partly hidden in a fiery explosion.

1. Launched the rocket over Florida
2. As the pilot watched tensely
3. The ship's whirring, spinning dials
4. Until the fire died away at last
5. Because a mistake would destroy the whole program
6. Millions of dollars and thousands of hours of work
7. All the people in the control room
8. When her voice could be heard through the static
9. Hoped their work would not be wasted
10. A safe landing, right on target

Hint: To be sure each group of words you write is complete rather than a fragment, ask the following three questions:
Does the group of words have a complete subject?
Does the group of words have a complete predicate?
Does the group of words express a complete thought?

A fragment most frequently occurs because the writer omits a subject or a predicate.

See Phrase, p. 457

Sentence fragments may be phrases. The most common are prepositional phrases and participial phrases.

EXAMPLES

FRAGMENT *Across the flat, open prairies of the American Far West*
[This fragment, which is a prepositional phrase, can be corrected by adding a subject and a predicate.]

COMPLETE SENTENCE Conestoga wagons traveled seemingly endless miles *across the flat, open prairies of the American Far West.*

FRAGMENT *Slashing with his teeth at the enemy*
[This fragment, which is a participial phrase, can be corrected by adding a subject and a predicate.]

COMPLETE SENTENCE *Slashing with his teeth at the enemy,* Buck drove off the furious wolves.

See Clause, p. 441

Sentence fragments are sometimes dependent clauses. The dependent clause usually needs an independent clause to make a complete sentence. Therefore, to make a dependent clause fragment into a complete sentence, add an independent clause to it.

EXAMPLES

FRAGMENT *While Eddie Ming was in the market*

COMPLETE SENTENCE *While Eddie Ming was in the market,* two men brushed past him.

FRAGMENT *If only the manager would come out*

COMPLETE SENTENCE The men might not get away *if only the manager would come out.*

Some sentence fragments lack a complete verb.

EXAMPLE

FRAGMENT *The men gone before the manager appeared*
[This fragment lacks an auxiliary verb to make the verb *gone* complete.]

COMPLETE SENTENCE The men *had gone* before the manager appeared.
or
The men *were gone* before the manager appeared.

See Auxiliary Verb, p. 440

The complete verb in a sentence tells the action or the state of being of the subject. The complete verb also tells the tense, or time, of the action or condition. Fragments lacking a complete verb often fail to show time.

Examples of incomplete verb form fragments:

Chickens being plucked and drawn for market
The gizzards and livers wrapped separately
These stuffed back inside the empty chickens

Examples of verb forms completed to make sentences:

Chickens *were being plucked* and *drawn* for market.

The gizzards and livers *were wrapped* separately.
These *were stuffed* back inside the empty chickens.

EXERCISE 2 Each of the following word groups is a sentence fragment. On a sheet of paper write each fragment as a complete sentence. Add whatever words are needed.

EXAMPLE Before steamships were invented
The American clippers were the fastest cargo ships before steamships were invented.

1. In the days of fast sailing ships
2. Danced on the water like a mermaid
3. Five rows of sails
4. With her skysails spread
5. *Sea Witch, Flying Cloud,* and *Westward Ho*
6. Speeded across the Pacific in less than a hundred days
7. Started with the China tea trade
8. Hundreds of gold-seekers in 1849
9. These swift, graceful ships
10. Through terrible storms

Another cause of sentence fragments is incorrect punctuation. A dependent clause is sometimes separated by mistake from the independent clause with which it belongs.

EXAMPLE The chickens are shipped. After they are frozen.
[The first group of words is an independent clause. The second group of words is a dependent clause. It should be attached to the independent clause to form a single sentence.]

The chickens are shipped after they are frozen.

Hint: If your sentence begins with the dependent clause, use a comma between it and the independent clause. If it begins with the independent clause, do not use a comma.

See Punctuation, p. 317

EXERCISE 3 Each of the following dependent clauses is a fragment. Add an independent clause to each fragment and write the complete sentence on a sheet of paper.

EXAMPLE Because of the daring of men and women

Alaska became settled because of the daring of men and women.

1. When gold was found in Alaska
2. Who had never been a miner before
3. Before they staked their claims on the river

4. Until they bought enough warm clothes
5. Which made them rich overnight
6. So that she could start a new life
7. As if the trees wore skins of ice
8. Because Alaska was a new, exciting frontier
9. Whom they had met in Fairbanks
10. As soon as they bought food and other supplies

RUN-ON SENTENCES

6b A run-on sentence is two or more sentences incorrectly joined.

EXAMPLES Cretta Bullwinkel tried to raise turkeys she wanted to make money selling them.
The feed cost her more than she had figured she lost money.

In general, there are four basic methods for correcting run-on sentences.

Method 1: The separate thoughts in a run-on sentence may be divided into separate sentences.

RUN-ON SENTENCE Debbie Accardo bought a turkey for Thanksgiving she didn't know how to cook it.

CORRECTED SENTENCES Debbie Accardo bought a turkey for Thanksgiving. She didn't know how to cook it.

See Punctuation, p. 318; Conjunction, p. 443

Method 2: The separate thoughts in a run-on sentence may be correctly joined by adding a comma and a coordinating conjunction. A coordinating conjunction alone may sometimes be enough.

RUN-ON SENTENCE The roasting pan was too small for the turkey Debbie decided to wrap it in foil.

CORRECTED SENTENCE The roasting pan was too small for the turkey, **but** Debbie decided to wrap it in foil.

Method 3: Some run-on sentences may be corrected by making one part into a dependent clause.

See Clause, p. 441

RUN-ON SENTENCE She was ready to put the turkey in the oven she discovered she had forgotten to stuff it.

CORRECTED SENTENCE When she was ready to put the turkey in the oven, she discovered she had forgotten to stuff it.

If you put the dependent clause first, remember to separate it from the main clause with a comma.

EXAMPLE After searching the kitchen, she found the stuffing in a bowl in the refrigerator.

Method 4: Some run-on sentences may be corrected by means of a semicolon.

See Punctuation, pp. 323–324

RUN-ON SENTENCE The turkey got very hot the fat dripped all over the oven.

CORRECTED SENTENCE The turkey got very hot; the fat dripped all over the oven.

EXERCISE 4 Rewrite correctly the following run-on sentences on a sheet of paper. Use one of the methods discussed earlier.

EXAMPLE Sojourner Truth was an American leader in the fight for human rights she fought with ideas and words.

Sojourner Truth was an American leader in the fight for human rights. She fought with ideas and words.

1. A tall Black woman was one of the most striking speakers of nineteenth-century America she called herself Sojourner Truth.
2. She walked through the country speaking about Black people's rights she spoke about women's rights, too.
3. She began as a slave named Isabella she was raised by a Dutch family in New York.
4. Religion was very important to her she joined several different churches.
5. Some women's rights leaders did not want to be associated with the antislavery cause they did not want Sojourner Truth to speak to them.
6. Sojourner spoke anyway she made everyone listen.
7. She said that women and Blacks had some of the same problems they both were often treated unjustly.
8. At last all the slaves became free Sojourner thought at one time they should start a new state of their own.

9. Sojourner spoke with force and humor no one could argue her down.
10. Sojourner Truth lived for almost a century hundreds of people came to her funeral.

MISPLACED AND DANGLING MODIFIERS

6c A misplaced or dangling modifier is a phrase or clause that seems to modify the wrong person or thing.

A modifier that seems to relate to the wrong word is a *misplaced modifier.* A modifier that relates to no word at all is a *dangling modifier.* Be sure that modifiers refer to the person or thing they name and are placed next to it.

EXAMPLE *Eating hungrily,* the turkey was enjoyed by Carl and his family. [The modifying phrase *eating hungrily* seems to relate to the turkey. However, the turkey is not eating. It is Carl and his family who are eating the turkey. The confusion comes about because the modifying phrase is misplaced. It should be next to *Carl and his family.*]

Here are some examples of misplaced modifiers.

MISPLACED After finishing their desserts, Carl suggested that his family help him clean the oven. [*After finishing their desserts* refers to Carl's family, not to Carl.]

CORRECTED Carl suggested that, after finishing their desserts, his family should help him clean the oven.

MISPLACED Not wishing to appear ungrateful, the oven was cleaned with the help of his family.
[The oven cannot appear ungrateful.]

CORRECTED Not wishing to appear ungrateful, his family helped him clean the oven.

MISPLACED Carl read them the instructions for cleaning an oven on the box of cleaner.
[The oven was not placed on the box of cleaner.]

CORRECTED Carl read them the instructions on the box of cleaner for cleaning an oven.

The modifier that dangles has nothing to attach itself to. It needs a word or words to relate to.

EXAMPLES Reading out loud, the instructions said to brush the cleaner on the inside of the oven.
[Who did the reading aloud? The sentence doesn't say.]

Following directions carefully, it was hoped the oven would come clean.
[Who is following the directions? The sentence doesn't say.]

Correct dangling modifiers by putting the word or words they modify next to them.

EXAMPLES Reading the instructions out loud, Carl said to brush the cleaner on the inside of the oven.
Following directions carefully, his family hoped the oven would come clean.

EXERCISE 5 The following sentences contain misplaced modifiers. Rewrite each sentence on a sheet of paper. Place the modifiers in their correct positions.

EXAMPLE Bending down to look in the oven, the edge of the counter bumped Carl on the head.
Bending down to look in the oven, Carl bumped his head on the edge of the counter.

1. Reeling back, his mother kept him from falling.
2. Someone said they should put him down in a loud voice.
3. Feeling faint, his father held Carl up.
4. After discussing this among themselves, Carl was helped by his family to a chair.
5. Feeling better quickly, the chair was just the right place for Carl.
6. Having forgotten about the cleaner, the oven was ignored by everyone.
7. After they made sure he was all right, Carl said goodbye to his family.
8. Still waiting to be cleaned, Carl realized he had no one to help with the oven.

EXERCISE 6 The following sentences contain dangling modifiers. Rewrite each sentence on a sheet of paper. Supply the words to which the modifiers can relate.

EXAMPLE Scrubbing hard, it was slow work.
Scrubbing hard, Carl found the work slow.

1. While on his knees scrubbing, the telephone in the next room began to ring.
2. Rushing to answer the phone, the oven was left open.
3. While on the phone with his mother, the doorbell rang twice.
4. His mother was asked to wait with the sound of the doorbell in his ears.
5. The doorbell was heard again leaving the phone off the hook.
6. Seeing his brother had returned to help him, he came in.
7. Saying he wanted to help finish cleaning his oven, Carl accepted the offer.
8. With his brother to help him with the work, his mother was forgotten.
9. Because her son didn't answer, Carl later found the phone was disconnected.
10. Explaining about the confusion, his mother accepted the apology.

NONPARALLEL STRUCTURE

6d Nonparallel structure is the incorrect use of different grammatical forms to express similar ideas.

Similar ideas in a sentence belong in structures that are grammatically parallel. Parallel ideas not in parallel grammatical structure confuse your reader.

EXAMPLES

NONPARALLEL VERBS Bluebeard *stomped* up and down the deck, *searched* the horizon for sight of land, and *cursing* any sailor within ten feet of him.

PARALLEL VERBS Bluebeard *stomped* up and down the deck, *searched* the horizon for sight of land, and *cursed* any sailor within ten feet of him.

NONPARALLEL PHRASES He ordered men *to the top of the masts, to the bow of the ship,* and *to swing over the side.*

PARALLEL PHRASES He ordered men *to climb to the top of the masts, to rush to the bow of the ship,* and *to swing over the side.*

NONPARALLEL CLAUSES His orders were *that every man should look for land* and *the first sight rewarded.*

PARALLEL CLAUSES His orders were *that every man should look for land* and *that the first one who sighted it should get a reward.*

EXERCISE 7 On a sheet of paper rewrite each of the following sentences containing nonparallel constructions. Make your constructions parallel.

EXAMPLE Advertising helps our economy by informing people of new products, telling of their advantages, and the competition.

Advertising helps our economy by informing people of new products, telling of their advantages, and stimulating competition.

1. People buy new products, try them out, and finding them to their satisfaction.
2. Some products catch on, some products last only a few years, and some poor products on the market.
3. Someone famous once said that you can fool some of the people some of the time, but not fooling all the people all the time.
4. A bad product may sell at first, and people will use it, but in time they stopped buying it.
5. Good products are widely accepted, enjoy popularity, and returning a fair profit to the company.
6. Experience shows that bad products are rejected and that companies often making them too fast.
7. Whenever you find shoddy materials, refuse to buy them or returning them to the manufacturer.
8. By doing that, you will show that quality is important and advertising that fact.

(1) Make compared or contrasted ideas grammatically equal and complete.

Sometimes you compare or contrast ideas in the same sentence. When you do, include all the words necessary to make the ideas grammatically complete.

EXAMPLES

CONFUSING Americans have proved themselves not only inventive but they work hard, too.
[The adjective *inventive* is compared with the clause *they work hard, too.* The clause should be another adjective to make it grammatically equal to *inventive.*]

CORRECTED Americans have proved themselves not only *inventive* but *industrious.*

CONFUSING Speaking as an individual is as important as to speak as a member of a group.
[The gerund *speaking* is compared with an infinitive *to speak.* They should both be gerunds or both infinitives.]

CORRECTED *Speaking* as an individual is as important as *speaking* as a member of a group.
or
To speak as an individual is as important as *to speak* as a member of a group.

CONFUSING Marguerita Diaz is not only the captain of the soccer team but also of the swim team.

CORRECTED Marguerita Diaz is the captain not only of the soccer team but also of the swim team.

CONFUSING She showed not only she could lead her teams but played well, too.

CORRECTED She showed she could not only lead her teams but play well, too.

EXERCISE 8 On a sheet of paper rewrite each following sentence containing compared ideas that are grammatically unequal. Make the compared ideas grammatically equal.

EXAMPLE Young people learn not only the modern dances but also they often dance some old-fashioned ones.

Young people learn not only the modern dances but also some old-fashioned ones.

1. Waltzing had been more popular at one time than to dance a two-step.
2. In Austria in the mid-1800's the older people not only waltzed but also the young people.
3. Waltzing became more popular than to dance any other way.
4. Ballrooms were not only filled with dancers but also musicians played.

5. Not only did they not have electronic music but no mechanical music machines.
6. Sometimes as many as four orchestras played in a large ballroom while hundreds of couples dancing.
7. Imagine not only the swirling mass of waltzing couples but also the musicians played.
8. Would you prefer waltzing to the music of live musicians or to dance in a discotheque?

REVIEW EXERCISE A **Sentence Fragments**

Each of the following words groups is a sentence fragment. On a sheet of paper write a complete sentence using each fragment. Use whatever words are necessary to do this.

EXAMPLE When he started swimming
When he started swimming, he felt fine.

1. The chilling current and the brisk wind
2. The distance to the point
3. Swam steadily onward
4. If he didn't get a cramp
5. Seeing a dark object in the water
6. Something to keep himself afloat
7. Tiring fast
8. Headed toward it
9. The last fading light of the day
10. Only a shadow

REVIEW EXERCISE B Run-on Sentences

Following is a group of run-on sentences. On a sheet of paper rewrite correctly the run-on sentences.

EXAMPLE There are three kinds of stages in modern theaters they are the proscenium stage, the theater-in-the-round, and the platform stage.

There are three kinds of stages in modern theaters. They are the proscenium stage, the theater-in-the-round, and the platform stage.

1. The proscenium stage has a curtain that can be drawn any changes of scenery can be hidden.
2. Members of the audience watch a play on the proscenium stage only from the front they see the play as if through a frame.
3. The curtain may be dropped when a scene is over it may be dropped to show that time has passed.
4. The theater-in-the-round, or arena, has no stage at all the play is performed at floor level.
5. The audience sits in seats all around the actors they can see the actors' expressions better.
6. There is no curtain little scenery can be used.
7. What scenery there is must be low enough the audience must be able to see over it.
8. The open stage is a raised platform it has seats arranged around three sides of it.

9. It is more like a proscenium stage than the theater-in-the-round it brings the actors closer to the audience.
10. It has a large area for the actors to use it can accommodate a greater number of actors.

REVIEW EXERCISE C Dangling or Misplaced Modifiers

Rewrite the following sentences, correcting the misplaced or dangling modifiers. You may have to add a few words of your own to do this.

EXAMPLE Although dead, a good taxidermist can make a lion look lifelike.

A good taxidermist can make a lion, although dead, look lifelike.

1. As though alive, taxidermy is the art of preserving dead animals.
2. Taking careful notes, the skin of the dead animal is measured.
3. The taxidermist makes a drawing of the animal's posed body after calreful calculations.
4. Serving as a guide for the finished product, he makes a model.
5. Using wire, plaster, or other materials, the model must be accurate.
6. Placing the skin on the model, it is sewn together.
7. Globes must be placed in the eye sockets of hollow, painted glass.

8. Adding other necessary items, the eyes and tongue are put in.
9. Museums used to have taxidermy departments for mounting animals in many towns.
10. Using many skills, a wide range of knowledge is needed by the taxidermist.

REVIEW EXERCISE D **Nonparallel Structure**

Each of the following sentences contains an example of nonparallel structure. On a sheet of paper rewrite each sentence to make all parts parallel. Some sentences contain nonparallel verbs. Some contain nonparallel phrases. Some contain nonparallel clauses.

EXAMPLE Anyone can go to a library, request a library card, and finding out important information.

Anyone can go to a library, request a library card, and find out important information.

1. If you want information about motorcycles, look in the card catalog, find a subject card, and then to get the book it names.
2. Certain magazines print articles not only about motorcycles but also list the best features of various machines.
3. Some bikes are used just for transportation; others for sport riding.
4. Riding in a race is as thrilling as to do any other sport, motorcyclists claim.
5. Successful racing requires not only skill but to be strong.

UNIT TWO

COMPOSITION

Paragraphs
Guidelines for Writing
Letter Writing

CHAPTER

7

PARAGRAPHS

A *paragraph* is a group of sentences which develops a single idea, or *topic*. The topic of a paragraph usually is stated in a single sentence. Other sentences in the paragraph then expand upon this idea.

The first sentence of a paragraph is indented. This is the signal that shows that the sentences that follow are organized around one idea.

As you study this chapter, you will learn ways to build better paragraphs.

DEVELOPING PARAGRAPHS

7a A paragraph is a series of sentences that tells about a single idea, description, or action.

When you write a paragraph, keep clearly in your mind what topic you are developing. Suppose, for example, you are telling about some event or happening. Every sentence in the paragraph should deal with something related to that event. Or you might describe a person or a place. If so, make each sentence you write add something to your description about that person or place. Possibly your paragraph will present your opinion about something. In that case, use each sentence in the paragraph to support or relate to your opinion.

Study the examples of paragraphs that follow. Note that the topic of each is clear, and that the rest of the sentences in each paragraph deal with the single topic.

> Example of a paragraph explaining something:
>
> Pop art tries to make people really look at things in the everyday world. One Pop artist made a soup can out of bronze and put it on a base, as if it were a Greek statue. Another artist made a typewriter out of soft cloth like a stuffed toy. Still another makes comic strip pictures several feet high. Some Pop art sculptures are machines that whir and flap and even blow themselves apart. By making common things a bit different, Pop artists make us think about what these things are really like.

> Example of a paragraph describing a place:
>
> Nine thousand feet below the surface of the sea, the water is cold and dark. Little, if any, life is there. But in special spots in the Galapagos Rift Zone near South America, the story is very different. Volcanoes are active in this zone, and fountains of warm water spurt

up through cracks in the undersea rocks. All kinds of sea creatures cluster around these fountains. Foot-long clams cling to rocks near the warm water. A little farther away, sea anemones and sea lilies wave their "petals" in the warm currents. Fish bask like sunbathers a few feet above them. Yet only several hundred feet away, the lava rock is cold and bare of life.

Example of a paragraph stating an opinion:

Pollution is ruining our waters. Spilled oil and industrial chemicals poison fish or other water life. That's only part of the problem, however. Other chemicals hurt the water ecology because they make food for tiny water plants called algae. The algae grow too fast and cover the water's surface. This cuts off the oxygen needed by the fish below. Even clean water can kill—if it is a little too hot. Some manufacturing plants put heated water into rivers. The temperature of the rivers goes up just a few degrees. This small change can stop fish from breeding and destroy the balance of plant and animal life in the water.

You can understand what each of the above paragraphs is about because its purpose is expressed clearly in a *topic sentence.* A topic sentence often begins a paragraph, as it does in each of these examples.

7b State the main idea of a paragraph in a topic sentence.

Write a clear topic sentence for each paragraph you compose. In fact, you will benefit by writing the topic sentence *before* you write the paragraph. Then you can study it to see whether it says just what you mean. Once you are satisfied with your topic sentence, relate the rest of your sentences to it.

You need not always place the topic sentence at the beginning of its paragraph. However, if you sometimes have difficulty keeping to the subject in your writing, plan to start each paragraph with a topic sentence.

Study the following paragraph. Note the way the opening sentence—the topic sentence—sets forth the main idea. The sentences that come after it treat some aspect of the main idea.

> *Your first name can make a difference in the way people react to you.* Scientists have found that the most popular children in school are often the ones with the most common names. Children with well-liked names such as Gregory or Susan thought better of themselves than did children with unpopular names. They did better in school, too. At least, they seemed to. Part of that might be the teacher's doing. Some teachers in an experiment gave better grades to an essay signed "Linda" or "Steve" than they did to the same essay signed "Bertha" or "Horace."

Here is another example of a paragraph with the topic sentence at the beginning.

> *The War between the States—the American Civil War—was a war of the young.* Mostly boys fought in the armies of the Union and the

Confederacy. Complete records are not available, but the majority of soldiers were less than twenty-one years of age. Many were only fifteen or sixteen. Even some of the generals were still in their twenties.

Remember that every paragraph you write needs a clear topic sentence.

EXERCISE 1 The following three paragraphs are missing topic sentences. Six possible topic sentences are listed after the paragraphs. Choose the best topic sentence for each paragraph. Write the numbers 1, 2, and 3 on a sheet of paper. Next to each number write the topic sentence that belongs with that paragraph.

1. (Topic sentence missing) When her husband became ill aboard the ship he captained in the 1850's, Hannah Burgess of Massachusetts navigated their large sailing ship all the way from Peru to Valparaiso, Chile. Margaret Longfellow brought her three children in an open boat from Nova Scotia to Maine in 1778 to escape the British. Two women, Mary Read and Anne Bonney, not only went to sea but became pirates. In 1969 Sharon Sites Adams sailed across the Pacific Ocean alone in a small boat.

2. (Topic sentence missing) The colonies would be shaped like giant tin cans. They would spin end over end to make a little gravity for the people inside. Parts of them would be giant factories. Taking advantage of the low gravity that makes things weigh less, people would put together materials to make more colonies. But the colonies' main business would be capturing the

sun's energy and beaming it back to earth. Solar energy would let the colonies make their own heat and grow their own food.

3. (Topic sentence missing) The paintings are part of a healing ceremony that may last nine days. The designs in the paintings represent spirits. When a painting is finished, the sick person sits in the middle of it. The healer sings over the sick person, asking the spirits for help. At the same time, the healer puts sand from the painting onto the person's body. The Navajos believe that the paintings and ceremonies will help the sick person come back into harmony with the world. Then the person will be healthy again.

1. The Navajo people of the American Southwest believe that paintings in colored sand can help to make a sick person well.
2. Women who sail the seas must study navigation.
3. Scientists have worked out plans for the United States to have self-contained colonies in space.
4. The open sea has usually been thought of as "a man's world," but many brave women have sailed the sea.
5. The space age has polluted space with tin cans.
6. The Navajo people in the American Southwest have a special talent for painting in sand.

7c Keep every sentence in a paragraph on the topic.

Once you have written a clear topic sentence, make sure the rest of the sentences in the paragraph develop the topic. Each sentence should relate to the topic in some way. Sentences in a paragraph of narration should carry along the action. Sentences in a paragraph of opinion should support or explain some aspect of the argument.

Occasionally you may accidentally include in a paragraph a sentence that does not deal with the topic. Because this sentence will seriously weaken the paragraph, it should be changed or taken out altogether.

Study the following paragraph. One of the sentences does not refer to the topic of the paragraph. If you can find it here, you can recognize a misplaced sentence in your own writing.

> (1) Among the Quechua people of Bolivia, weaving is part of everyday life for all members of the family. (2) Both men and women weave from earliest childhood. (3) Women weave at home. (4) Men spin yarn as they walk along, carrying heavy loads. (5) Even little children have toy spindles and small looms that they work with their toes. (6) The children have few commercial toys. (7) The Quechua weave almost everything: clothes, blankets, carrying bags, even string for magic charms and braided rope for slingshots. (8) When a Quechua man asks a woman to marry him, he gives her a belt he has woven himself. (9) If she accepts him, she gives him a little woven bag.

The topic of this paragraph is stated in the first sentence: *The Quechua people weave a great deal.* All the sentences but one relate to that topic. Sentence 6, *The children have few commercial toys,* does not relate to the topic. This sentence says nothing about the Quechua practice of weaving. As a result, it weakens the paragraph. The writer should take it out or change it to make it refer to the topic.

Here is another example of a paragraph with an odd sentence in it. See if you can find it.

> The world's largest windmill is an American device built to convert wind power into electricity. Its tower is forty-five meters high with two fiberglass blades spanning sixty meters. The blades rotate thirty to forty times per minute in winds up to thirty-two kilometers per hour. Winds sometimes blow more than a hundred and sixty kilometers. In a wind averaging twenty-nine kilometers per hour the windmill will generate enough electricity to supply five hundred homes with power.

You can see that the next-to-last sentence—*Winds sometimes blow more than a hundred and sixty kilometers per hour*—does not belong in the paragraph. That sentence should come out to make the paragraph stronger.

Learn to keep such unrelated sentences out of paragraphs you write.

EXERCISE 2 Each of the following paragraphs contains two sentences that are not on the topic of the paragraph. Write the sentences that do not belong in each paragraph.

1. If a company cheats you, your best solution is to tell the world. Most businesses hate bad publicity. A story on a radio or television program about a company's unfair ways can do more harm than a lawsuit. More lawsuits are being filed every year. People will hear the story and

stay away from that company. It may lose money. Even threatening to "spill the beans" in this way can make a company start listening to you. Some years ago in San Francisco people planned a "lemonstration"—a parade of all the bad cars that car dealers had sold but would not fix. San Francisco is located on the Pacific Coast. Many car dealers suddenly decided to fix the cars rather than see them—with the dealers' names on them—take part in the "lemonstration" parade.

2. A "bandage" of a tropical fruit may be the best cure for wounds that won't heal. The fruit is called the papaya, or pawpaw. Chemicals in it can make flesh soft. That is why its juice is sometimes used in meat tenderizers. Many markets sell meat tenderizer. That might sound like it would make wounds worse, but it does just the opposite. It may kill germs that infect the wounds. A papaya tree may produce a hundred pounds of fruit in one season. African healers have used papaya on wounds for many years. Now doctors have shown that this folk medicine really works.

7d A paragraph may be developed with details, examples, or reasons.

By using details in a paragraph, you fill out the picture in the mind of your reader. Suppose your paragraph tells about something that has happened. Your description of the event needs details to complete the scene and the action.

Here is an example of a paragraph telling about people in an open boat in a rough sea. Notice the several details in the paragraph that help you see clearly what is taking place.

> The little boat seemed to bounce at the peak of every wave, jostling the people inside who desperately tried to row. Each time the boat kicked up, several oars would splash water and one or two would completely miss the surface. The frustrated rowers could keep no rhythm; their oars knocked about at odd angles. The sunlight caught the wet, shiny shafts of uplifted oars dipping and lifting and sometimes crossing over one another. The choppy waves and wind gave more thrust to the boat than did the efforts of the rowers.

The next paragraph is not describing anything. Instead, it expresses an opinion, which is stated in the first sentence, the topic sentence. An opinion needs examples or reasons to back it up. The sentences following the topic sentence all support the argument by giving examples or reasons.

> The "good old days" were not always so good. Most people who want to go back to other times are the ones who never had to live through them. Some young people today wish they had lived in the 1950's, when Elvis Presley was king of rock and roll. They don't know how people then worried about the Cold War. Others would like to go back to the 1930's, when families stuck together, and divorce was less common. They don't realize that in those

depression days, sticking together was sometimes the only way to survive.

EXERCISE 3 Choose one of the following topics. Write a paragraph about the topic. Develop your paragraph by using details, examples, or reasons.

1. A crew of working people trying to accomplish a task
2. Cheerleaders at an athletic contest trying to get cheers from the fans
3. Being ten years old is fun
4. Being ten years old is not fun
5. A good athlete has an easy time of it in high school
6. A good athlete does not have an easy time of it in high school
7. Carbonated soft drinks are good thirst-quenchers
8. Carbonated soft drinks are not good thirst-quenchers.

7e A paragraph may be developed through comparison and contrast.

When one thing is compared to another, both things become clearer because of the comparison. The contrast between the two sharpens the image of each.

Example of a paragraph developed by comparison and contrast:

A few hundred years ago, the Polar Eskimos thought they were the only people in the world. They had even lost contact with other Eskimos. Today they see people from Denmark and the United States very often. Now there are more Polar Eskimos than there used to be, but fewer of them stay home and follow the traditional way of life. The life of a hunter used to be the only proper one for a Polar Eskimo man. The young men of today would rather be government clerks. The Polar Eskimos still wear clothes of polar bear fur and sealskin. They still live on the meat and fat of the animals they kill. But their children go to school and learn new ways. Slowly but surely, the old ways of the Polar Eskimos are being forgotten.

EXERCISE 4 Make a list of points about two items from the following eight topics. In your list, include points that show the comparison and contrast between the two items.

1. Two similar sports (such as soccer and water polo)
2. Two similar articles of clothing (such as jackets and shirts)
3. Two similar appliances (radios or dryers, for example)
4. Two similar food dishes (casseroles and desserts, for example)
5. Two similar customs (holidays in different cultures or traffic systems, for example)
6. Two similar popular musical groups
7. The eyes of two people
8. Two similar pieces of furniture important to you

EXERCISE 5 Use the information you listed in Exercise 4. Write a composition of one to three paragraphs comparing and contrasting the items you selected.

7f A paragraph may be developed by cause and effect.

Pairs of events are related. One event happens, and right away another happens. In fact, the first event often causes the second one.

In the summer of 1977, for example, lightning struck an electric power station near New York City. Within minutes the electric power for the city had been cut off. More than ten million people were without electric power. The lightning storm caused a power blackout. This is an example of cause and effect.

Events related in this way belong close together in your writing. Often they belong in the same paragraph. Show the relationship of causes and effects so that your reader understands them better.

Example of a paragraph developed by cause and effect:

A Pennsylvania banker came up with a new way to make sure he gets back the money people borrow from him; he found them jobs. Bank president John Carr learned that his bank was losing money because some people could not pay back their loans. They could not pay the money because they had lost their jobs. Carr realized that threatening them would not make them—or his bank—any richer. But getting them jobs might. So Carr talked to business people in his town. Some of them had jobs to give. Carr put them in touch with the people who needed work. Because of Carr's new idea, many of his jobless loan customers were jobless no longer. They became happy and made Carr happy, too.

EXERCISE 6 Choose one of the following topics and write a paragraph or two. Show cause and effect in your paragraphs.

1. Why hail is formed
2. A whirlwind
3. How popcorn pops
4. How a yo-yo works
5. The rising of bread
6. Sonar

7g Events in a paragraph may be organized by time.

Events occur in time. Events may occur at the same time, or they may happen one after the other. In your writing, it is important to describe events in their actual time frame. You need to tell your reader which events happen first and then which events follow. By doing this, you give your reader a better understanding of how the events are related.

Example of a paragraph organized by time:

To win a bet, Captain Allardyce Barclay of Scotland walked a thousand miles in a thousand hours during the summer of 1809. Or rather, he walked the same mile over and over, once each hour, day and night. At the beginning of his long task, Barclay covered each mile in less than fifteen minutes. Later, he was dragging out the time to twenty minutes. He would walk two miles together, one at the end

> of the first hour and the other at the beginning of the next hour. That way, he had an hour-and-a-half rest between walks. Even so, the lack of sleep and the hot summer sun finally wore him down. He barely completed the walking nearly six weeks after he had started.

In this paragraph several references to periods of time show the time framework within which the events occurred—one thousand hours, or "nearly six weeks."

Additional terms help show time relationships. Examples are *at the beginning of, later,* and *finally.* From these your readers can gain a better picture of what happened when.

EXERCISE 7 Choose one of the following topics and write one or two paragraphs about it. Show how events are related in time.

1. Being half awake and half asleep
2. Preparing to do my homework
3. Unplugging a stopped drain
4. Caring for a house plant
5. Cleaning a carpet

7h A paragraph may be organized by space.

Whenever you describe someone or something, it helps your reader if you show where important things are located. The details of space relationships help your reader develop a mental picture of whatever you are describing.

Example of a paragraph with details organized by space:

In the twenty-two hours he was trapped in the tiny, dark room, John Dore got to know every inch of it. The room was part of an offshore oil rig that had turned over and sunk. What had been the top of the room became the bottom for John. A pipe near what had been the ceiling was handy for him to stand on so he could reach the floor over his head. That was important because the upper part of the room—formerly the floor—was where the air was. The lower part of John's body was in water, but as long as he could keep his head in that big bubble of air, he knew he was all right.

Notice in this paragraph the words that help show the location of details. Prepositional phrases such as *top of the room* and *over his head* help give a good picture of the space relationships. Instead of being confused, the reader understands the location of important details.

EXERCISE 8 Choose one of the following sentences as a topic sentence for a paragraph. Or think of one of your own. Write a paragraph of five or six sentences. Organize your paragraph by time or by space.

1. Just an hour ago the world seemed all in order.
2. The kitchen looked like the inside of a garbage truck.
3. We had passed the midpoint of the race.

4. The last ten minutes of the class period crawled at a worm's pace.
5. The accident began and ended before anyone realized what had happened.
6. The band was on stage as the spotlights came on.

7i A paragraph may be organized by a combination of time and space.

The following paragraph combines details of time and space to relate an event. See how each action follows the one before it. You also can tell where the actions take place because the writer keeps the focus on important locations.

> As the low clouds began to lift from the airfield, the pilot made her way from the hangar to the single-engine plane parked near the runway. She checked its engine and tapped its wings and tail before opening the cockpit door and climbing in. Inside, she strapped herself to the seat, adjusted a number of controls on the panel in front of her, and started the engine. The two-bladed propeller kicked over and then whirled into a circular blur, sending vibrations through the plane. Within a minute the pilot had eased the plane onto the end of the runway and turned it to face the long expanse of asphalt. For a short time she raced the engine while holding the plane in place with its brakes on. Finally, releasing the brakes, she gunned the engine. The plane leaped forward,

gained speed, and in a swift, bird-like swoop lifted from the ground, flying free toward the clouds.

7j Link the sentences of a paragraph together by connecting words.

Certain words help to show the relationship between ideas. These words serve as links in sentences. Without them, sentences in a paragraph may seem disconnected.

Compare the following two short paragraphs. Paragraph A has no connecting words. In paragraph B the relationship between the ideas is made clear.

PARAGRAPH A

Pioneers settled the North American great central plains slowly. A few lonely hunters and trappers followed the courses of major rivers. The tales of their adventures caused other daring people to explore the territory. Whole familes ventured into the Great Plains and set up clusters of homes. The people somehow withstood the trials of the frontier and established the beginnings of towns and cities. The railroads crossed the plains, bringing the quantities of people and material needed to build today's Midwest.

PARAGRAPH B

Pioneers settled the North American great central plains slowly. *At first,* a few lonely hunters and trappers followed the courses of the major rivers. *Afterward,* the tales of their adventures caused other daring people to explore the territory. *Following this,* whole families ventured into the Great Plains and set up clusters of homes. The people somehow withstood the trials of the frontier and established the beginnings of towns and cities. *At last,* the railroads crossed the plains, bringing the quantities of people and material needed to build today's Midwest.

You can see that the sentences in Paragraph A are not tightly linked in their time relationships. In Paragraph B the connecting words show the time links.

Examples of words that show time relationships are listed here.

at first	finally
after (that)	then
afterward	at last
next	in time
following this (that)	

Several connecting terms help show space relationships in a paragraph. Here are a few common terms.

around	near
above	at the right (left)
between	inside
next to	under
over	

To help show comparison or contrast in a paragraph, the following terms are helpful.

compared with (to)	however
in contrast to	on the one hand
in the first place	on the other hand

7k Use a paragraph to show the words of a new speaker.

An indentation at the beginning of a paragraph marks the words of a speaker. If you quote someone's words in a passage, begin the quotation by indenting the first line.

The following example shows how quotations are indented. Anna and Dolores are twin sisters who look so much alike that few people can tell them apart.

> Late one evening before falling asleep, Anna and Dolores lay in their bunk beds whispering.
>
> "Anna."
>
> "What?"
>
> "I have an idea."
>
> "Well?"
>
> "Do you ever get tired of being called by the wrong name?"
>
> "Yes. Most people are too busy to notice how different we are in many ways."
>
> "What are we going to do about it?"
>
> "You and I should trade places! Let's see how many of our teachers and friends we can fool tomorrow at school."
>
> The following day Anna and Dolores prepared for school. They dressed differently wearing each other's clothes. They even remembered to exchange the bracelets engraved with their names.
>
> "Dolores, do you really think our little trick will fool anyone?"
>
> "Yes, if we follow each other's class schedules and try not to be seen together at the same time."

"All right, Dolores, good luck."
"Thanks, but today my name is Anna!"

REVIEW EXERCISE A Paragraphs

Number a sheet of paper 1–13 and write each of the following topics next to each number. Then write *I* if the topic refers to an idea, *D* if it refers to a description, or *A* if it refers to an action. Finally, choose five of the topics and write your own topic sentence for a paragraph about each.

EXAMPLE The beauty of the coast of Maine

D
The craggy, wild coast of Maine is a magnificent sight.

1. How to make a candle
2. My idea of a beautiful person
3. How to hunt a deer
4. How to repair a broken window
5. A piece of clothing I have designed
6. A terrible sight
7. A wonderful sight
8. Why I like my favorite comic strip
9. People should live differently
10. Improvements the school should make
11. How to make up your face
12. Preparing a menu
13. Life on a ranch

REVIEW EXERCISE B Keeping Sentences on the Topic

Each of the following paragraphs has one or two sentences that do not relate to the topic. Number a sheet of paper 1–3. Next to each number write the number of the sentence or sentences in the paragraph that do not relate to the topic.

1. (1) More and more people are beginning to appreciate the nutritional value of brown rice. (2) For centuries, the people of China and India ate brown rice. (3) In India, curry is also a popular dish. (4) There was little malnutrition in these countries until the British introduced modern milling techniques. (5) Since these techniques remove the hull and bran layer of rice, they strip it of much of its food value. (6) What is left is white rice, which is much less nutritious than brown rice.

2. (1) On May 10, 1869, a great silver sledge hammer came down on a gold spike at Promontory Point, Utah. (2) The transcontinental railroad was finished. (3) It had taken a little more than three years to build. (4) Finally, after twenty thousand workers had toiled to lay almost two thousand miles of track, the East and West met. (5) Many of the men who labored on the railroad were Chinese. (6) The days of the covered wagon were over.

3. (1) Alcatraz Island is a deceptively beautiful place. (2) "The Rock," as it is called, lies in the middle of blue, sparkling San Francisco Bay. (3) San Francisco Bay meets the ocean nearby, close

to the Golden Gate Bridge. (4) But Alcatraz Island is the site of a notorious prison. (5) Stories of the harsh life of the prisoners there and the impossibility of escape are legend. (6) For several years, prisoners were forbidden to speak to one another. (7) The cold, damp, lonely cells were full of despairing men locked in their loneliness. (8) In 1969, a group of Native Americans occupied Alcatraz and laid claim to it.

REVIEW EXERCISE C Ways of Developing Paragraphs

Following is a list of topics for paragraphs. Choose three topics and write them as three headings across a sheet of paper. Then choose one of the following ways to develop each topic: *Details, examples, or reasons; comparison and contrast; cause and effect*. Do not choose the same way twice. Write the method you choose beneath each topic. Then list four points that you could use in developing the topic by this method.

EXAMPLE Making cheese

Making cheese
Cause and Effect
1. If milk is allowed to sour, lumpy curds form.
2. Adding rennet separates the curds from the whey.
3. Cutting, heating, straining, and pressing the curd helps to form the cheese.

4. Aging develops flavor and ripeness in cheese.

1. Why I like this city
2. Why I dislike this city
3. Television vs. movies
4. Two similar years in history
5. Why the sky is blue
6. How a car's ignition works
7. An interesting coincidence
8. Cooking with microwaves
9. The mineral malachite
10. Two people who look alike
11. A beautiful pair of boots

CHAPTER

8

GUIDELINES FOR WRITING

Composition is putting thoughts together. Every time you say or write something you are composing because, whether you speak or write, you are expressing what is in your mind.

The goal of composition is successful communication. This chapter provides important guidelines for putting your thoughts together. By following them carefully, you can increase effective communication with others.

CHOOSING YOUR TOPIC AND YOUR AUDIENCE

8a Write about what you know.

Knowing something about your subject can make composing much easier than if your topic is unknown to you. For this reason, be careful in choosing a topic. Select something you know well or can find out about. Your own experiences and feelings often are the easiest to write about.

If you don't know enough about a topic, find out about it before you begin writing. Read about it or ask others who know more than you do.

See Sources of Information, pp. 401–419

Choosing the right topic is the first step to preparing an interesting composition. The best topic is the one you know the most about. Then make a list of the most important items related to it.

EXERCISE 1 List five topics about which you could write a short composition.

8b Choose a topic to suit your audience.

Whenever you write a composition, think clearly about your *audience*—the person or persons who probably will read it. If you are not sure who will read what you write, you may have a hard time choosing your words and putting them together.

When you are talking to a person, you choose words and phrases that suit that person. Follow the same practice in writing. Write almost as though you were speaking to that person or persons.

EXERCISE 2 Choose one of the following topics to write about. Think about how you would write about it to someone you know well and who is your age. Then think about how you would write about it to an adult you do not know well. Choose either of these audiences. Then write at least one paragraph about your topic for that audience.

1. How I feel about people who talk too much
2. How I feel about people who never listen
3. That person was really rude
4. That person was really thoughtful
5. The time our pet was mistreated
6. I love to get dressed up
7. I hate to get dressed up
8. The person I respect and admire the most

EXERCISE 3 Rewrite the composition you wrote for Exercise 2. This time write your new composition for the audience you did not choose earlier.

ORGANIZING YOUR WRITING

Organization is the overall structure of your writing. Without it, your readers will find it hard to follow your reasoning. First choose a topic and an audience. Then decide how you will present your topic. For example, you might be able to treat it humorously rather than seriously. The effect you hope to achieve will largely determine the words you choose.

Next, make sure you can deal with the topic you have chosen.

8c Limit the topic you choose to write about.

A topic that is too broad will be difficult to fit into a composition. One example of an overly broad topic is "Food." Food has many aspects: growing it, preparing it, selling it, eating it. Think about all the different aspects of food and which ones interest you. Which ones do you know about? A limited topic within one of those aspects will be small enough to write about in a composition of a few paragraphs. Here are some possible examples.

How to cook a spicy dish
Why junk food is called "junk"
Food for a late night snack

EXERCISE 4 Think about some aspect of the broad topic of food. All of the following topics deal with food. However, some are still too broad to be treated in a composition of three or four paragraphs (300–500 words). Which of the topics that follow is best suited for a composition of three or four paragraphs? Write the topics on a sheet of paper.

1. The most unusual dish of food I ever ate
2. Spices of the world
3. The best restaurant meal I know
4. Elaborate menus
5. The fanciest dessert
6. How to barbecue steak
7. Preparing to roast a turkey
8. How to please with a hamburger

EXERCISE 5 The following topics are all too broad to be useful as topics for compositions of three or four paragraphs. On a sheet of paper write the numbers 1–8. Next to each number write at least three limited topics related to the broad topic. Each of the limited topics should be suitable for a composition of three or four paragraphs in length.

EXAMPLE Airplanes

The basic principle of a jet engine; The world's most dangerous airplane route; The thrill of my first take-off

1. Professional basketball
2. Mountain climbers
3. Hats
4. American holidays
5. Diseases still to be conquered
6. A home garden
7. Solar energy
8. The history of money

See Speaking and Listening, pp. 363–364

8d Organize events under major subtopics.

After you have chosen a topic, list the most important points you want to tell about it. Then see whether any of these major points, or subtopics, can be grouped together. Usually you can write one paragraph about each subtopic or each group of subtopics.

For example, suppose you chose the topic "A soccer maneuver." You can probably describe the entire maneuver in a single paragraph. If you chose the limited topic "A talent show," however, you may organize your description under three major subtopics: the contestants, the judges, and the decision. You may also have a fourth subtopic, the winner. Each of these subtopics could be treated in one paragraph in your composition.

EXERCISE 6 For each of the following topics, think of two or three subtopics. Number a sheet of paper 1–5. Skip three lines between numbers. Next to each number, write three subtopics you would include in a composition about the topic.

EXAMPLE The beach party
1. Planning the menu
2. Packing the car
3. Gathering firewood

1. The healthiest exercise
2. The challenge for today's farmer
3. A home aquarium
4. The perfect disco
5. Shopping for shoes
6. Binoculars

8e Relate events in the order they happen.

When you write about a number of related events in the sequence in which they occurred, you are writing a *narrative*. Narrative writing tells of experiences, or things that happen. Successful narrative writing requires that you keep events in the order they occurred.

Suppose you are relating the events leading up to a special trip you have taken. Begin at the beginning. When did you first learn you were going on a trip? How did you get the information? What were your first thoughts? What did you do to prepare for your trip? What happened as you finally departed?

A good way to remember all these events is to write them in a list before you begin writing. Then check over your list and put each incident in chronological order.

You may want to divide your list into a *beginning,* a *middle,* and an *ending.* This will save you and your readers much trouble because it will help you and them see the natural sequence clearly. It will also help you decide how many paragraphs you will need to cover all the events.

EXERCISE 7 Following is a list of connected events. Only the first and last event are in order, however. On a sheet of paper write the letters of the events in the order the events probably happened.

A. A tree cutter marked a tall tree to be felled.
B. The cutters sawed the trunk into logs.
C. The branch trimmer started the power saw.
D. The branch trimmer climbed down the bare trunk.
E. The logs were strapped on the truck.
F. The branch trimmer sawed off the top of the tree.
G. The branch trimmer strapped on climbing gear.
H. The cutters felled the bare trunk.
I. The branch trimmer trimmed all but the topmost branches.
J. The branch trimmer picked up a power saw.
K. The branch trimmer climbed higher.
L. The branch trimmer trimmed the lower branches.
M. The branch trimmer climbed to the lowest branches.
N. The truck hauled the logs to the sawmill.

8f Tell about the setting of events.

Writing successfully about anyone or anything depends in part upon your creating a complete picture in the mind of your reader. To show the importance of an event, you must tell where it happens. The place where it happens is its *setting*.

Striking a match can be relatively unimportant if it's done in your kitchen. The same act can be extremely significant if it is done in a field of tall, dry grass.

In describing a setting, choose only those features that help make it special. On the one hand, one or two features are not enough to distinguish it. On the other hand, you do not need to include every feature. Too many features begin to overload the image you are creating.

Following is an example of a description of a setting that does not include enough features. Following that is a description of the same place with colorful features that are well chosen.

> Dawn began to show light in the east, although overhead the stars shone in a dark sky. The mountains to the east were outlined by the dawn. Carla looked with one eye but, feeling cold, retreated deeper into her sleeping bag. Not being sleepy, she looked out again. Everything was the same as before: the pine trees and the odor from their needles. Another day had begun.

> Slowly the light of dawn filled the eastern sky, faint blue against the darker, star-specked expanse above. The low range of mountains to the east appeared more sharply outlined

against the soft light with each brightening span of time. Carla partly opened one eye and peeped at the flush of light, but she felt the cold air on her face and quickly snuggled deeper within her green cocoon of a sleeping bag. But she couldn't fall asleep again, and soon she lifted her face into the open and turned her head from side to side. Nothing had changed since yesterday. The pine trees stood guard over her. The perfumed aroma of their needles scented the still air. Another day in the wilderness had begun.

EXERCISE 8 Describe a place where you had a special experience. Tell how features of the place are situated in relation to one another. You can choose an experience from the following list. Or you may wish to choose another experience.

1. The most beautiful scene I remember
2. The ugliest scene I remember
3. The place I'd like to forget
4. The memory lingers on
5. An ant's eye view
6. The street from the highest window
7. In the darkest night
8. A mysterious place

8g Tie events together by causes and effects.

Life is a series of related events, events that cause other events to happen. In your writing it is important to show how one event leads to another.

Sometimes you have to study how events are tied together so that you can write clearly about them. You may need to tell your readers that the events are connected before you can make the relationship clear.

EXAMPLES

UNCONNECTED EVENTS Sally ran into the street. Her mother was angry.

CONNECTED EVENTS Sally ran into the street. As a result, her mother was angry.

EXERCISE 9 Following is a list of events. Something caused each to happen. Think of a possible cause for each event. Number a sheet of paper 1–8. Write the possible cause next to the number of each event.

EXAMPLE A tree's branch breaks.
A heavy person climbs out too far on the branch.

1. A window pane is broken.
2. Moss grows on a rock.
3. The edge of a cup is chipped.
4. A small stone is very hot.
5. A stain shows on the tablecloth.
6. A hole appears in the blanket.
7. A car's fender is dented.
8. The ceiling has a wet spot.

The English language contains words called *connectors* that connect causes and effects. They will help you show the relationship between events.

See Conjunction, p. 443; Adverb, p. 438; Preposition, p. 458

Examples of such words are *because* and *then.* Connectors may be conjunctions, adverbs, or prepositions.

Here are some examples of connectors.

as a result	Elena left her money at home; *as a result,* she had to walk.
because	*Because* the street was torn up, all traffic was detoured.
since	The motorcycle won't start *since* there is no gas in the tank.
therefore	Loretta found her wallet; *therefore,* she doesn't have to borrow any cash.
thus	The decorations were finished in time; *thus,* the party was a great success.
whenever	You can be sure friends will help *whenever* an emergency comes up.

EXERCISE 10 Following are pairs of sentences that can be combined as causes and effects. On a sheet of paper write each pair as one sentence. Use connectors to show the relationship of cause and effect. Underline the connectors you use.

EXAMPLE A cat crept across the grass. A squirrel scolded from a tree branch.

Whenever the cat crept across the grass, a squirrel scolded from a tree branch.

1. Suds foamed over the top of the washing machine. Phil had poured in too much soap.
2. Trash lay near the garbage can. A stray dog had tipped over the can.
3. A soaring glider stays aloft. A strong, steady wind blows.
4. The goalie moved too slowly. The ball sailed into the goal.
5. Rhonda received mostly money as birthday gifts. She was able to buy herself a purse and shoes.

EXERCISE 11 Write a composition of two or three paragraphs about an experience you had or an event you know about. Show the relationship between at least three causes and three effects. Use connectors to show how the causes and effects are related and underline the connectors.

CHOOSING YOUR WORDS

8h Use words and phrases that appeal to the senses.

See Phrase, p. 457

The meanings people give to words are closely related to their experiences. The words you use in your compositions should remind your readers of experiences that they have had. This will help them understand the meanings your words intend to convey.

Words that are most successful are ones that appeal to your reader's senses of sight, hearing, touch, taste, and smell. They make your writing come alive.

The first sentence here lacks sensory appeal. The second sentence adds words that appeal to the senses.

1. Babs picked up the sea snail and dropped it.
2. Babs gingerly picked up the moist, sand-covered sea snail and, noticing its sour odor, quickly dropped it.

In the second sentence you see words that appeal to the senses. *Gingerly* tells how Babs picked up the sea snail. It suggests that she will quickly drop it, which she does. The words *moist* and *sand-covered* appeal to the senses of touch and sight. The sense of smell is affected by the phrase *sour odor.*

As you describe events and objects, think how you can appeal to the senses of your reader by choosing sensory words.

EXERCISE 12 Following is a list of words that appeal to the senses. Choose ten words from the list. Use those words in ten sentences of your own construction. Underline the sensory word you use in each sentence.

EXAMPLE rumble

We heard the rumble of distant trucks on the highway.

frizzle	roasted	cackle
ripped	orange	peppery
flapping	sandy	grimy
blunt	pungent	fiery
rustle	damp	splat
crunch	blinding	worn

EXERCISE 13 Each of the following sentences lacks words that appeal to the senses. Rewrite each sentence on a sheet of paper. Add words that appeal to the senses. You may also change some words. Do not change the basic meanings.

EXAMPLE The hawk circled in the air.

The giant hawk, teetering from wing to wing, swung in easy circles on invisible drafts of air.

1. A foghorn sounded in the distance across the bay.
2. At the top of the tower a light blinked on and off.
3. The seal swam along the edge of the pool; then it came out of the water.
4. Shinji rested under a tree that summer afternoon.
5. Lucia opened the bakery door and entered.
6. We were alone in the snow under a cloudy sky.
7. The furnace in the steel plant gave off heat and light.
8. A lone ant walked along the edge of the box.

8i Use comparisons to improve your descriptions.

Comparisons can be especially useful in your writing. You often can describe one person or thing more clearly and more interestingly by comparing it to another person or thing. The object of comparison does not have to be just like the one you are describing. It may have only certain qualities in common with your topic. Nevertheless, the similarity will help create a complete picture of your topic.

Suppose, for example, you describe the crowd at a sporting event. You describe how the crowd becomes angry because of something that happens. You might compare the angry crowd to a hive of bees.

EXAMPLE The angry crowd buzzed, as noisy and restless as bees when their honeycomb is disturbed.

Bees are not people, of course. But something about the action of angry bees suggests the disturbance in a crowded grandstand.

See Common Confusions, p. 282

In many cases the word *like* or *as* begins the wording of a comparison. When either does, the comparison is a *simile*.

EXAMPLE The big dog charged *like* a maddened bull.
Rena stood stiff *as* an icicle.

To create a comparison, think how one person, place, or thing is like some other. Then place the two together, using *like* or *as* if one of those words helps the two to fit.

EXERCISE 14 List A contains objects or qualities. List B contains comparisons. Number a sheet of paper 1–5. Next to each number write the item from List A. Then write the best comparison from List B. The first one is done for you as an example.

EXAMPLE Red
Red as blood running from a cut

A	B
1. Red	like the underfeathers of a baby bird
2. White	as polished marble
3. Weightless	as a freshly laundered sheet drying in the sun
4. Smooth and hard	as bits of dust seen floating in a shaft of light
5. Soft	as blood running from a cut

EXERCISE 15 The items listed here need comparisons to make their descriptions more interesting. Write each of them on a sheet of paper. Add your own comparison to each.

EXAMPLE unsteady

Unsteady as the legs of a newborn colt

1. A head of hair
2. A glass eye
3. A squirrel's tail
4. The petal of a flower
5. Smooth
6. Warped
7. Noisy
8. A moving locomotive
9. Stiff
10. Tasteless

EXERCISE 16 Choose one of the following topics. Or choose a topic from Exercise 1 on page 191. On a sheet of paper write at least one paragraph describing what you have chosen. Include comparisons in your description.

1. The soup I dislike
2. The best kind of music
3. Hair I would like to have
4. I saw a picture of an attractive man
5. I saw a picture of an attractive woman
6. An unusual dog
7. An unusual cat
8. The outfit of clothes I would like to have
9. The most ridiculous costume
10. A special flower arrangement

See Paragraphs, pp. 174–175

8j Support your ideas with specific details, examples, or reasons.

Broad statements, or *generalizations,* are made every day. You hear someone say, "Florida is the best place to vacation." But you probably hear few reasons to back up the claim. People also generalize when they say "New Yorkers are friendly" or "Joggers never die of heart attacks."

Generalizations usually refer to a broad fact or opinion. Often they ascribe to a whole category of persons or things qualities that more often belong only to individuals. Their weakness lies in their lack of specific details, examples, or reasons to prove what they say. What they need is specific information.

A generalization may sometimes serve as the title of a composition or as a topic sentence.

EXAMPLE College football is better than professional football.

This topic sentence is a generalization. It needs specific details, examples, and reasons to back it up.

College football is better in what particular ways? The generalization gives no particulars.

A general statement is strengthened if it is supported with specific information. When you write a composition based upon a generalization, think of specific evidence to back up your statement. List your facts before you begin writing.

EXERCISE 17 The following list of ideas is general statements. They need supporting details, examples, or reasons to make them stronger. Choose one of the generalizations. Write the complete statement on a sheet of paper. You may reword it if necessary. Write down at least four supporting details, examples, or reasons to support the statement.

1. (Name of a TV show) is the best comedy on television.
2. (Name of a TV show) is the worst show on television.
3. (Name of a movie) is the best horror movie ever made.
4. The funniest movie sequence ever filmed is (name of movie).
5. The most romantic story ever told is (name of story).
6. (Name of a singer) is the best singer today.

EXERCISE 18 Write a composition of 150–300 words about the generalization you chose in Exercise 17. Use the supporting details, examples, or reasons you listed. Also remember to use words that appeal to the senses. Make comparisons where you can.

8k Show clearly how your ideas are linked together.

See Connector, p. 444

Connectors help to show how ideas are linked together. The ideas may be in separate sentences or they may be in separate paragraphs.

See Pronoun, p. 458

Pronouns, for example, when carefully used, sometimes can show the relationship of ideas.

EXAMPLE A visit to the movies can be fun. *It* is one way of escaping life's realities. [*It* repeats the phrase *a visit to the movies*. The pronoun *it* ties the two sentences together.]

See Adverb, p. 438

Some adverbs show the relationship of events in time.

EXAMPLE Christina picked up the diamond bracelet. *Then* she uttered a gasp of dismay.
[*Then* shows the time relationship between the picking up of the bracelet and the uttering of a gasp.]

Other kinds of words also work as connectors. Here is a list of common ones.

After that (or *this*) is used to show what follows an event.

The shark circled closer. *After that,* I decided to get to the surface.

As a result is used to tell of the effect of some action.

As a result of my motions, the shark seemed more curious.

At first, at last, are used to begin or end a series of items related in time.

At last we arrived at the bridge.

Besides is used to introduce an additional point.

No one wanted to go swimming. *Besides,* we had left the swim fins behind.

Finally is similar to *at last.*

For example (for instance) is used to introduce a specific point that supports a general statement.

Hunger seems a powerful force. *For instance,* timid fish will, when hungry, eat right out of my hand.

Furthermore is used to show that another point is coming.

We met their charge head on. *Furthermore,* we were prepared for an attack on our flank.

Hence is used to show that something is a result of some action or thought.

The motion has been passed. *Hence,* we can continue making progress in our meeting.

However is used to tell of a contrast.

Most lawyers are skilled in argumentation. *However,* they don't always get their way in a family fight.

In addition is used to show that more is coming.

The lawn has been cut. *In addition,* its edges are trimmed.

In conclusion is used to begin a final point.

In conclusion, the awards committee deserves congratulations.

Instead is used to tell of a contrasting action or point.

The pilot could have landed. *Instead,* she flew around the field.

Later is used to show a time relationship.

Georgette spoke with fury. *Later* she would have a chance to apologize.

Meanwhile is used to tell about something else that happens at the same time.

The sailors struggled to bring in the jib. *Meanwhile,* the mainsail had torn in the wind.

Moreover is similar to *in addition.*

Nevertheless is similar to *however.*

On the other hand is similar to *however.*

Therefore is similar to *hence.*

Thus is similar to *hence.*

EXERCISE 19 Each pair of the sentences that follow needs a connecting term to show how the ideas are related. Write each pair of sentences on a sheet of paper and include the best connecting term in its most suitable position.

EXAMPLE The police officer let her off without a ticket. She was furious at herself for going through the red light.

The police officer let her off without a ticket. Nevertheless, she was furious at herself for going through the red light.

1. José continued the meeting. The crowd kept yelling in the hall.
2. The windows have been washed. The sills are clean.
3. We carefully tended the little garden. Green shoots began to poke through the soil.

4. The high diving board looks dangerous. The low one seems safe enough.
5. Red might have chosen to go with Pete. He decided to accept Valerie's invitation.

REVISING YOUR WRITING

8l Revise your writing to improve its effectiveness.

Good writing means rewriting. Few writers can make their writing say what they mean the first time. You should be prepared to revise your writing a second or even a third time. You may leave something out or state a point in an unclear way. By revising, you can add anything missing. You can reword a point to make it stronger.

Before revising, give yourself at least a few hours' rest. This will allow you to take a fresh look at your work. With a fresh eye, you often can spot careless errors.

For additional help in improving your composition, try reading it aloud to another person. Or have someone else read it aloud to you.

At least read your composition aloud to yourself to see whether it sounds sensible. Stop reading when you hear something that sounds out of place or disconnected and correct it.

8m Check the mechanics of your writing.

See Mechanics, pp. 294–339

Give your completed composition a final reading. Look for mechanical errors. Are words spelled correctly? Did you put capitals where they belong? Are your marks of punctuation correctly used?

Check your paragraph against the Composition Checklist.

COMPOSITION CHECKLIST

1. Do you know enough about your topic?
2. Have you an audience clearly in your mind?
3. Does your topic suit your audience?
4. Is your topic limited so that you can deal with it?
5. Have you organized the events in time and place?
6. Have you used the words and phrases that appeal to the audience?
7. Have you used comparisons?
8. Have you supported general ideas with specific details?
9. Have you used connectors clearly?
10. Does each paragraph develop an idea or an event?
11. Are your words, phrases, and sentences the most effective for putting across your ideas?
12. Have you left any phrases or clauses separated from complete sentences?
13. Have you checked the mechanics to the best of your ability?

PREPARING A COMPOSITION

Follow these guidelines when you put your composition in its final form, unless your teacher directs you otherwise.

1. Write or type on good quality white paper 8½-by-11 inches in size. Handwritten compositions should be on lined paper. Typewritten compositions should be on unlined paper.
2. Use blue or black ink in a pen or a black ribbon in a typewriter. Write on only one side of each sheet. Double-space typewritten lines.
3. Keep margins even, about 1½ inches top and left. The right and bottom margins may be narrower for handwritten than for typewritten papers. Indent paragraphs another inch from the left margin. Avoid crowding.
4. Center the title at the top of the first page only. Use no quotation marks or underlining in a title unless another title is part of your title.
5. Include your name and the date as directed by your teacher.
6. Never put a comma, a semicolon, a colon, or any end punctuation at the beginning of a line. Do not put beginning quotation marks or a parenthesis at the end of a line.
7. Divide words at the end of a line between syllables. However, do not end or begin a line with only one letter of a word. For example, do not break *a-part, e-mit, luck-y.*
8. In most cases, divide words between two consonants. For examples, *trap-per, thun-der.* However, do not divide double consonants that stand for one sound. For example, do not divide *gop-her, as-hes.*
9. Write or type neatly. Avoid making a mess when erasing or marking over mistakes. Draw a single straight line through a mistake or unwanted word. When inserting a letter or word, mark the point of insertion on the line with a

caret (∧). Write the inserted letter or word above that point.

10. Keep papers from being crumpled, torn, or dirty. Plan ahead so that you hand them in on time and in their best form.

REVIEW EXERCISE A Topic and Audience

Match each of the following numbered topics with its most appropriate audience. Number a sheet of paper 1–6. Next to each number write the topic and the letter of the audience that goes with that topic. Next, choose one of the topics. Write at least five points that relate to the topic and that can be used in a composition. The first one is done for you.

EXAMPLE Siamese cats

Siamese cats – f
1. Probably of Eastern origin
2. Have unusual coat pattern
3. Great voice range
4. Kittens born white; acquire color
5. Sociable and entertaining

TOPICS	AUDIENCE
1. Siamese cats	a. Your classmates
2. A notorious criminal	b. Young parents
3. A famous popular singer	c. The Police Officer's League
4. How to succeed in high school	d. Potential dancers
5. A child's first year	e. Most younger music lovers
6. How to do a popular dance	f. Pet lovers

REVIEW EXERCISE B Limiting the Topic

Following are two lists. One of these is a list of broad topics, and the other is a list of more limited topics. Number a sheet of paper 1–10. Next to each number write the broad topic from the first list and the more limited topic from the second list that relates to it.

EXAMPLE Painting

Painting – How to Mix Colors

BROAD TOPICS

1. Playing music
2. Sports
3. Dancing
4. Acting
5. A typical week
6. Working with clay
7. Making candy
8. Athletic uniforms
9. Cooking vegetables
10. Crocheting

LIMITED TOPICS

Applying stage makeup to the eyes
Making a pair of gloves
Happy Friday
Perfect steamed asparagus
Some ballet exercises
Old-fashioned fudge
How to control the puck in ice hockey
High notes on the flute
Football pads for players
The potter's wheel

REVIEW EXERCISE C Writing a Composition

Choose one of the limited topics in Review Exercise B and write a composition of 150–200 words about it. If you prefer, write about another topic that is similar.

REVIEW EXERCISE D Cause and Effect

Following is a list of effects. Number a sheet of paper 1–5. Next to each number write a cause that would lead to the effect given.

EXAMPLE I wore earmuffs in July.

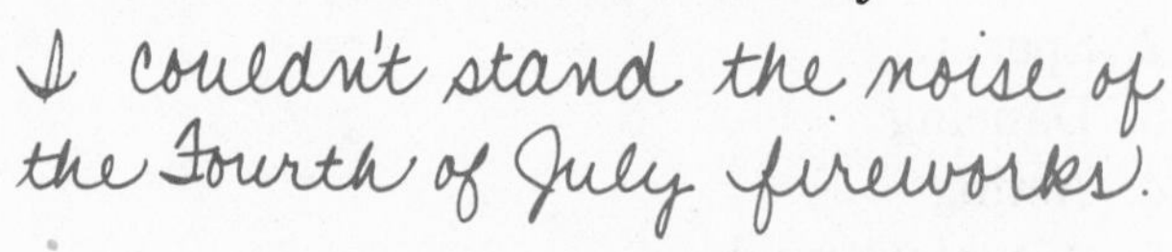

I couldn't stand the noise of
the Fourth of July fireworks.

1. And that is why the giraffe has a long neck.
2. The door suddenly flew open and a man ran out.
3. Thus the town got its name.
4. I will always hate the color blue.
5. Everything seemed to turn a different color.

REVIEW EXERCISE E Choosing Words

Following is a list of ten words or phrases. Number a sheet of paper 1–10. Next to each number write a sentence using the word or phrase. Include in your sentence one of the following items: a comparison, words that appeal to the senses, or a word used to show a connection between two ideas.

EXAMPLE Crisp

The crisp skin of the roast duckling looked deliciously brown.

1. like a great white globe
2. although
3. greasy
4. a small, round object
5. the corners of her mouth
6. because
7. fragrant
8. like a sinister swamp
9. his brown, freckled hand
10. since

CHAPTER

9

LETTER WRITING

For most people, composing letters is probably the most important kind of writing they do. But even if you do other kinds of writing in your life, you will find that writing effective letters is an extremely handy tool to have. You may write a letter asking for a job. Or you may write a letter to explain something of great importance. Perhaps you will write a letter to someone that will strongly influence that person's feelings toward you. Whatever the occasion, learning how to write effective letters will benefit you greatly.

The two main kinds of letters are *personal,* or *friendly, letters* and *business letters*. Both kinds put across their meaning in both their *content* and their *form.* The content is what you write. The form is how your letter appears.

This chapter gives guidelines for writing both personal and business letters.

PREPARING THE LETTER

9a Follow the five guides for letter writing.

(1) Think ahead before you write.

Ask yourself what information you want the reader of your letter to have. Ask also what action, if any, you want your reader to take. If you are writing a personal letter, you may be telling of your experiences. It will help if you jot down the high points before you start writing. Then you can refer to them as you write.

If you want your reader to take some action, you must state exactly what that action should be. In a business letter that requests or orders something, you must be very clear. Otherwise you may get something you do not want. Or you may get nothing at all.

(2) Use the best paper and writing equipment.

Your stationery represents you to your reader. If you write neatly on clean paper, you create one kind of impression. If you use smudged or torn paper, you give a different impression.

The kind of pen or typewriter you use will also make a difference. Clean, straight letters look better than letters that are scratched and blurred.

It is best to type business letters. If you must write your business letters by hand, be sure you use pen rather than pencil.

(3) Follow standard form.

Use the standard form illustrated in this chapter when writing a business letter.

Make sure the names and addresses you use are correct. If a business person receives a letter that is incorrectly addressed, he or she wonders whether the information in the body of the letter is also incorrect.

Your return address and the date are important parts of your letter. They are used for reference purposes and for contacting you.

Sign your name in ink in the closing, even if the letter is typewritten.

(4) Use standard grammar, spelling, and punctuation.

Letters with careless errors are far less effective than those that are error free. Check your writing closely to catch any mistakes you may have made.

(5) Read over your letter before you send it.

Reading a letter through will help you find any errors. If the letter is really important, write it and then put it aside for a time. Later, when you come back to read it over, read it aloud to yourself. Put yourself in the position of the receiver. Does your letter convey the meaning you want it to?

In most cases, a few simple corrections can be made on the letter itself. Place a single clean line through an error. Write your correction just above the error. Of course, if too many errors make the letter look sloppy, copy it over.

THE BUSINESS LETTER

9b Use the standard form in a business letter.

Follow the standard form of a business letter carefully. People in business are in the habit of reading letters that follow a certain form. They are accustomed to looking for information in certain places. If you send a business letter that doesn't follow the form, it may not get the attention you want.

Notice the six parts of the business letter.

HEADING

452 Carolina St.
Lansing, MI 48915
November 15, 1980

INSIDE ADDRESS

Spengler's Department Store
1600 Hathaway St.
Lansing, MI 48910

SALUTATION

Dear Sir or Madam:

BODY

On October 3 I bought a pair of hiking boots in your store and charged them to my account. (My Spengler's charge card number is 0419-623-785.) The boots cost $39.95.

Yesterday I received the bill from your store; but instead of the $39.95 charge for the boots, I was charged $72.56 for a lounge chair. I am afraid that my account has been confused with someone else's, as I never purchased a lounge chair at your store.

I am enclosing a copy of my bill and a copy of my receipt for the hiking boots. Could you please check your records and remove this charge from my next bill? Please call me at 485-2209 if you have any questions.

CLOSING

Sincerely,

SIGNATURE

Coretta Washington

Coretta Washington

The main kinds of business letters are the *letter of application* or *request,* the *order letter,* and the *letter of adjustment* or *complaint.*

The Letter of Application

A letter of application usually asks for a job. Many firms require you to fill out a standard application form. As a result, you may not have to write a letter if the application form is sufficient. This is not always the case, however, so knowing how to write a letter of application for a job is a useful skill to have.

A letter of application should do at least five things:

1. State how you came to know of the company or the job.
2. State that you are seeking a job with the company.
3. List your qualifications and any experience or special skills that you have. You may want to say why this job interests you.
4. Give the name and address of at least one person who can supply a good reference. This person may be a former employer, a teacher, or anyone else who can give information about your character and qualifications.
5. You may also want to ask for an interview appointment.

Here is an example of a letter of application.

421 Apple Lane
Oak Grove, NY 11702
April 29, 1980

Manager, Pet-Vet Kennels
29 Elm Street
Genesee, NY 11835

Dear Sir:

I read in the Times that you are seeking a young person to assist part-time at the Pet-Vet Kennels. I would like to apply for that job.

For several years I not only have cared for my own pets--two dogs, several cats, and a sheep, but also have taken care of neighbor's pets while their owners have been away.

I am experienced in training animals and in treating them when they get sick. I learned how to do these things from my aunt, who once worked as a veterinarian.

For more information on my qualifications for the job, you may contact her.

Katherine C. Thompson
The Four Elms
Oak Grove, NY 11702

I hope you will consider me for the job.

Sincerely,

Lorna Alhouse

Lorna Alhouse

The Request Letter

As its name states, this kind of business letter asks for something. You may be searching for information. Or you may want a copy of some printed material. Whatever you are seeking, the neatness and correctness of your letter will help you get it.

It is a good idea to send a return envelope with your request letter. Fill out your name and address on the envelope and add the correct amount of postage if you know it.

Here is an example of a request letter.

10041 Gila Rd.
Phoenix, AZ 85001
September 20, 1980

American Friends Service Committee
2160 Mesa Boulevard
Tucson, AZ 85705

Dear Sir or Madam:

My high school guidance counselor has told me that you have special programs for students who want to live and go to school in foreign countries.

I am a fourth-year Spanish student and would like to improve my Spanish by living with a family and attending high school in Central or South America. Could you please send me information on your programs there? I would also appreciate it if you would give me the names and addresses of other organizations that sponsor students in Spanish-speaking countries. I am enclosing a stamped, self-addressed envelope.

Thank you.

Sincerely,

Alison Malinsky

Alison Malinsky

EXERCISE 1 Look in the newspaper for a job for which you might be qualified. Write a letter of application. Do not send the letter unless you are serious about applying for the job.

EXERCISE 2 Write a letter to an organization requesting information. Ask for any catalogs, brochures, publications, or other printed material. You can also ask for prices of items for sale. Do not send the letter unless you really need the information.

The Order Letter

Ordering by mail is a common way of buying goods. However, in your order letter you must take great care to describe exactly what you are buying. Otherwise you might get the wrong materials.

In order to avoid confusion between you and the supplier, ask yourself the following questions when you order by mail:

1. Do I have the right name of each item and its catalog number?
2. Are the prices and totals correct?
3. If I must prepay, have I included the correct amount in a check (if acceptable) or money order?
4. If the postage is required, have I included it?
5. Is my correct return address included?
6. If a choice of shipping is requested, have I stated how I want material sent?

An example of an order letter follows on the next page.

2115 Aviation Blvd.
San Diego, CA 92106
January 10, 1980

J & D Publications
Box 3063
Bethlehem, PA 18017

Sirs:

I understand that you have a program for a person with a camera to make extra money taking pictures. I would like to order your instruction booklet.

In addition to the booklet, please send me the full information telling me how I can get into this work.

I own a 35 mm. camera and have experience taking both portrait pictures and action shots. Also, I do my own photo processing.

Enclosed is my money order for $3.25 and a self-addressed envelope with postage. I am also enclosing some samples of photos I have taken and processed.

I look forward to hearing from you.

Sincerely,

Jose Rivera

Jose Rivera

EXERCISE 3 Write a business letter ordering the following:

1 Wall and Mirror Stencil Kit #11245 with stencils, brush, paint, and instructions @ $14.99

1 Bathtub Decal Kit #10142 in red and blue @ $6.95

1 Decorator's Guide booklet (free)

The company is Better Homes, Dept. 2VA, Box 374, Des Moines, IA 50336. You enclose a money order or a check for $21.94.

The Letter of Adjustment or Complaint

Something you have bought by mail is damaged or is not what you ordered. Perhaps there is a mix-up in the amount of money you are charged for whatever you have bought. These situations require a letter of adjustment.

An example of a letter of adjustment follows.

1022 Front St.
Quincy, MA 02764
December 16, 1980

Nord-Viscount Corp.
Dept. HR-56
Brooklyn, NY 11230

Dear Sir or Madam:

On November 29 I ordered two quarts of your "World's Finest" Auto Glaze at $7.50 per quart. I sent you $15.00 plus $2.00 for postage, or $17.00 total.

On December 12 I received one quart of what I ordered and one can of Gumout Jet-Spray, which I did not order. I will be happy to return the Gumout Jet-Spray, which I have not used; but I would like the other quart of Auto Glaze.

Would you please send me the Auto Glaze I ordered? I will return the Gumout.

Thank you for your attention to this matter.

Sincerely,

Janet Holum

Janet Holum

A letter of complaint is like a letter of adjustment, although it may not correct an error in buying or selling something. Instead, the letter of complaint calls attention to something you find wrong. An example follows.

118 Grandview Rd.
Ardmore, PA 19003
June 4, 1980

Manager
Purebest Food Market
Lancaster Square
Ardmore, PA 19003

Dear Sir or Madam:

I would like to call your attention to a problem in the parking lot in back of your store, which I can see from my home. Twice each week for several months someone has been piling trash on the lot against the back of your building a day or two before the trash collectors haul it away.

In that pile of trash is something that gives off a strong smell, especially during these warm days. Moreover, I have seen stray dogs pulling the trash apart. Often the trash is spread around the lot.

I do not think you would want this condition to continue if you knew of it, so I am writing to let you know. I hope you can correct the situation.

Sincerely,

Theodore Sammit

Theodore Sammit

EXERCISE 4 Write a letter of complaint or a letter of adjustment regarding some matter that you believe an organization should correct. For example:

a. You live near an airport. Lately the landing pattern for airplanes has been changed so that incoming planes fly low over your house. You write a letter to the chief traffic controller at the airport complaining about the noise.
b. You bought a scarf from Art Crafts, Inc., Box 21, Flagstaff, Arizona. You sent $11.50 plus fifty cents postage. You received a hat by mistake. Write a letter saying you are returning the hat and would like the scarf you ordered.
c. You live in the country near a large farm that is sprayed by airplane. During the spraying you notice that some of the spray falls outside the crop area. You write the farmer who owns the cropland, warning about the misplaced spray.

MAILING THE LETTER

9c Use standard form in addressing an envelope.

The following form is standard for addressing a business letter envelope.

Coretta Washington
452 Carolina St.
Lansing, MI 48915

Spengler's Department Store
1600 Hathaway St.
Lansing, MI 48910

EXERCISE 5 Prepare a piece of paper as though it were the front of an envelope. Write the correct form for addressing an envelope for sending one of the model business letters on pages 221–228.

REVIEW EXERCISE A Standard Form for Business Letters

Following is an outline of a business letter with numbers where its various parts should be. Number a sheet of paper 1–6. Next to each number write the letter of the correct part from the list that corresponds with the number on the outline.

STANDARD PARTS

a. The heading
b. The closing
c. The inside address
d. The salutation
e. The body of the letter
f. Your signature

1. ______

2. ______

3. ______

4. ______

5. ______

6. ______

Sandra Gomez

REVIEW EXERCISE B Kinds of Business Letters

Each of the following directions relates to one of these kinds of business letters: *the letter of application, the request letter, the order letter,* or *the letter of adjustment or complaint.* Number a sheet of paper 1–12. Next to each number write *AP* if the statement relates to a letter of application, *R* if it relates to a request letter, *O* if it relates to an order letter, or *AC* if it relates to a letter of adjustment or complaint.

EXAMPLE State how you came to know of the company or the job.

AP

1. Ask for information.
2. Include the correct name of each item and its catalog number.
3. Include information about your choice of shipping.
4. State what your qualifications are.
5. State the problem or error clearly.
6. State that you are seeking a job with the company.
7. Ask for a copy of some printed material.
8. Include correct prices and totals.
9. State what you want done about the problem or error.
10. Include a check or money order if prepayment is necessary.
11. Include a self-addressed, stamped return envelope.
12. Give the name of a reference.

REVIEW EXERCISE C Order Letters and Letters of Adjustment or Complaint

Following is a list of subjects for order letters or letters of adjustment or complaint. Choose one or use your own subject and write a business letter. Make sure you follow standard form.

1. Order: 1 pint lady bugs, price $4.00 per pint; 2 praying mantis egg cases, price $1.25 per case, and a free copy of "The Organic Gardening Guide" from the Bug Ranch, RFD 3, Happy Trails, OR 97369. Postage is $2.00 regular mail, $6.00 airmail.
2. The searchlight advertising the new gas station down the block shines directly into your bedroom window all night, and your curtains do not shut out the light. You want Save-U-Gas, 460 Maple St., New York, NY 10023, to do something about it.
3. You ordered two copies of *How To Cut Toenails Properly,* by Dr. J. Bunyon, Harper and Millan Publishing Co., 720 Oak St., New York, NY 10045. You enclosed a check to cover the $4.50 cost of each book plus $1.00 postage. However, they sent you two copies of *Are you Crazy?* by Y. Yak rather than the book you ordered.
4. You would like to order: 3 5″×7″ prints of negative #3 at $1.00 each, 1 8″×10″ print of negative #6 at $2.50, and 10 wallet-sized photos of negative #9 at $.20 each. Postage is $.75 regular mail and $1.50 airmail. The company is Negative Attitudes, 5523 East 52nd St., New York, NY 10036.

UNIT THREE

USAGE

Using Parts of Speech
Common Confusions

CHAPTER

10

USING PARTS OF SPEECH

Usage in English means which words and which forms of words you choose to convey your meaning to your listener. You choose a particular word in a sentence because you have heard it used that way before. You form the word in a certain way because you believe that form is the correct one to use in that instance. In both cases, you need to be sure you have made the best choice.

Which words to use and when to use them are questions all people using English in formal situations must consider. For example, a newscaster speaks to a large radio or television audience. He or she must choose words with great care. The forms of those words must be correct. When a political leader addresses an audience, his or her language must be correct. The same is true for all people who communicate in situations where exact language is necessary.

Correct usage, therefore, is partly defined by the situation in which language is used. What is correct or appropriate in one situation may or may not be the same as in another situation. But you do not have to use formal language if you are not in formal situations. Only if you are aware of all the rules, however, can you choose which ones are appropriate in a given situation. Of course, the basic rules of usage must be maintained. Otherwise your listeners will not understand what you are trying to say.

AGREEMENT OF SUBJECTS AND VERBS

10a A verb must agree with its subject in number.

See Verb, p. 462; Subject, p. 460

Every verb in the present tense takes a singular form if its subject is singular and a plural form if its subject is plural.

Only in the third person singular in the present tense does the verb add the **s** or **es** to the infinitive form.

EXAMPLES Maria Torres swim**s** daily.
She relax**es** in the water.
It feel**s** good.

The first and second persons in the singular and the three persons in the plural do not add **s** or **es.** Instead the infinitive form of the verb is used.

The following list shows how the ending of a regular verb changes in the present tense.

	SINGULAR	PLURAL
First Person	I like	we like
Second Person	you like	you like
Third Person	she he } likes it	they like

EXERCISE 1 Number a sheet of paper 1–10. Choose the correct verb for each sentence. Write the verb next to the number of each sentence.

EXAMPLE Life in the oceans (take/takes) many forms.

1. The oceans (hold/holds) a wide variety of plant and animal life.
2. Bright-colored coral (cover/covers) the bottom of tropical seas.
3. Tiny animals (float/floats) on the surface.
4. Sea lilies (wave/waves) gently in the underwater garden.
5. A cold ocean current (change/changes) the life pattern.
6. Divers (explore/explores) the ever-changing undersea world.
7. A sharp-toothed eel (hide/hides) in a cave.
8. Schools of tiny fish (hurry/hurries) through the water.
9. A shark (pass/passes) overhead.
10. A sunbeam (vanish/vanishes) in the depths of the ocean.

10b A linking verb agrees with its subject.

The linking verb sometimes causes problems in agreement. The linking verb ties a subject completer to the subject. If the subject completer is not the same number (singular or plural) as the subject, a question of verb agreement arises.

See Linking Verb, p. 453; Subject, p. 460; Completer, p. 442

EXAMPLES

INCORRECT AGREEMENT	The sixteenth year *were* times of success and times of failure. [The subject is *year,* which is singular. The verb cannot be plural.]
CORRECT AGREEMENT	The sixteenth year *was* times of success and times of failure.
INCORRECT AGREEMENT	Youth *are* days for dreaming. [The subject is *youth,* which is singular. The verb cannot be plural.]
CORRECT AGREEMENT	Youth *is* days for dreaming.

Hint: Make the linking verb agree with the subject, not the completer.

If you are not sure of subject-verb agreement when using a linking verb, change the sentence.

EXAMPLES The sixteenth year was a time of success.
Youth is made up of days for dreaming.

Some sentence constructions place the subject after the verb with *There is/There are* or *Here is/ Here are* at the start of the sentence. When the subject follows the linking verb, make the verb agree with the subject.

EXAMPLES

INCORRECT AGREEMENT	There *is* the logs we cut.
CORRECT AGREEMENT	There *are* the logs we cut.
INCORRECT AGREEMENT	Here *is* some nails to use.
CORRECT AGREEMENT	Here *are* some nails to use.

Be careful when using the contractions *there's* and *here's*. They are the same as *there is* and *here is*.

EXAMPLE

INCORRECT AGREEMENT	There's two glasses of juice for Janet Ono.
CORRECT AGREEMENT	There are two glasses of juice for Janet Ono.

EXERCISE 2 Choose the correct term in parentheses. Write the correct choice on a sheet of paper.

EXAMPLE Here (is/are) the dates of the calendar.

are

1. A year (is/are) four seasons.
2. Spring (is/are) for hopes and dreams.
3. There (is/are) few warm days in winter.

4. Here (come/comes) short days and long nights.
5. Summer (is/are) golden hours of recreation.
6. Fall (is/are) cooler days and nights.

10c The verbs *be* and *have* use special forms to show agreement with their subjects.

The irregular verbs *be* and *have* do not change their forms the same way other verbs do. Pay special attention to the irregular formation of these two verbs. They are used often in speaking and writing.

	The Verb *Be*		The Verb *Have*	
	PRESENT TENSE		PRESENT TENSE	
	SINGULAR	PLURAL	SINGULAR	PLURAL
First Person	I am	we are	I have	we have
Second Person	you are	you are	you have	you have
Third Person	he is she is it is	they are	he has she has it has	they have

	PAST TENSE		PAST TENSE	
	SINGULAR	PLURAL	SINGULAR	PLURAL
First Person	I was	we were	I had	we had
Second Person	you were	you were	you had	you had
Third Person	he was she was it was	they were	he had she had it had	they had

EXERCISE 3 Number a sheet of paper 1–10. Next to each number write the correct form of the verb in parentheses.

EXAMPLE Chimpanzees in the wild (does/do) not use visual symbols.

do

1. Now, however, some of them (is/are) being taught in laboratories.
2. In one lab, two chimps (was/were) kept in glass rooms next to each other.
3. One (was/were) taught to ask for food by pressing a special button she (have/had).
4. The second chimp could watch which symbol (was/were) flashed on a screen when the button (was/were) pressed.
5. The second chimp (have/had) a button with the same symbol.
6. He must have thought, "I (have/has) a button like the one she (has/have)."
7. "I (am/is) hungry; so if I press the button with that symbol, it (is/am) a way to get food."
8. Soon the two chimps (was/were) flashing symbols to each other to ask for food.
9. One chimp (have/had) fifteen different kinds of food, including orange drink and jelly sandwiches.
10. The other chimp flashed a symbol for what she wanted and (was/were) given the food by her friend.

EXERCISE 4 The following sentences give you a choice between two verbs in the parentheses. Only one agrees with the subject. Number a sheet of paper 1–8. By each number write the verb that agrees with the subject.

EXAMPLE How (am/is) I to answer Lucy?

am

1. I think that the subject of statistics (are/is) dull, especially when you have the measles.
2. "Even a speech about politics (are/is) more interesting," I told my sister Lucy.
3. "You (is/are) wrong," said Lucy, who (is/am) always right, "because statistics tells us some fascinating things."
4. "For example, did you know that the French eat six million snails a year? That (is/am) a statistical fact."
5. "Many snails (is/are) needed for the French," I said.
6. "I (is/am) able to tell you more," said Lucy; "I hope you (is/are) listening."
7. "If all those snails (was/were) put end to end, they would circle the world one and a half times," she said.
8. It (is/are) hard having the measles with Lucy around.

10d A compound subject joined by *and* usually takes a plural verb.

EXAMPLES Coffee and tea *are* more expensive now.
The gas and the air *mix* in the carburetor.
Maria and Jed *have left* the area.

Sometimes a compound subject joined by *and* is considered one combination. In that case, it takes a singular verb.

EXAMPLE My name and address is printed on the package.

EXERCISE 5 Some of the following sentences have compound subjects. Some have simple subjects. Number a sheet of paper 1–10. After each number write the correct choice of the verb in parentheses.

EXAMPLE The South and the North (is/are) engaged in a terrible war.

are

1. Both the North and the South (think/thinks) they have good reason to fight the Civil War.
2. Slavery and states' rights (is/are) some of the issues.
3. President Lincoln (worry/worries) about what will happen to the country.
4. Even brothers (argue/argues) about who is right.
5. Shiloh and Gettysburg (name/names) battles as well as towns.
6. Jefferson Davis (lead/leads) the Confederacy in the South.
7. Young boys and old men (join/joins) the warring armies.
8. Ulysses S. Grant (gain/gains) fame as a general and is later elected president.
9. Lincoln (write/writes) the Gettysburg Address about the men who died to save the Union.
10. War wounds and sad memories (take/takes) a long time to heal.

10e When a compound subject is joined by *or, nor, either . . . or,* or *neither . . . nor,* the verb agrees in number with the nearer subject.

EXAMPLES Either Penny or Sasha *has* the keys.
[The two proper names make up the compound subject: *Penny* and *Sasha.* They are separated by the conjunction *or.* Therefore the verb must agree with *Sasha,* which is closer to it.]

Ms. Dunwiddie or her sisters *have* planned to be at church.
[The nearer subject is *sisters.* Therefore, the verb *have* is plural.]

EXERCISE 6 Look at each pair of verbs in parentheses. Choose the one which agrees with the subject of the sentence. Number a sheet of paper 1–10 and write the correct verb by each number.

EXAMPLE Witchcraft or spirits (do/does) not frighten me.
do

1. Either a brownie or a leprechaun (is/are) a helpful spirit.
2. Gold or jewels (lie/lies) in the cave in Secret Mountain.
3. The magic words or Alzanor's wand (lets/let) you in.
4. Either a white mark on this deer's forehead or a silver hair on her tail (tell/tells) you that she is really a princess.

5. Neither money nor power (turn/turns) away the curse.
6. A sneer or a cross word to the old man (make/makes) you into a frog.
7. Only the wizard or his cat (know/knows) the way out of the forest.
8. Neither magicians nor warlocks (has/have) the key.
9. The warrior maid or her mother (defend/defends) the castle.
10. Either the dragons or the prince (win/wins).

10f When a group of words comes between the subject and the verb, the verb still agrees with the subject.

Sometimes extra words come between the subject and its verb. Do not be misled, even if one of the extra words is a noun. Be sure the verb agrees with the subject, not with the extra words of a different number.

EXAMPLES

INCORRECT AGREEMENT	The spoons in the drawer *needs* polishing.
CORRECT AGREEMENT	The spoons in the drawer *need* polishing. [The subject is *spoons*.]
INCORRECT AGREEMENT	Each person without extra blankets *have* to pick them up at the office.
CORRECT AGREEMENT	Each person without extra blankets *has* to pick them up at the office. [The subject is *person*.]

Check carefully to see which word is the subject of the sentence. Then make the verb agree with that subject.

EXERCISE 7 In the following sentences choose the correct form of the verb in parentheses. Number a sheet of paper 1–10. Next to each number write the correct form.

EXAMPLE Workers who do something well (need/needs) continuing support.

need

1. The weavers of Harris tweed (live/lives) on an island near the mainland of Scotland.
2. This special kind of woolen cloth (is/are) a famous British export.
3. The weavers, working at home, (weave/weaves) the cloth on foot-powered looms.
4. Islanders, who number about six hundred, (work/works) at making the cloth.
5. A change in their ways of working (was/were) suggested a few years ago.
6. Dealers, unhappy with differences in the pieces of cloth, (want/wants) the workers to work in a factory.
7. Cloth from a factory (don't/doesn't) show any difference.
8. The people of the island (has/have) voted against the factory idea.
9. Freedom from rules and time clocks (is/are) very important to them.
10. The results of their work (prove/proves) they are right.

10g Certain nouns and phrases that name a quantity may appear to be plural, but they take a singular verb.

EXAMPLES The *news brings* too much unhappy information.
Two *cents is* all I will give you for that.

10h Collective nouns are singular in form but may be singular or plural in meaning.

Examples of collective nouns are *class, club, crowd, family, group, herd, school,* and *team.*

A collective noun that is used to mean the separate members of a group takes a plural verb.

EXAMPLE The *family were* taking turns gathering firewood.

In most cases the collective noun will take a singular verb.

EXAMPLES The *crowd* usually *breaks* up before midnight.
The *herd is* restless.

EXERCISE 8 Number a sheet of paper 1–8. Write the correct form of the verb in the parentheses.

EXAMPLE Their company (make/makes) moving pictures.

makes

1. The news (is/are) that the company (is/are) making a movie about Plodzilla, the baby monster.
2. Its family (live/lives) on an island near Japan.

3. A crowd of sightseers (arrive/arrives) by boat to see Plodzilla.
4. The group (has/have) heard about the monster from a press release.
5. Fifty dollars (was/were) the cost of the boat ticket.
6. The movie company (is/are) not being honest about Plodzilla, because it does not exist.
7. When they found that out, the group (was/were) angry, disappointed, or unhappy.
8. The money (was/were) repaid to them.

10i Indefinite pronouns that are singular in meaning take the singular form of the verb.

See Pronouns, p. 16

EXAMPLE *Everybody wants* to go.
Nobody expects to be left out.
Everyone hopes for good weather.
Either of the twins *plays* first base.

Be especially careful about extra words that come between the pronoun subject and the verb, as in the last example. Make the verb agree with the pronoun subject no matter which extra words come between them.

EXAMPLES

INCORRECT AGREEMENT *Someone* behind the trees and boulders *are* shouting.

CORRECT AGREEMENT *Someone* behind the trees and boulders *is* shouting. [*Someone* is the singular subject.]

INCORRECT AGREEMENT *Everybody* who had blueberry pancakes for breakfast *have* to go without blueberries for lunch.

CORRECT AGREEMENT *Everybody* who had blueberry pancakes for breakfast *has* to go without blueberries for lunch.
[*Everybody* is the subject. It is singular.]

EXERCISE 9 Number a sheet of paper 1–6. Write the correct form of the verb or verbs from the parentheses in each sentence.

EXAMPLE Everyone whose last name begins with L (is/are) excused.
is

1. Somebody who is underweight (need/needs) to eat more.
2. Someone losing pounds (is/are) usually happy for awhile.
3. Anybody who (has/have) traveled abroad (has/have) eaten unusual food.
4. Someone traveling in France (find/finds) good restaurants along the road.
5. Anyone visiting Germany (learn/learns) about their special dishes.
6. Either of the countries (offer/offers) delicious food.

10j The indefinite pronouns *all, any, most, none,* and *some* take either a singular or a plural verb depending on the reference.

An indefinite pronoun refers to one or more living or nonliving things. A pronoun that refers to only one thing takes the singular form of the verb. A pronoun that refers to more than one thing takes the plural verb.

EXAMPLES *All* of the stamps *have* been used. [*All of the stamps* means more than one.]

All of the postage *is* in the box. [*All of the postage* means one batch.]

Most of the apples *were* rotten. [*Most* means more than one apple.]

Most of the food *was* gone. [*Most* means a part of the food.]

EXERCISE 10 Number a sheet of paper 1–7. Next to each number, write the correct form of the verb in parentheses.

EXAMPLE Any of the dresses (look/looks) good on you.
look

1. All of the styles (seem/seems) to suit you.
2. None of the styles (suit/suits) me.
3. Some of them (bulge/bulges) in the middle.
4. Most of them (appear/appears) too long.
5. Most of the stock in the store (is/are) too expensive, too.
6. None of my money (is/are) going to be spent here.
7. (Is/Are) any of the dresses on sale?

SPECIAL VERB PROBLEMS

Active and Passive Verbs

10k An active verb tells of action done by the subject of a sentence. A passive verb tells of action done to the subject.

See Sentences, pp. 130–133

See Voice, p. 462

Examples of verbs in the active voice:

The enemy *started* the attack.
[It was the enemy that acted.]

They *jumped* over the walls early in the morning.
[The jumping was done by the enemy—*they.*]

Examples of verbs in the passive voice:

The attack *was started* by the enemy.
[The attack had the action done to it.]

The walls *were jumped* by the enemy.
[The walls had the action done to them.]

See Auxiliary Verb, p. 440

Hint: The passive form of the main verb takes an auxiliary verb.

EXAMPLES *was* started
were jumped

EXERCISE 11 Five of the following sentences have verbs in the active voice. The others have passive verbs. Number a sheet of paper 1–10. After each number write the complete verb. Next to the verb write the word *active* or *passive* to tell its voice.

EXAMPLE A famous circus was run by a clever man named P.T. Barnum.

was run, passive

1. Barnum fooled his customers out of their money many times.
2. Usually Barnum's tricks were just enjoyed by people.
3. One day a sign was hung over the door at one end of the big top.
4. The words on the sign said, "To the egress."
5. Hundreds of people walked out the door under that sign.
6. Certainly, a sign about an "egress" must advertise a strange and frightening creature!
7. The curious people found only the empty field outside the circus tent.
8. Each of them was charged fifty cents to get back into the circus.
9. Later, the word "egress" was explained to them.
10. It was defined as "exit" in spite of its unusual sound.

Tense

10l Learn the main tenses of verbs.

See Tense, pp. 37–39

The tenses of verbs help tell *when* action occurs or something exists.

(1) Present tense tells of present action or existence.

EXAMPLES She *works* at Tony's store.
Rae *is* my neighbor.

The present tense can also show action that goes on regularly.

EXAMPLE The bus *runs* every hour down Cedar Street.

(2) Past tense tells of past action or existence that has stopped.

EXAMPLES The can *floated* past the rock.
It *landed* on the shore.

(3) Future tense tells of action or existence that is coming.

EXAMPLES Paula *will learn* the song tonight.
Tomorrow she *is going to sing* it for us.

(4) Present perfect tense tells of past action or existence that may or does continue.

EXAMPLES Rory *has run* in the marathon.
I *have been training* for the next race.

(5) Past perfect tense tells of past action or existence completed before some other action or existence is mentioned.

EXAMPLE After Leslie *had closed* the vault, the teller asked for more cash.

(6) Future perfect tense tells of future action or existence which will be finished before some other future action or existence.

EXAMPLE When Jodie gets through, she *will have done* fifty sit-ups.

EXERCISE 12 Rewrite each of the following sentences. Change the tense of the verb as instructed in the parentheses.

EXAMPLE Japanese customs will develop over many generations. (present perfect)

Japanese customs have developed over many generations.

1. Japanese tradition directed everyone's social behavior. (present)
2. People will show unusual politeness. (past)
3. Strangers say little to each other. (future)
4. They choose their words carefully. (present perfect)
5. People practiced respect. (past perfect)
6. The world will benefit from their example. (future perfect)

Irregular Verbs

Irregular verbs do not add **d** or **ed** as regular verbs do to show past tense. Instead, irregular verbs show past tense in special ways.

See Irregular Verbs, pp. 39–40

10m Irregular verbs form their past tense in special ways, without adding *d* or *ed.*

EXAMPLES

PRESENT TENSE	PAST TENSE
see	saw
swim	swam
fight	fought

Following is a list of the most common irregular verbs in their present, simple past, and present perfect forms.

COMMON IRREGULAR VERBS

PRESENT	SIMPLE PAST	PRESENT PERFECT
bear	bore	(have) borne
begin	began	(have) begun
bind	bound	(have) bound
blow	blew	(have) blown
break	broke	(have) broken
bring	brought	(have) brought
buy	bought	(have) bought
catch	caught	(have) caught
choose	chose	(have) chosen
come	came	(have) come
dive	dived, dove	(have) dived
do	did	(have) done
draw	drew	(have) drawn
drink	drank	(have) drunk
drive	drove	(have) driven
eat	ate	(have) eaten
fall	fell	(have) fallen
fight	fought	(have) fought
fly	flew	(have) flown
freeze	froze	(have) frozen
give	gave	(have) given

go	went	(have) gone
grow	grew	(have) grown
hang	hung	(have) hung
keep	kept	(have) kept
know	knew	(have) known
lay	laid	(have) laid
lead	led	(have) led
lie	lay	(have) lain
lose	lost	(have) lost
make	made	(have) made
mean	meant	(have) meant
ride	rode	(have) ridden
ring	rang	(have) rung
rise	rose	(have) risen
run	ran	(have) run
see	saw	(have) seen
seek	sought	(have) sought
send	sent	(have) sent
shake	shook	(have) shaken
shine	shone, shined	(have) shone (have) shined
sing	sang	(have) sung
sleep	slept	(have) slept
speak	spoke	(have) spoken
spin	spun	(have) spun
spread	spread	(have) spread
steal	stole	(have) stolen
swear	swore	(have) sworn
swim	swam	(have) swum
swing	swung	(have) swung
take	took	(have) taken
teach	taught	(have) taught
tear	tore	(have) torn
throw	threw	(have) thrown
wear	wore	(have) worn
write	wrote	(have) written

Hint: Develop the habit of saying aloud the right verb in a standard sentence frame. This will help you when you write the form.

PRESENT Today I *(choose)* .....
SIMPLE
PAST Yesterday I *(chose)* .....

EXERCISE 13 Number a sheet of paper 1–10. Next to each number write the complete subject and the correct form of the verb.

EXAMPLE Some of Vic's passengers have (rode/ridden) with him for years.
Some of Vic's passengers have ridden

1. Vic has (drove/driven) a bus for twenty years.
2. Sometimes he wishes he had (did/done) some other kind of work.
3. He has (saw/seen) a lot of strange things during his days as a bus driver.
4. He (chose/chosen) to stay on the job because he felt that his work was important.
5. Lately more people have (began/begun) to ride the bus.
6. A woman with crutches (rang/rung) the bell to get off, and Vic helped her out.
7. Vic has (took/taken) thousands of people to work or to their homes.
8. Sometimes Vic feels that his job has (wore/worn) him out.

9. People who have (rode/ridden) with Vic say he is a fine driver.
10. He always (knew/known) exactly what he was doing.

SPECIAL PRONOUN PROBLEMS

Personal Pronouns

The pronouns *she* and *her* both refer to a female person. Their different forms are determined by the way each is used in sentences.

See Pronoun, p. 458

Personal pronouns also change form depending upon their use in sentences. Learn the forms and uses of personal pronouns. One form is called the *subjective case*. Another is called the *objective case*.

See Case, p. 440

10n A personal pronoun is in the subjective case when used as a subject and in the objective case when used as the object.

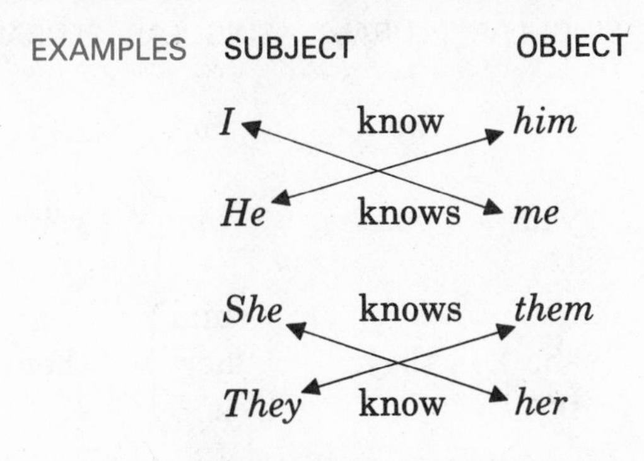

[These personal pronouns change form in the subjective and objective cases.]

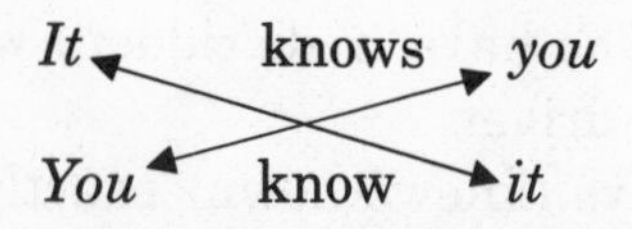

[The pronouns *it* and *you* do not change form in the subjective and objective cases.]

When a pronoun is the object of a verb, it is in the objective case. When it is the object of a preposition, it is also in the objective case.

EXAMPLES

OBJECT OF A VERB

The company forced *her* to take the watch.
The driver dropped *him* at the corner.

OBJECT OF A PREPOSITION

The river rushed under *us* as we stood on the bridge.
The call came in for *him.*

Here is a list of subjective and objective case forms of personal pronouns:

	SUBJECTIVE CASE		OBJECTIVE CASE	
	SINGULAR	PLURAL	SINGULAR	PLURAL
First Person	I	we	me	us
Second Person	you	you	you	you
Third Person	he she it	they	him her it	them

Most people have very little trouble with the case of pronouns when only one pronoun appears in a sentence. However, when two pronouns or a noun and a pronoun serve as the subject or object of a sentence, errors can occur.

EXAMPLES

INCORRECT The chef will show you and *I* how to clean up.

CORRECT The chef will show you and *me* how to clean up.

INCORRECT Sadie and *me* will wash the wall.

CORRECT Sadie and *I* will wash the wall.

Hint: To check yourself on your use of the pronoun in sentences like those above, do the following: Leave the pronoun that is giving you difficulty. Remove the other noun or pronoun and the conjunction. Say the sentence with the remaining pronoun.

EXAMPLE The chef will show *me* how to clean up.
[Correct.]

Me will wash the hall.
[Incorrect. The sentence should be "I will wash the hall."]

Strictly formal usage requires that the subject completer used after the linking verb *be* should be in the subjective case. For example, *It is I*. However, general usage now allows the objective form to be used. For example, *It's me*. (It is *me*.) It's *us*. (It is *us*.) It's *them*. (It is *them*.)

EXERCISE 14 Number a sheet of paper 1–8. Next to each number write the correct form or forms of the pronouns from the parentheses.

EXAMPLE The coach asked Barry, Zelda, and (I/me) to practice swimming.

me

1. Barry arrived ahead of Zelda and (I/me) at the pool.
2. Other swimmers had come ahead of Barry and (we/us).
3. The coach gave instructions to (they/them) and (we/us).
4. Barry and (I/me) had to get kickboards.
5. Our coach worked with Zelda first and then with Barry and (I/me).
6. In fact, the coach is depending on (she/her) to score points in meets.
7. Zelda gives pointers to the other swimmers and (I/me).
8. (We/Us) swimmers need more practice before our first meet.

10o A pronoun must agree in number and sex with the noun or pronoun to which it refers.

EXAMPLES Any *woman* who is late loses *her* chance.
Women who are late lose *their* chances.

Reflexive Pronouns

A reflexive pronoun is a form of a personal pronoun combined with the word *self* or *selves*. Be careful to use *himself* instead of *hisself* and *themselves* instead of *theirselves*. *Hisself* and *theirselves* are considered poor usage today.

See Pronouns, p. 16

Relative Pronouns *Who* and *Whom*

The pronouns *who* and *whoever* show the objective case form by adding the letter **m.** The two forms are used in much the same way as *he* and *him*. However, widespread usage allows for the use of *who* and *whoever* in many cases where the rule would call for *whom* or *whomever.*

See Pronouns, p. 15

EXAMPLES
STRICTLY CORRECT *Whom* do you want?
WIDELY USED *Who* do you want?
STRICTLY CORRECT For *whom* did you vote?
WIDELY USED *Who* did you vote for?
STRICTLY CORRECT Vote for *whomever* you want.
WIDELY USED Vote for *whoever* you want.

PROBLEMS WITH ADJECTIVES AND ADVERBS

10p Use an adjective after a linking verb to refer to the subject.

See Linking Verb, p. 453; Subject, p. 460

Remember that an adjective describes or modifies a noun or a pronoun but not a verb or another

See Adjective, p. 438; Adverb, p. 438

adjective. An adverb does not describe a noun or a pronoun. It modifies an action verb, an adjective, or another adverb.

See Common Confusions, p. 283

EXAMPLE

INCORRECT It's a *real* funny movie.
[*Real* is an adjective. It cannot modify the adjective *funny* that follows it.]

CORRECT It's a *really* funny movie.
[The adverb *really* should be used to modify the adjective *funny.*]

See Common Confusions, p. 278

Hint: Be especially careful not to confuse the adjective *good* with the word *well*. *Well* is either an adverb or an adjective, depending on its use in a sentence. *Good* is only an adjective.

EXAMPLE

INCORRECT Nanda plays the piano *good*.

CORRECT Nanda plays the piano *well*.

EXERCISE 15 Number a sheet of paper 1–6. Rewrite any sentence in which an adjective or adverb is incorrectly used.

EXAMPLE Alfreda knows how to skate good.
Alfreda knows how to skate well.

1. Good players come along once in a while.
2. If she plays good, get her on the team.
3. She drives a real hard shot.

4. It is really tough to stop.
5. It is real good to have more players who hit good.
6. A real good one is rare.

The Double Negative

10q Avoid using a double negative.

Negatives are *no, not, never, none, nothing, no one,* and *hardly.* When one of these is used in a sentence, another should not be used.

EXAMPLES

INCORRECT She won't come here no more.
CORRECT She won't come here any more.
or
She will come here no more.

INCORRECT Vera hasn't learned nothing today.
CORRECT Vera hasn't learned anything today.
or
Vera has learned nothing today.

INCORRECT There wasn't nothing to learn.
CORRECT There wasn't anything to learn.
or
There was nothing to learn.

EXERCISE 16 Number a sheet of paper 1–5. Next to each number write the correct word from the parentheses in each sentence.

EXAMPLE We don't see the ocean (any/no) more.

any

1. In recent years we (can't/can't hardly) see out to the island on a clear day.
2. These days we never see (anything/nothing) much beyond the shore.
3. The smog never lifts (no/any) more.
4. None of us can remember (nothing/anything) so bad.
5. We are afraid we won't see the island (ever/never) again.

REVIEW EXERCISE A Subject-Verb Agreement

Number a sheet of paper 1–10. Next to each number write the correct form of the verb in parentheses.

EXAMPLE The crowd (murmur/murmurs) its approval as the balloon is readied for the ascent.

murmurs

1. The balloonist and her associates (climb/climbs) into the basket.
2. The ropes holding the balloon (is/are) untied.
3. Slowly the mushroom-shaped craft (rise/rises).
4. Balloons filled with gas (float/floats) because the gas is lighter than the air.
5. Neither the wind nor other air forces (affect/affects) the balloon's flight.
6. It (feel/feels) the effects of air turbulence, however.
7. The balloon with its occupants (ride/rides) as a part of the air mass.

8. The group (drop/drops) ballast to make the balloon rise.
9. Free balloons (travel/travels) hundreds of miles in a good wind.
10. The news on evening television (tell/tells) about the flight.

REVIEW EXERCISE B More Verb Usage

Number a sheet of paper 1–10. Next to each number write the correct form of the verb in parentheses.

EXAMPLE Nobody (knows/know) for certain exactly what to expect at death.

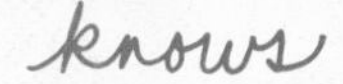

1. People who have been close to death (say/says) that it is not a fearsome experience.
2. Many (describe/describes) a feeling of peace and serenity.
3. Some (tell/tells) about floating outside their bodies and watching other people around them.
4. Some people who come close to dying (are/is) able to describe what others around them were saying at the time.
5. Many scientists (are/is) baffled by these experiences.
6. None (are/is) able to explain them completely.
7. What (do/does) all these experiences really mean?
8. Most of the world's religions (teach/teaches) that we live on after death.

9. Can it be that there (is/are) a life after death?
10. Philosophers and religious leaders (tries/try) to make the answer clear.

REVIEW EXERCISE C Irregular Verbs

Following is a list of irregular verbs in their present tense. Number a sheet of paper 1–10. Next to each number write the simple past and the present perfect form of the verb. Then write a sentence using either tense of the verb.

EXAMPLE choose
chose, have chosen
She has chosen to study forestry.

1. go
2. blow
3. spin
4. ride
5. keep
6. know
7. teach
8. spread
9. run
10. ring

REVIEW EXERCISE D Pronoun Usage

Number a sheet of paper 1–10. Next to each number write the correct form of the pronoun in parentheses.

EXAMPLE She and (I/me) were going to go shopping.
I

1. "Don't tell Alice, Judy, and (she/her)," Loretta said.
2. I don't want to go with her and (they/them).
3. All (they/them) will want to do is look in the windows.
4. But if you and (I/me) go alone, we'll get more done.
5. (We/Us) can look for a present for my mother.
6. I'm not sure what to get for (she/her).
7. My sister and (she/her) have the same birthday.
8. I guess I'd better look for something for both of (they/them).
9. My father asked me to try to find them a gift from (he/him).
10. My sister and (he/him) always have trouble buying presents.

REVIEW EXERCISE E Adjective and Adverb Usage

Number a sheet of paper 1–10. Next to each number write *C* if the sentence given is correct. If the sentence uses an adjective or an adverb incorrectly, rewrite it and correct the error.

EXAMPLE Zena Jones has a real hard job.

Zena Jones has a really hard job.

1. She has to judge which pie is the best among some really good pies.
2. Most of the contestants bake good.
3. A real well-baked pie should have a flaky crust.

4. It should not have nothing soggy or heavy about it.
5. The filling should use good ingredients.
6. Real home-baked flavor can't be bought.
7. Zena will have a real tough time choosing.
8. I'm afraid her own mother won't speak to her no more if she doesn't win.
9. Fortunately for Zena, she won't know who none of the contestants are.
10. I hope she does the job good.

CHAPTER

11

COMMON CONFUSIONS

Many words and forms in English are so similar to others that it is sometimes hard to know which are appropriate in which situations.

This chapter lists alphabetically the English words and forms that are most commonly confused and provides definitions or explanations that clarify the questions.

Many examples and short exercises will help you see clearly how to use some of the terms you may wonder about.

ALPHABETICAL LISTING

Accept/except: The word *accept* is a verb that means "to receive."

EXAMPLES Tracy will *accept* the prize.
All gifts for charity will be *accepted* at the counter.

Except is most often a preposition meaning "leaving out."

EXAMPLES The day was perfect *except* for the rainstorm.
All *except* Carlos got wet.

EXERCISE 1 Write the following sentences on a sheet of paper. Fill each blank with either *accept* or *except.*

1. Judy has come to ______ the fact she is thin.
2. Everyone ______ Judy thinks that is desirable.
3. Weight is easy to lose ______ for the last few pounds.
4. Most people ______ the truth about weight loss.

Advice/advise: *Advice* is a noun meaning "an opinion or suggestion."

EXAMPLES Your *advice* is much appreciated.
We need some *advice* before acting.

Advise is a verb that means "to give an opinion."

EXAMPLES How would you *advise* Charlene?
Her counselor *advised* her not to go.

EXERCISE 2 Write the following sentences on a sheet of paper. Fill each blank with a form of either *advice* or *advise.*

1. ______ seems to come cheaply.
2. Please ______ those fools to stay away from here.

3. The ______ we heard last night makes sense.
4. The king was ______ not to go to war.

Affect/effect: *Affect* is a verb meaning "to influence."

EXAMPLES The loss of his dog *affected* him deeply.
The silence *affected* her noticeably.

Effect is a noun. It means "the result." Occasionally *effect* is used as a verb to mean "to bring about or change."

NOUN You can see the *effect* that has on her.
VERB The council will *effect* a change in the rules.

EXERCISE 3 Write the following sentences on a sheet of paper. Choose the correct form of the word in parentheses.

1. Try not to allow the appearance to (affect/effect) your judgment.
2. The (affect/effect) is sometimes startling.
3. However, the fact that the furniture is unpainted should not (affect/effect) your decision.
4. With a little paint we can (affect/effect) a real change in its appearance.

All right: Always write *all right* as two separate words. It should not be written as *alright* since English has no such word. When spoken, the two words "all right" sound like one word. They are not.

Almost/most: *Almost* means "nearly" or "all but."

EXAMPLES They were *almost* home.
Almost every bit of the money was gone.

Most has these meanings: "More than anything else," "the greatest amount," or "nearly all."

EXAMPLES Roberta chose the *most* expensive car.
Most of the days were sunny.
Most people try to save energy.

Do not use *most* as a short form of *almost.*

WRITE The hour is *almost* over.
not
The hour is *most* over.

EXERCISE 4 Some of the following sentences use *most* where *almost* should be used. On a sheet of paper rewrite correctly each sentence that uses *most* incorrectly.

1. *Most* of the old cats have gone.
2. Trixie *most* shouted when she saw the dog.
3. It was *most* after midnight when she awoke.
4. The dog seemed *most* crazy racing around the yard.

Already/all ready: *Already* means "before now."

EXAMPLES Mei-Ying *already* knew the answer.
She had *already* studied for the exam.

All ready are two words that mean "fully ready."

EXAMPLES Winnard got the apartment *all ready* for visitors.
Each chair was *all ready* to be covered.

When you mean that something is completely ready, use the words *all* and *ready.*

WRITE The paper was *all ready* for wrapping the fish.
not
The paper was *already* for wrapping the fish.

EXERCISE 5 Write the following sentences on a sheet of paper. Fill each blank with either *already* or *all ready.*

1. Josina thought she was ______ for the dance.
2. It was ______ past time for Greg to pick her up.
3. He was ______ on his way to her place.
4. He was ______ to ask her the big question.
5. She ______ knew the answer.

All together/altogether: *All together* is a two-word term meaning "everyone (or everything) combined."

EXAMPLE The ranchers brought their cattle *all together* at the roundup.

Altogether is an adverb meaning "completely" or "entirely."

EXAMPLE The sailboat took an *altogether* different course.

Am not, are not, is not/ain't: *Ain't* sometimes is heard in very informal conversation, but it should be avoided in more formal situations. *Ain't* is a poor substitute for *am not, are not,* or *is not.*

Among/between: These two words mean about the same thing, but *among* is used when three or more persons or things are involved.

EXAMPLES None *among* us was willing to volunteer.
Among the members of the class are some lazy students.

Between is used when only two persons or things are involved.

EXAMPLES There is no love lost *between* her and me.
It is hard to tell the differences *between* the twins.

Between can also mean "the space or time that separates two things."

EXAMPLES The days *between* Sunday and Saturday don't go fast enough for me.
The cracks *between* the boards are too wide.

Between can also mean "something shared by *two* people or things."

EXAMPLES *Between* us, Joan and I can get the job done.
We have six hours *between* us to finish it.

Use *between* when talking about only two of anything. Use *among* when talking about three or more.

WRITE I can't choose *among* the many kinds of jobs.
not
I can't choose *between* the many kinds of jobs.

EXERCISE 6 Decide whether to fill each blank with *among* or *between*. Write each sentence on a sheet of paper.

1. One sports car ______ the many on the lot caught my eye.
2. It was parked ______ a two-door sedan and a station wagon.
3. ______ the several cars, this was the best-looking.
4. Do you and I have enough money ______ us to buy it?

At: *At* is a preposition that sometimes is used when it is not needed, as in the sentence *Where is she at?* The sentence should be *Where is she?* The word *where* includes the idea of place. For this reason, *at* is unnecessary.

Beside/besides: *Beside* means "next to."

EXAMPLES The shoes are *beside* the bed.
Put the spoon *beside* the knife.

The word *besides* can be either a preposition or an adverb.

Besides as a preposition means "in addition to."

EXAMPLES *Besides* the sourdough bread, we had rye bread.
We can get dessert *besides* the main course.

Besides as an adverb means "as well."

EXAMPLE They were ready to do the yard. *Besides,* they had the tools.

EXERCISE 7 Write the following sentences on your paper. Put *beside* or *besides* in each blank.

1. ______ the lake is a little cabin.
2. For recreation there is canoeing ______ plenty of swimming.

3. The dock has a roped area ______ it for swimmers.
4. ______, there is a pool next to the cabin.

Burst/bust: The word *burst* is acceptable as a verb meaning "to break open." *Bust,* however, is slang and should not be used in formal speech or writing.

WRITE The bubble *burst.*
not
The bubble *busted.*

Can/may: *Can* means "be able."

EXAMPLES This is what you *can* do for her.
Few *can* rise to that height.

May means "to have permission."

EXAMPLE You *may* drive the car home.

Can hardly/can't hardly: *Hardly* means "barely." *Can hardly* means "can barely."

EXAMPLE They *can hardly* finish in an hour.

See Double Negative, p. 263

Do not use *can't hardly.* It is a double negative.

WRITE We *can hardly* lift this.
not
We *can't hardly* lift this.

Continual/continuous: *Continual* means "happening again and again."

EXAMPLE The *continual* interruptions made concentration difficult.

Continuous means "happening steadily."

EXAMPLE The horn was stuck and gave a *continuous* blast.

Could have/could of: There is no such term as *could of.* Use only *could have,* as in *I could have been wrong.* Because people say "could have" quickly, it sometimes sounds like "could of." However, *could of* makes no sense in English.

WRITE She *could have* done it.
not
She *could of* done it.

Data/datum: The word *data* means "several pieces of information." *Datum* means only one piece of information. Sometimes you hear people say "the data is correct." This should be either "the datum is correct" or "the data are correct."

Disinterested/uninterested: A *disinterested* person is a person who does not stand to benefit from a situation. It does not mean a person who has no interest in the situation. A person with no interest is *uninterested.*

EXAMPLES The *disinterested* judge listened intently to both arguments.
The *uninterested* judge dozed on the bench.

Drowned/drownded: *Drown* is the verb meaning "to die in the water." Its past tense adds **ed** only. There is no such word as *drownded.*

WRITE Two sailors *drowned* in the storm.
not
Two sailors *drownded* in the storm.

Fewer/less: *Fewer* means "not so many separate items." *Less* means "a smaller amount of a substance."

EXAMPLES Vince had *fewer* friends than Alice did.
Today brought *less* rain than yesterday.

WRITE This shirt has *fewer* buttons than that.
not
This shirt has *less* buttons than that.

Good/well: *Good* is an adjective that means "better than usual."

EXAMPLE This seemed a *good* way to end it.

Well is an adverb that means "in a fine manner."

EXAMPLE He drives *well*.

WRITE Zelda sings *well*.
not
Zelda sings *good*.

Well can also describe the health of an individual.

EXAMPLE No longer sick, I can say I am *well* now.

EXERCISE 8 Write the following sentences on a sheet of paper. Fill in the blanks with *good* or *well*.

1. It's a ______ day for flying, thought Alissa.
2. My balloon seems to be flying ______ these days.
3. I think it would be a ______ idea to fill it with hot air.
4. I must plan my trip ______.
5. The last trip was enough to make me airsick, but I'm ______ now.

See Reflexive Pronouns, p. 261

Himself/hisself: Do not use *hisself* for *himself*. Many years ago some people thought *hisself* was correct. It is no longer considered correct.

I/me/myself: These words all refer to the speaker, but they should be used only in certain positions in sentences.

I refers to the one doing the action. *Me* is used when the action is received by the speaker. *Myself* is used to repeat the *I* or emphasize it.

EXAMPLES *I* will drive the car first.
Juan will drive *me* in the car.
I myself will drive it later.

Do not use *myself* in place of *me*.

WRITE Drive Juan and *me* in the car.
not
Drive Juan and *myself* in the car.

Imply/infer: *Imply* means "to suggest."

EXAMPLE The senator *implied* in her speech that her opponent was a crook.

Infer means "to understand or interpret."

EXAMPLE I *infer* from what you say that you think I am a crook.

Its/it's: These two words are *homonyms,* that is, they are words that sound the same but are spelled differently. *Its* is a single word, a possessive pronoun. This pronoun does not take an apostrophe.

EXAMPLE The cable car lost *its* power.

It's is a contraction for *it is* or *it has.*

EXAMPLE *It's* lost power.

EXERCISE 9 Write the following sentences on a sheet of paper. Put *its* or *it's* in each blank.

1. ______ a long way home.
2. Our car has lost ______ headlights.
3. We think ______ too dangerous to drive.
4. The night has lost ______ glamor.

Kind/kinds: *Kind* is singular. *Kinds* is plural. When speaking or writing about several kinds of anything, use the word *kinds*.

EXAMPLE These *kinds* of accidents are costly.

WRITE The *kinds* of opportunities you have are limited.
not
The *kind* of opportunities you have are limited.

Lead/led: These two spellings can be homonyms. When they are, *lead* is a word that names a metal.

EXAMPLE The sinker on a fishing line is made of *lead*.

Led is pronounced the same way. But it means "guided."

EXAMPLE In the past, people were *led* to commit errors.

Learn/teach: *Learn* is a verb meaning "to gain knowledge."

EXAMPLE You can *learn* to drive a tractor.

Teach is a verb meaning "to give knowledge."

EXAMPLE She had trouble *teaching* her dog a new trick.

EXERCISE 10 Choose either *learn* or *teach* to fill each blank in the following sentences.

1. Can you ______ your pet raccoon a trick?
2. It will ______ from you if you reward it.
3. To ______ it how to come to you, hold out a pellet.
4. It will have to ______ which is the pellet and which is your finger.

Leave/let: *Leave* means "to go away."

EXAMPLE We will *leave* on the trip this Saturday.

Let means "to allow."

EXAMPLE *Let* Pepe come with us.

Lie/lay: *Lie* means "to recline."

EXAMPLE The wires *lie* right across the roof.

Lay means "to put something down."

EXAMPLE *Lay* the knife on the table.

These two verbs are often confused because the past tense of *lie* is *lay* (the same word as the present tense of *lay*). The principal forms of the two verbs are as follows:

INFINITIVE	SIMPLE PAST	PAST PARTICIPLE
lie	lay	(have) lain
lay	laid	(have) laid

EXERCISE 11 Write on your paper the correct forms of *lie* or *lay* that belong in the blanks.

1. ______ the boards on the sidewalk.
2. Let the other tools ______ in the shed.

3. When you are tired, ______ down.
4. After you have ______ down a while, you should feel rested.
5. Pick up the boards you ______ there.

Like/as: *Like* is a preposition that takes an object.

EXAMPLES She swam *like* a fish.
But she breathed *like* a human.

See Clause, p. 441

As is a conjunction. It relates a dependent clause to an independent clause.

EXAMPLES She hesitated *as* she came to the wall.
Her legs curled up *as* she made the turn.

As may also be used as a preposition.

EXAMPLE The package came wrapped *as* a time bomb.

Like is sometimes used informally as a conjunction. Its use as a conjunction is not recommended in formal speech or writing, however.

WRITE Lennie made pancakes *as* he was taught.
not
Lennie made pancakes *like* he was taught.

OK, O.K., okay/all right: All of the three spellings of *okay* are common. In writing usually it is better to use *all right* instead of *okay*.

Practicable/practical: The word *practicable* means "probably workable."

EXAMPLE It seemed like a *practicable* plan.

The word *practical* means "useful." Anything practical has already proved itself in practice.

EXAMPLE The modern sewing machine is a highly *practical* mechanism.

Real/really: *Real* is an adjective.

EXAMPLE That was not *real* snow in the movie.

Really is an adverb.

EXAMPLE The *really* young birds stay in the nest.

Avoid using *real* as an adverb in formal speech or writing.

WRITE The *really* sick people need help.
not
The *real* sick people need help.

Set/sit: *Set* as a verb means "to put something down." It also tells of a bird's action on a nest of eggs. It does not tell of the action of a person on a chair.

EXAMPLES The waiter *set* the table.
The hen *sets* on the nest nearly all the time.

Sit means "to be seated." People and animals *sit*.

EXAMPLE The judge *sits* on the bench.

WRITE Let's all *sit* down.
not
Let's all *set* down.

EXERCISE 12 Write the following sentences on a sheet of paper. Fill each blank with the correct form of *set* or *sit*.

1. Bluebeard ______ the treasure chest on the beach.
2. "Whew!" he grunted, "I think I'll ______ this here for a minute."
3. "Maybe I'll ______ on it for a short rest before we bury it."
4. He turned to his men and said, "______ your shovels down, men, while I ______ on the chest. We'll bury it soon."

Shall/will: No one needs to make a distinction between these two words. *Will* is perfectly correct in all verb forms showing future action or intention.

WRITE I *will* go.
or
I *shall* go.

About two hundred years ago some English grammarians tried to separate the use of *shall* and *will*. They stated that *shall* should be used in the first person to show simple future tense and in the second and third persons to show firm intention. They also stated that *will* should be used just the other way around. Today, most people ignore these rules.

Should have/should of: *Should of* is not correct English. Some people write it by mistake because the contraction "should've" sounds like "should of" when it is spoken quickly.

WRITE I *should have* known better.
not
I *should of* known better.

Their/there/they're: These three words sound alike in speech. They are homonyms. However, they are spelled differently and mean different things.

See Spelling, p. 393

Their is a possessive noun.

EXAMPLE *Their* team won.

There points out a place. It also is used in the subject position in a sentence.

EXAMPLES
PLACE She left the gloves *there.*
SUBJECT POSITION *There* is a new window in the building.

They're is a contraction of the words *they* and *are.*

EXAMPLE *They're* all done with the work.

EXERCISE 13 Write the following sentences on a sheet of paper. Put in the correct form of *there, their,* or *they're.*

1. The money was left ______ on the table.
2. ______ was no one who came in the room.
3. ______ are mysterious ghosts at work.
4. They left ______ traces when the money disappeared.
5. ______ looking everywhere for the money.

This/this here: Do not use *this here. This* is the only word needed. The same is true for *that there* and *these here.*

WRITE Did you include *this* coin?
not
Did you include *this here* coin?

WRITE Have you got *that* money?
not
Have you got *that there* money?

WRITE We didn't count *these* coins.
not
We didn't count *these here* coins.

Those/them (there): *Them* and *them there* are not substitutes for *those.*

WRITE Look at *those* acrobats.
not
Look at *them there* acrobats.

To/too/two: These short words get confused in writing. They are homonyms.

To is a preposition.

EXAMPLE They gave the towel *to* Jenny.

Too is an adverb. It means "also" or "more than enough."

EXAMPLE It was *too* dirty.

Two means "one plus one."

EXAMPLE She'll need *two* towels.

EXERCISE 14 Write the following sentences on a sheet of paper. Fill each blank with *to, too,* or *two.*

1. Little Willie is ______ years old.
2. He has grown ______ the size of a bull.
3. He is ______ big to be called "Little Willie" anymore.
4. We plan ______ call him "Big Will."
5. It takes ______ of us to get him into his corral.

Try to/try and: You should usually use *try to* in speech and writing.

WRITE *Try to* push that button in.
not
Try and push that button in.

Note that it is correct to say or write, "People will *try and try* to do something too hard. Many people *try and* fail." In these cases you mean two actions. The first is *try*. The second is whatever verb comes next.

We/us: Some people make the mistake of saying "*Us* people" in a sentence such as, "*We* people know what's good for us." The pronoun *us* should not be used as part of the subject of a verb.

WRITE *We* athletes get special training.
not
Us athletes get special training.

Who/whom: *Who* and *whom* are different forms of the same word. *Who* is in the subjective case. *Whom* is in the objective case.

See Case, p. 440

EXAMPLES *Who* looks at the speedometer?
Who follows the speeders?
Whom did you follow?

Whom should be used after a word like *to, from,* or *for.*

WRITE to *whom,* for *whom,* from *whom*
not
to *who,* for *who,* from *who*

Whose/who's: These two words are homonyms. *Whose* is a form of *who* that shows ownership or possession.

EXAMPLES *Whose* house is on the corner?
This is the reason we need to know *whose* book it is.

Who's is a contraction of *who* and *is*. The apostrophe (') takes the place of the *i* in *is*.

EXAMPLE *Who's* going to go?

Remember to use *who's* only when you mean *who is*.

EXERCISE 15 Rewrite each of the following sentences that has a *whose/who's* error in it.

1. Whose sorry now?
2. This came from the lady whose standing by the counter.
3. I don't know whose this is.
4. Toss it to the man whose on the stairs.

Your/you're: These two words are homonyms. *Your* is the possessive form of *you*. It shows ownership.

EXAMPLE This is *your* idea.
Your thanks are appreciated.

You're is a contraction of *you* and *are*.

EXAMPLE *You're* the one chosen.
She thinks *you're* the greatest runner.

EXERCISE 16 Rewrite each sentence that has a *your/you're* error in it.

1. Is this you're cheetah?
2. Your going to get into trouble with that cat.
3. If you're sure it won't bite, I'll come near.
4. You're cat acts more like a wild dog.

REVIEW EXERCISE A Word Usage

Number a sheet of paper 1–10. Next to each number write the correct word in parentheses.

EXAMPLE It was (most/almost) impossible for Anne Hutchinson to avoid clashing with the Puritan authorities.

almost

1. In the early seventeenth century, the Massachusetts Puritans would not (accept/except) any views but their own.
2. The (affect/effect) of this narrowness was to create fear among the colonists.
3. (Besides/beside) being a Puritan, Anne Hutchinson was a broad-minded person.
4. She held weekly meetings (among/between) her friends and acquaintances to discuss the sermons and the preachers.
5. She believed that the Bible as interpreted by the church elders was not the only source of (real/really) religious inspiration.
6. Against the (advise/advice) of the church elders she continued to state her views.
7. Many people were (all ready/already) convinced by her before the authorities denounced her.
8. They convicted her of heresy and treason and banished her from the colony (beside/besides).
9. Anne Hutchinson (could have/could of) despaired, but she, her family, and a group of followers moved to an island in Narragansett Bay.
10. They established the town of Portsmouth and eventually helped found the colony of Rhode Island, which guaranteed (continual/continuous) freedom from religious persecution.

REVIEW EXERCISE B More Word Usage

Following is a matching exercise. Match the words in the list with the blanks in the sentences. Number a sheet of paper 1–10. Next to each number write the letter of the correct word from the list.

a. really
b. disinterested
c. infer
d. uninterested
e. can
f. should have
g. real
h. may
i. imply
j. kinds
k. your

EXAMPLE Henry was ______ in a jam.

a

1. "What ______ I do?" he thought.
2. When I told Jennifer I'd drive her to the dance, I didn't mean to ______ that I'd be her date.
3. I've been planning to ask Gail to go with me for months; my love for her is true and ______.
4. If I tell that to Jennifer, she'll be hurt; but if I don't ask Gail if I ______ take her, I'll be hurt.
5. I ______ thought of this earlier.
6. Maybe a ______ observer could give me some advice.
7. "You look worried, Henry. What's ______ problem?" asked Henry's father.
8. Henry described how Jennifer came to ______ that he meant to go to the dance with her.
9. "I don't mean to appear ______, but I don't know how to advise you," his father said.

10. "Your brother is good at these ______ of things."

REVIEW EXERCISE C Common Confusions

Number a sheet of paper 1–10. Next to each number write the correct word from the parentheses in each sentence.

EXAMPLE (Sit/set) your package over there on the table.

set

1. Now (sit/set) down.
2. I (should have/should of) talked to you sooner.
3. You have been (like/as) a son to me.
4. June and (I/myself) have always loved you.
5. But (there/they're) is something I must tell you.
6. (Your/You're) father came here today to see you.
7. He wants to (try and/try to) buy a small house.
8. He feels that his health has improved, and (it's/its) good enough to allow him to work.
9. He wants to try selling real estate; he thinks that's a (practicable/practical) scheme.
10. He wants to know if (your/you're) willing to help him.

REVIEW EXERCISE D More Common Confusions

Number a sheet of paper 1–10. Next to each number write the correct word from those in parentheses.

EXAMPLE The Imperial Palace in Peking, China, has stood in (it's/its) present place since 1407.

its

1. The palace was built by an emperor (who's/whose) plan was to reestablish the capital of the empire at Peking.
2. (It's/Its) surrounded by a moat.
3. (It's/Its) walls are over thirty-five feet high.
4. The last emperor (whose/who's) family lived there was Henry Pu-Yi.
5. (Their/They're) lives in the palace's private apartments were prisoners' lives.
6. The emperor (himself/hisself) wrote his memoirs and described the experience.
7. (Less/Fewer) walls surround the palace than formerly.
8. (They're/Their) presence held back the flow of traffic, and they were almost all removed.
9. If (your/you're) ever able to travel to Peking, visit the Imperial Palace.
10. (We/Us) Westerners have little knowledge of the magnificent treasure to be seen there.

UNIT FOUR

MECHANICS

Capitalization
Punctuation

CHAPTER

12

CAPITALIZATION

A capital letter stands out from the letters that surround it because it is larger than the rest. For this reason, a capital letter is used at the beginning of a special word to set it apart from other words in your writing. The first word in a sentence is capitalized, for example, Capital letters are used in other ways as well. This chapter is about the many uses of capital letters.

CAPITAL LETTERS

12a Capitalize the first word in a sentence and the first word in a direct quotation.

Be sure you have a capital letter on the first word of every sentence. Sentences in quotations also have the first word capitalized.

EXAMPLES **Two** hundred years ago some women wore fancy hairdos.

Elisha said to her hairdresser, "**Give** me the fanciest hairdo you can create."

12b Capitalize the pronoun *I*.

EXAMPLE "When you are done, **I** want to attract lots of attention," she said.

Only the pronoun *I* is capitalized when it comes in the middle of a sentence. Do not capitalize other pronouns unless they are at the beginning of a sentence.

EXAMPLE **You** may be right, but **you** should take care to be sure.

12c Capitalize proper nouns and proper adjectives.

See Proper Nouns, p. 5

Proper nouns name particular persons, places, or things. A proper adjective is formed from a proper noun. Every proper noun and proper adjective begins with a capital letter.

EXAMPLES
PROPER NOUNS **S**outh **A**merica, **E**urope, **J**uanita **K**reps
PROPER ADJECTIVES **S**outh **A**merican, **E**uropean

(1) Capitalize the names of particular people and animals.

EXAMPLES "You're wrong," insisted **M**avis. "**M**ark **T**wain never had a jumping frog named **S**pringer."

(2) Capitalize the words for family members when they are used as proper nouns.

The words that name the members of a family should be capitalized if they are used in place of those people's names.

EXAMPLE I bought **M**other a birthday present. [But: I bought *my mother* a birthday present.]

(3) Capitalize the names of particular places.

EXAMPLES

Cities, Towns	**H**ouston, **V**icksburg, **M**iddletown
States, Counties	**D**elaware, **T**exas, **O**range **C**ounty
Countries	**L**ibya, **N**orway
Continents	**A**sia, **N**orth **A**merica
Special Regions	the **N**ortheast, the **B**ermuda **T**riangle [Do not capitalize *the*.]
Bodies of water, Islands, Points of land	**B**ar **H**arbor, **M**t. **D**esert **I**sland, **L**and's **E**nd
Parks	the **E**verglades, **D**isneyland
Roadways, Waterways	**I**nterstate 80, the **P**anama **C**anal

Do not capitalize directions.

EXAMPLE When leaving Boston, the traveler going westward crosses seemingly endless land; but going eastward there is nothing but water.

EXERCISE 1 Each of the following sentences needs capital letters. Number a sheet of paper 1–6. Write each word needing capitals. Put in the necessary capitals.

EXAMPLE the panama canal connects the atlantic and the pacific.

The Panama Canal, Atlantic, Pacific

1. american history begins before the landing of christopher columbus.
2. he landed on san salvador in the caribbean sea.
3. however, ancestors of earlier americans had probably come from asia to what is now alaska.
4. both eskimos and native americans arrived before the europeans.
5. for that matter, polynesians settled hawaii many hundreds of years ago.
6. the asians, the europeans, and the africans all helped to make the culture of the united states.

(4) Capitalize important words in the names of organizations, institutions, businesses, and branches of government.

EXAMPLES

Organizations — Society for the Prevention of Cruelty to Animals (SPCA), the North Atlantic Treaty Organization (NATO)

Institutions	the University of North Carolina, Northwestern University, Church of Good Faith, Lincoln High School
Businesses and their products	General Mills, Post Toasties, Chrysler, Colgate soap
Branches of government	Central Intelligence Agency (CIA), House of Representatives, the Supreme Court

(5) Capitalize subjects taught in school when they name particular courses.

EXAMPLES The first class in the morning is Homemaking II, followed by Mathematics III.

Do not capitalize the name of a general field of study.

EXAMPLE The study of history doesn't interest Jody, but science does.

(6) Capitalize the names of nationalities, races, and religions.

EXAMPLES Mexican, Methodist, Chinese, Muslim, Sudanese

(7) Capitalize the name of God and other beings worshipped by people.

EXAMPLES God, Buddha, the Supreme Being

(8) Capitalize the names of the days of the week, months of the year, and special holidays.

EXAMPLES **M**onday, **J**anuary, the **F**ourth of **J**uly, **M**emorial **D**ay

Do not capitalize the seasons: summer, fall, winter, and spring.

EXERCISE 2 Each of the following items needs capitals. Write each item on a sheet of paper and put in the capitals where they belong.

EXAMPLE the harrison street neighbors
The Harrison Street neighbors

1. monday is labor day
2. the united states
3. the university of virginia
4. autumn in san antonio, texas
5. cadillacs from general motors
6. english and french
7. The title of the course is civics for americans.
8. the god of love in greek mythology is eros.
9. Many muslims live in the near east.
10. the security council of the united nations

(9) Capitalize the names of historical events and documents.

EXAMPLES the **M**agna **C**arta, **W**orld **W**ar II, the **B**attle of **B**ull **R**un

(10) Capitalize the first word and every important word in the titles of people, books, magazines, newspapers, movies, television shows, and other works people produce.

EXAMPLES

People	**M**ayor **S**korsky, **L**ieutenant **P**erez, **A**unt **E**lena
Books, Stories, Poems	***T****he* ***S****hame of the* ***C****ities* (book), "**A**n **O**ccurrence at **O**wl **C**reek **B**ridge" (story), "**T**o a **W**aterfowl" (poem)
Newspapers, Magazines	the **S**eattle ***T****imes,* the **N**ew **Y**ork ***P****ost,* ***S****urfing* ***T****oday,* ***N****ewsweek*
Movies, Plays, TV shows	***T****he* ***B****ride of* ***F****rankenstein* (movie), ***I****diot's* ***D****elight* (play), "60 **M**inutes" (TV show)
Works in music, art, architecture	Remington's "**B**ronco **B**uster" (sculpture), the **G**olden **G**ate **B**ridge (structure)

EXERCISE 3 The following items need capitals. Number a sheet of paper 1–10. Capitalize each item correctly.

1. the declaration of independence
2. the hundred years war
3. major trumble
4. *gone with the wind* (book)
5. "wide world of sports" (TV show)
6. the henry hudson bridge
7. the *chicago sun-times* (newspaper)

8. "to an athlete dying young" (poem)
9. *u.s. news and world report* (magazine)
10. aunt trixie

REVIEW EXERCISE A Capitalizing Names and Places

Some of the following sentences contain words that should be capitalized. Number a sheet of paper 1–10. Next to each number rewrite any word that needs a capital letter and capitalize it. If the sentence is correct as it stands, write *C*.

EXAMPLE I have a horse named clea.
Clea

1. She is an appaloosa.
2. The nez perce are credited with developing the appaloosa breed.
3. The name "appaloosa" is not the horse's original name.
4. Palouse is the name of a river in the country of the Nez Perce, and the horses were called Palouse horses.
5. This land was in the northwestern united states.
6. It included parts of oregon, washington, and idaho.
7. The horses are said to have come from Mexico, where the Spaniards brought them.
8. Horses with markings like the Appaloosa's are seen in ancient chinese and persian art.
9. Distinctive round colored spots and white hindquarters are some of the Appaloosa's markings.

10. they also have striped hooves, wispy tails and manes, and a white marking around the eye.

REVIEW EXERCISE B Capitalizing Important Words

Number a sheet of paper 1–10. Next to each number rewrite correctly any word that needs a capital letter. If the sentence is correct as it stands, write *C*.

EXAMPLE This is senator John Gooley speaking.

Senator

1. I am speaking on behalf of the concerned citizens committee.
2. We believe that the Department of the Interior should join with private businesses and interested groups to help clean up the air.
3. Courses called "how to have a cleaner environment" are being carefully designed by our committee.
4. They will be presented to interested people throughout this great state of idaho.
5. Part of the cost will be borne by amalgamated noodles, inc. of this city.
6. Students at the Idaho state college of teachers have agreed to donate their time.
7. Civic leaders, including mayor Johnson, are planning to take the course.
8. I would like to see everyone—including the italian community, the chinese community, the

black community—unite to make this project a success.

9. What can be more important to Americans and to the world than the air we breathe?
10. Sister Josephine of St. Mary's Church, Rabbi Cohen of the Temple Beth-El, and Dr. Brown of the United Church of Christ will each speak to you now.

REVIEW EXERCISE C More Capitalization

Certain words in the following sentences need capital letters. Number a sheet of paper 1–6. Next to each number write all the words from the sentence that need capital letters. Add the capital letters.

EXAMPLE the constitution of the united states guarantees free speech.

The Constitution, United States

1. ancient civilizations, such as the one in greece, had systems of law.
2. the egyptians before the time of christ made laws based on their religion.
3. the greeks thought it was the god zeus who ruled from mount olympus.
4. the romans worshipped many gods, such as jupiter, juno, and minerva.
5. laws based on religion were common in the countries near the mediterranean sea.
6. however, by the time of julius caesar in rome, civil laws were separated from religious laws.

CHAPTER

13

PUNCTUATION

End Punctuation, Commas

Punctuation marks seldom were used in writing several hundred years ago. Their absence made reading difficult. Punctuation marks signal the reader when to pause. Without those pauses it is hard to tell which words are grouped together. In time, punctuation was developed to help the reader keep meanings clear.

Look at the following sentence:

To Joann Wilson meant little.

Is this a proper English sentence? It makes little sense. Yet it is correct—except for punctuation. Place a comma in the sentence and it reads correctly.

To Joann, Wilson meant little.

This example illustrates the importance of punctuation in establishing meaning. End punctuation works to make meaning clear in similar ways.

In some cases, punctuation marks are used only because of custom. An example is the use of the period after an abbreviation, as in *Dr.*

To make your writing clear in meaning, follow the rules and customs of punctuation. This chapter will help you understand how important punctuation can be.

END PUNCTUATION

A sentence always ends with a mark of punctuation. The mark may be a *period* (.), a *question mark* (?), or an *exclamation mark* (!). Each punctuation mark serves a different purpose.

The Period

13a A period is used to mark the end of a statement or a request.

EXAMPLES The waffles were brown and crisp.
Please take off your hat in here.

13b A period is used after some abbreviations.

EXAMPLES Mt. Hood Rte. 5
P. O. Box Dr.

13c A period is usually used after an initial.

EXAMPLES Mr. Wm. O. Douglas was a justice of the U.S. Supreme Court.

Certain sets of initials often used together do not need periods.

EXAMPLES **HUD** (Housing and Urban Development)
NATO (North Atlantic Treaty Organization)

EXERCISE 1 Write the following sentences on a sheet of paper. Put in periods where they belong.

EXAMPLE The U S Postal Service operates from Washington, D C

The U.S. Postal Service operates from Washington, D.C.

1. Mt Everest is approximately 9,700 meters high
2. The *N Y Times* is printed on Forty-Third St in Manhattan
3. Mr S I Hayakawa was the oldest junior senator elected from California to the U S Senate
4. On Aug 12, 1977, NASA flew the first space shuttle
5. T H Kiami, M D began practicing medicine Oct 10, 1961, in Detroit, Mich, at Mercy Hospital

The Question Mark

13d A question mark is used at the end of a sentence that asks a question.

EXAMPLES Can you ride a motorcycle?
Do you have one?

EXERCISE 2 Copy the following sentences on a sheet of paper. Put a period after each statement or request. Put a question mark after each question.

1. The sun shines brightly when the sky is cloudless
2. Are there often rainstorms at night
3. When will we be able to have a picnic
4. The weather can change our plans for outdoor activity
5. Let's take a softball and bat to the park
6. Are sports a major pastime of Americans
7. Do you like baseball
8. Everyone needs a hobby or activity
9. Don't try to interest me in team sports
10. Do you ever enjoy watching a good football game

The Exclamation Mark

13e An exclamation mark is used at the end of a sentence that shows shock or surprise.

To give special emphasis to a written sentence, the exclamation mark is used instead of a period.

EXAMPLES What a way to go!
You have won the grand prize!
She really earned it!

Use exclamation marks sparingly. Putting in too many takes away from their value in expressing shock or surprise.

EXERCISE 3 Number a sheet of paper 1–10. After each number put the mark of end punctuation that goes with each sentence.

1. Many seashells are extremely rare
2. Is this one expensive
3. Yes, the Spondylus Regius is not a common shell
4. Are you familiar with the purple coral found off Baja California
5. No, but please send me a specimen
6. Some people use seashells as a focal point of their house's decor
7. These are the most amazing colors
8. Look out, that sea urchin shell is very fragile
9. Are puka shells still popular
10. What a strange shell

INSIDE PUNCTUATION

Punctuation inside a sentence helps you see how the words are grouped together. This enables you to understand meaning more quickly.

The Comma

13f A comma is used between items in a series.

Words or groups of words sometimes appear in a series of three or more. The items should be separated by commas. The same is true for a series of letters or numerals.

EXAMPLES

WORDS In our history class we read about Washington, Jefferson, and Hamilton.

PHRASES We kicked off our shoes, loosened our ties, and began to wrestle.

CLAUSES Angie watered the petunias, I cut the grass, and then we both weeded around the hedge.

NUMBERS AND LETTERS The teacher instructed us to number our papers 2, 4, 6, 8, and 10.

Your teacher may instruct you to omit the comma between the last two items in a series. This style of punctuation is acceptable, but it should be followed regularly.

EXAMPLE We had juice, cereal and fruit for breakfast.

EXERCISE 4 The following sentences are missing commas. On a sheet of paper write the words just before and after a missing comma. Put a comma between them.

EXAMPLE The coastlines of New England are rocky its small mountains are rounded and its vegetation grows rich and green.

rocky, its
rounded, and

1. Connecticut Massachusetts Maine and New Hampshire are four of the New England states.
2. Men women children and animals sailed on the *Mayflower* to New England.

3. Some of the Native American tribes that the Pilgrims first met were Delaware Mohican and Narragansett.
4. New England was the home of Benjamin Franklin John F. Kennedy Henry David Thoreau and Henry Wadsworth Longfellow.
5. Some people like to fish for bass pickerel trout and salmon in the lakes and rivers of New England.
6. The state of Maine has towns named after such European cities and countries as Paris Norway Belfast and Dresden.
7. Riding horses picking fruit camping in the woods and climbing tree-covered hills are popular pastimes in the New England countryside.
8. Would you say that the men and women of early New England helped to establish our rights of life liberty and the pursuit of happiness?
9. New England the Mid-Atlantic states and Virginia contributed heroes in the Revolutionary War.

13g Commas are used to set off items that interrupt a sentence.

EXAMPLES Early pioneers, *the strong ones at least*, made a life for themselves in the wilderness. There were others, *however*, who could not survive.

(1) Commas are used to set off appositives.

See Noun, p. 454; Pronoun, p. 458

An appositive is a word or group of words that follows a noun or a pronoun and repeats its meaning. The appositive is set off by commas because it interrupts the sentence.

EXAMPLE The drive toward the Pacific, *the Westward movement*, brought about extreme changes in American life.

(2) Commas are used to set off words like *yes, no,* and *well* when they begin or interrupt a sentence.

EXAMPLES She could have taken it; but, *no*, she refused the offer.
This, *without doubt*, will cause trouble.

(3) Commas are used to set off transitional terms.

Words such as *however, nevertheless,* and *moreover* are called *transitional terms*. When used in sentences, transitional terms should be set off by commas.

EXAMPLES Worrell saw the rainstorm coming. *Nonetheless*, he kept the wagon moving. It would be long hours, *however*, before he could reach the fort.

(4) Commas are used to set off names used in direct address.

EXAMPLES His wife called to him, "Don't you reckon, *Worrell*, that we ought to stop?"
"Not yet, *Ellie*, 'cause we've got a piece to go yet," he answered. Then he turned to the oxen, "Git up, *Babe*! We'll make it."

Hint: A comma usually comes in a sentence where your voice pauses and drops in tone as you read the sentence aloud.

EXERCISE 5 The following sentences are lacking commas. Number a sheet of paper 1–10. Next to the number for each sentence write the words just before and after a missing comma. Put the comma between them.

EXAMPLE It was after all a rainy afternoon.

was, after all, a

1. Yes I think my hair is definitely too curly.
2. However straightening it weakens the hair shaft.
3. I should be glad to have so much hair I suppose.
4. I asked a friend, "George do you think I need something done to my hair?"
5. Really friends don't know much about my hair problems.
6. After all they don't have my hair.
7. One of my teachers a gray-haired older woman used to get her hair tinted blue sometimes.
8. The color looked fine however even though it made me smile.
9. Then again my wild curls a source of much embarrassment to me made others smile.
10. Do people in our society the critical ones spend too much time judging others by outward appearances?

EXERCISE 6 The following sentences are lacking commas. Number a sheet of paper 1–8. Next to the number for each sentence write the words just before and after a missing comma. Put the comma between them.

EXAMPLE I am as you can tell a busy traveler.
am, as tell, a

1. Driving from Los Angeles to Idaho a journey of 1500 miles requires that I rest now and then.
2. The trip is to say the least rather tiring.
3. However I usually overlook such drawbacks because I love to travel.
4. The Northwest a beautiful section of our country is one of my favorite vacation spots.
5. Indeed I lived there several years before moving on.
6. Summer I must add is my favorite time of year in that area.
7. The mountains' snow looking like great white crowns feeds into many rivers and lakes.
8. Without doubt the Northwest has a lot to offer people.

(5) Commas are used to set off nonessential phrases or clauses.

See Phrase, p. 457; Clause, p. 441

Any phrase or clause that is not necessary to the meaning of a sentence is called *nonessential.* The rest of the sentence would make sense without the nonessential phrase or clause.

EXAMPLES Jeremiah Spangenberg, *the richest settler here*, runs a ranch twice the size of mine.
[The phrase is not necessary for the sentence to carry its meaning.]

His wife Rosita, *who married him for his sense of humor*, now runs the ranch.
[This clause is not essential to the meaning of this sentence.]

Hint: To tell whether or not commas should be used to set off an inserted phrase or clause, ask: *Are these words necessary to know which particular person or thing is meant?* If your answer is no, the phrase or clause is nonessential. It should, therefore, have commas around it.

Following are some examples of essential and nonessential phrases:

ESSENTIAL PHRASE The two boys *brought up on the ranch* help out with the chores.
[This phrase tells which boys help out on the ranch.]

NONESSENTIAL PHRASE The Spangenberg ranch, *located over those hills*, covers about three hundred acres.
[This phrase adds information about the ranch but is not necessary to complete the meaning of the sentence. The

word *Spangenberg* already identifies clearly which ranch is meant.]

EXERCISE 7 Some of the following sentences contain nonessential clauses or phrases. On a sheet of paper write the words before and after the place for a comma. Add commas where they belong.

EXAMPLE Our town which is a quiet place has very little happening.

town, which place, has

1. The hotel maid who made up our room is from Iowa.
2. The denim jeans that have a patch on the knee are clean now.
3. My sister Nancy who has curly hair likes to read modern novels.
4. Our dog who seems to get fleas every summer has a very thick coat.
5. The old lady who lives next door tries to grow tomatoes on her porch.
6. The little restaurant that has a green door serves delicious omelettes.
7. Downtown Honolulu where lots of people go shopping shows the influence of many different cultures.
8. The little tree that the woodpecker pecked froze in the winter of 1972.
9. Our pet rock which cracked when Nancy dropped it was brown with red splotches.
10. The comma which looks like a period with a tail is grammatically essential.

13h A comma is used to separate adjectives not joined by the conjunction *and*.

See Conjunction, p. 443

EXAMPLES Grissom noticed the tired, gasping horse.
He yelled at the jumping, hooting boy to stop.

If the second of two adjectives is closely related to the noun it modifies, no comma is needed.

EXAMPLE The sparkling young girl skipped across the puddle.

EXERCISE 8 The following sentences need commas. Number a sheet of paper 1–6. Next to each number write the word before and after a comma that belongs in the sentence. Put in the missing comma.

EXAMPLE Much of our earth is covered by deep salty life-giving bodies of water.
deep, salty, life-giving

1. Seemingly endless noisy torrential rains fell upon the earth hundreds of millions of years ago.
2. These rains created our deep extensive silent seas.
3. The drying oceans left huge cavernous sand-filled rocky basins.
4. Many people could not live without tasty nutritious seafood to eat.
5. We must protect our precious limited life-giving water resources.
6. Without water, the world would be an empty dead desert.

13i A comma is often used to set off a dependent clause at the beginning of a complex sentence.

See Clause, p 441; Complex Sentence, p. 442

EXAMPLES Whenever Paco heard the coach, he ran into the street.
If anyone was aboard, he wanted to be the first to know it.

EXERCISE 9 Each of the following sentences needs a comma. Number a sheet of paper 1–10. After each number write the words before and after the place for a comma. Add the comma.

EXAMPLE As democracy developed in ancient Greece the people began to govern themselves.
Greece, the

1. When it is time for elections we see democracy in action.
2. If the governmental processes are unfair we can work toward changing them.
3. Because many countries are nondemocratic their people are allowed fewer freedoms.
4. Sometimes when minorities enjoy less freedom than the majority violent protests result.
5. When Mahatma Ghandi preached nonviolence he became a famous leader of India's people.
6. If people assemble peaceably more people are apt to listen to their ideas.
7. Even though there are more peaceful alternatives some people seem to make trouble when they try to bring about changes.

8. Because Communism demands a restricted life-style many people flee from Communist-ruled countries.
9. Even though we have a great deal of freedom in our democratic society some people prefer to live elsewhere.
10. While you can please some people you can't please all the people all of the time.

13j A comma is usually used before a coordinating conjunction joining the independent clauses in a compound sentence.

See Conjunction, p. 443; Compound Sentence, p. 443

EXAMPLES Sometimes the mail sacks were so empty they were limp, *but* other times they were bulging.
Jon longed for a letter for himself, *yet* he never had a piece of paper.

If each clause in a compound sentence has only a few words, commas may be unnecessary. Follow the directions of your teacher.

EXAMPLE Some weeks he was sad and others he was happy.

EXERCISE 10 Each of the following sentences needs a comma. Number a sheet of paper 1–8. After each number write the words before and after the place for a comma. Add the comma.

EXAMPLE Everyone learns to speak a dialect but some people can speak several.
dialect, but

1. Virginia Brandon lived in New York but she talked like a Texan.
2. Her father was raised in Texas and she learned to speak with a Texas accent.
3. People stared at her when she spoke but Virginia didn't take notice of them.
4. She reasoned that those people all have some odd habits and she felt better about being different.
5. Classmates in school teased Virginia but they soon learned to like her as a person.
6. As an older girl she moved to Texas but the people there mistrusted her New York ways.
7. Virginia learned to ignore other people's attitudes and she was able to become friendly with the people who accepted her.
8. Virginia knew how to make friends for she was not blocked by unimportant matters like an accent.

13k Commas are used in certain standard ways.

Commas have standard uses that are not just to clarify meanings. They also help to make reading easier. These standard uses are presented in the following pages.

(1) A comma is used before the quotation marks around the words of a speaker.

A comma sets off the exact words of the speaker from the rest of the sentence.

EXAMPLE Darlene whispered across the room, "Let me have your paper," as Emilie tried not to notice.

A comma always goes in front of the quotation marks.

EXAMPLES Darlene whispered louder, "Didn't you hear me?"

Emilie answered, "No," and went on reading.

EXERCISE 11 Number a sheet of paper 1–10. Write the following sentences. Put in commas where they belong.

EXAMPLE An aide reported to General Andrew Jackson "You sent for me, sir?"

An aide reported to General Andrew Jackson, "You sent for me, sir?"

1. "Yes" said Jackson "take this message to Colonel Bainbridge."
2. "Yes, sir" answered the aide "I'll deliver it at once."
3. "We can see the British now" said Jackson.
4. "We'll make our stand along the canal" he added "and force the British to cross it."
5. "Pile up sugar barrels" he went on "and bank mud against them."
6. "If General Pakenham tries an attack" Jackson continued "he'll have to swim and climb."
7. "Stand firm" ordered Jackson "as they come near."

8. "When they come within range" Jackson cautioned "hold fire until I order you to shoot."
9. "Now they're coming" said a lieutenant "but we're ready."
10. "This Battle of New Orleans" he murmured "may go down in history."

(2) A comma is used to separate items in dates and geographical names.

EXAMPLES The city of St. Louis, Missouri, is called the Gateway to the West. It was first settled on Feb. 14, 1764.

EXERCISE 12 Number a sheet of paper 1–4. Next to each number write each part of the following sentences that need commas. Add commas where they belong.

EXAMPLE Columbus died in the town of Volladolid Spain on May 20 1506.

Valladolid, Spain
May 20, 1506

1. Historians believe that Christopher Columbus was born in Genoa Italy about Aug. 25 1451.
2. The *Santa Maria,* the *Nina,* and the *Pinta* sailed from Palos Spain on Aug. 3 1492.
3. The *Santa Maria* was wrecked on a reef in the Carribean on December 24 1492.
4. Columbus returned to Spain on March 15 1493 and was given the title "Viceroy of the Indies."

(3) A comma is used after the greeting and the closing in a friendly letter.

EXAMPLES	Dear Frank,	Yours sincerely,
	Dear Uncle Joe,	Cordially,

REVIEW EXERCISES for Punctuation will be found at the end of Chapter 14.

CHAPTER

14

PUNCTUATION

Semicolons, Colons, Hyphens, Apostrophes, Dashes, Italics, Quotation Marks, Parentheses

This chapter continues the explanation of inside punctuation in Chapter 13. It introduces the remaining marks of inside punctuation—the *semicolon,* the *colon,* the *hyphen,* the *apostrophe,* and *italics (underlining).* Marks of enclosing punctuation—*quotation marks* and *parentheses*—are also presented.

INSIDE PUNCTUATION

The Semicolon

14a A semicolon is used between the clauses in a compound sentence that are not joined by a conjunction.

See Compound Sentence, p. 443; Conjunction, p. 443

EXAMPLES Roscoe likes a place where the weather is mild; Jean prefers the north country with its fierce cold.

Differences in climate may occur closely together; all one has to do is find a very high mountain in the tropics.

14b A semicolon is used between the clauses of a compound sentence when either clause has a comma in it.

EXAMPLE Mauna Kea is a high mountain on the island of Hawaii; its peak is snow-covered, but palms sway at its feet.

This rule applies even when a coordinating conjunction joins the two clauses.

EXAMPLE The morning sport can be skiing; but in the afternoon, after a trip down the slope, swimming is the sport.

14c A semicolon is used to separate items in a series having inside punctuation.

EXAMPLE Among the Hawaiian islands, Hawaii is the largest; Oahu, with the state capital of Honolulu, is the most heavily populated; and Kauai, called the Garden Isle, is the wettest.

14d A semicolon following a quotation goes outside the quotation marks.

EXAMPLE The god Pele begged, "Please release me"; but he was caught in the net and could not escape.

EXERCISE 1 The following sentences are missing semicolons. Number a sheet of paper 1–11. Next to each number write the words before and after the place where a semicolon belongs. Put in a semicolon.

EXAMPLE Captain James Cook, Hawaii's first English explorer, made friends with many Hawaiians but later, through a misunderstanding, he was killed by Hawaiian warriors.

Hawaiians; but

1. Hawaii, the Aloha State, is a beautiful group of islands but a majority of the people live on Oahu, the site of the state capital.
2. Most people stay near Honolulu where there are plenty of jobs the other islands are less inhabited.
3. The state bird, a goose, is called a *nene* the state flower is the hibiscus.
4. The chief agricultural products of Hawaii are cattle, chickens, pineapples, sugar cane, and dairy products and the chief fishing industry product is tuna.
5. The Hawaiians are descendants of the Polynesians, who settled the islands several hundred years ago but there are many other races who inhabit Hawaii, such as Filipinos, Chinese, and Portuguese.
6. As early as the 1500's, Spanish, Dutch, or Japanese explorers may have stopped at the Hawaiian Islands however, the world didn't hear much about Hawaii until James Cook landed in early 1778.

7. King Kamehameha I exported great quantities of sandalwood to China this provided money for ships, clothing, arms, and other goods.
8. The pineapple, brought from Jamaica, has been a thriving crop in Hawaii but a sudden change of soil conditions, which nearly killed the entire crop, has caused the death of many pineapple plants.
9. On August 21, 1959, Hawaii became the fiftieth state though in more than fifty years, a total of fifty-nine bills for statehood had been introduced in the U.S. Congress.
10. The Hula, a noted Hawaiian dance which involves swaying hips and waving arms, looks easy and flowing but when done for a long period of time it can be very exhausting to the dancer.
11. Most of the many volcanoes on the other islands are now extinct however Hawaii, the largest of the islands, has two active volcanoes today.

The Colon

14e A colon is used to introduce a list of items.

EXAMPLES Several things disturb me: barking dogs, howling cats, and the loud singing of birds at sunrise.

We have the following sizes in stock: 8A, 9A and 9B, and 10B.

14f A colon is used in numerals expressing time.

EXAMPLES At the chime, the time will be 5:30.
The next chime will be at 5:45.

14g A colon is used after the greeting in a business letter.

EXAMPLES Dear Ms. Farley:
Dear Madam:

EXERCISE 2 Colons are missing from the following sentences. Number a sheet of paper 1–5. Next to each number write the words or numbers needing colons after them. Put in the colons.

EXAMPLE The telephone is used for a number of purposes doing business, calling friends, and getting help.

purposes:

1. The ringing telephone awoke me at 320 A.M., and a recorded voice relayed this message "Hello, I hope you are sleeping well. If not, use Snoozeze sleeping capsules. Goodnight!"
2. Understandably, I was upset since I was supposed to wake up at 600.
3. I had many errands to do fixing my shoes, buying a bedspread, and having my hair cut and set.
4. At 515 when I finally returned home, I read in the newspaper the following item "If you receive a recorded phone message advertising sleeping capsules, call the Better Business Bureau because the company does not have a proper business license."

5. Now I have learned two things don't buy Snoozeze sleeping capsules, and don't answer the phone at 320 A.M. when you have to get up at 600.

The Hyphen

See Compound, p. 442

14h A hyphen is used to connect the parts of certain compound words and word numbers from twenty-one to ninety-nine.

EXAMPLES	pull-ups	father-in-law
	thirty-four	a movie stand-in

Check a dictionary if you are in doubt about the use of hyphens in compound words. Some compound words do not take hyphens.

EXAMPLES	watchman	suntan

14i A hyphen is used with a compound adjective that comes before the noun it modifies. No hyphen is used after an adverb ending in *-ly*.

EXAMPLES the well-run machine
[but not: The machine was well run.]

a too-tired horse
[but not: A horse, too tired from work, cannot gallop.]

a poorly planned party

14j A hyphen is used to divide a word between syllables at the end of a line.

EXAMPLES

CORRECT Felicia didn't enjoy the cele-
bration. She slept through the symphony.

INCORRECT Felicia didn't enjoy the celebr-
ation. She slept through the symphony.

EXERCISE 3 Number a sheet of paper 1–10. Copy each of the following items. Put in hyphens where they belong. For each single word, write the syllables separately. Put hyphens between the syllables to show how each word should be broken at the end of a sentence. You may use a dictionary.

EXAMPLE contagious

con-ta-gious

1. appetite
2. concentration
3. linguistic
4. encyclopedia
5. kindergarten
6. a well planned schedule
7. refrigerator
8. twenty two
9. gymnastics
10. mother in law

The Dash

14k The dash is used to set off certain interrupters in a sentence, especially those with inside punctuation.

EXAMPLE Their efforts to raise money for the hall—though, according to the lawyer, open to question on legal grounds—are worthy of support.

The Apostrophe

See Nouns, pp. 7–10

14l An apostrophe is used with nouns to show possession or close relationship.

EXAMPLES Henrietta's sister bought Miguel's car.
The car's muffler needs fixing.

(1) Most singular nouns form the possessive with an apostrophe and an *s*.

EXAMPLES the cow's milk
the storm's center
her brother's friends
Janis's letter

(2) A plural noun ending in *s* forms the possessive with an apostrophe only.

EXAMPLES The birds' nesting places had been destroyed by the wind.
Lawyers' arguments are usually logical.

Note that the apostrophe follows the **s**.

(3) A plural noun not ending in *s* forms the possessive with an apostrophe and an *s*.

EXAMPLES Children's toys become more expensive every year.
Deer's habits in the wild are little known.

EXERCISE 4 Some of the following sentences are correct. Others have errors in the use of the apostrophe to show possession. Number a sheet of paper 1–8. Write *C* for any sentence that is correct. Rewrite any incorrect sentence to show the correct use of the apostrophe.

EXAMPLE Our familys life is quite normal.
Our family's life is quite normal.

1. Our dogs tail often wags when it is happy.
2. Trixie likes to eat meat and bones.
3. When someone knocks on the door, we hold our cats collar so it will not run away.
4. Our neighbors house looks attractive with its brown shutters.
5. The childrens television show came on before dinner.
6. Rodneys hair is usually in tangles.
7. Melissas shoes get lost every week.
8. Our pets behave themselves when Dads eyes get a stern look.

14m An apostrophe is used to show that letters have been omitted.

Be sure the apostrophe appears in the exact spot where the omitted letters belong.

EXAMPLES wouldn't (would not)
hasn't (has not)
they'll (they will)
should've (should have)

Because these *contractions* are not formal, they appear more often in speech than in writing.

14n An apostrophe is used with the letter *s* to show the plural of letters, numerals, and special symbols.

EXAMPLES Schools in the district are supported by their PTA's.

The tally sheet had too many 10's for them and too many 0's for us. Of course we could not win.

EXERCISE 5 Number a sheet of paper 1–10. Next to each number write the form that shows the possessive. Use apostrophes where necessary.

EXAMPLE the wallet that belongs to Pam
Pam's wallet

1. the horse that belongs to Sandra
2. yokes that belong to oxen
3. toys that belong to children
4. the rake that belongs to the gardener
5. the icing that belongs on a cake
6. the point that belongs to a pencil
7. flowers that belong to a florist
8. rights that belong to the people
9. the yard that belongs to Ms. Harris
10. the pipe that belongs to Grandpa

EXERCISE 6 Rewrite the following items. Put in apostrophes where they belong.

EXAMPLE Whats it like in there?

What's it like in there?

1. shouldnt
2. Mom cant drive the car.
3. Hasnt Bruce called yet?
4. Ill write to you tomorrow.
5. Its too bad shes lost.
6. Mrs. Brown doesnt know that.
7. Dot the *i*s.
8. couldve
9. Dont wake the baby.
10. Lets have a little quiet.

Italics (The Underline)

14o Underlining is used for titles of books, movies, periodicals, ships, letters of the alphabet, and important works created by people. In printed matter these items are usually set in italics.

EXAMPLES One of the best horror movies was *Frankenstein*.
Beethoven's *Fifth Symphony* begins with four memorable notes.

14p Underlining is used to make special items and foreign words stand out.

EXAMPLES When approaching, *watch for flying sparks*.

No food or drink allowed inside the area.
All the Frenchman could say was, "*Alors.*"

EXERCISE 7 Number a sheet of paper 1–6. Write the parts of the following items that need underlining. Underline where necessary.

EXAMPLE Gone With the Wind is a famous book.

Gone With the Wind

1. Clark Gable starred in the movie Gone With the Wind.
2. He also was in It Happened One Night.
3. Articles about him have been in magazines such as Silver Screen and TV Guide.
4. He played Christian in a movie about a ship named Bounty.
5. Mutiny on the Bounty was the movie's name.
6. The book Mutiny on the Bounty was written by Charles Nordhoff.

ENCLOSING PUNCTUATION

Sometimes punctuation is used to enclose groups of words. Quotation marks, for example, enclose the exact words of a speaker. Parentheses also are useful in special cases for enclosing groups of words.

Quotation Marks

14q Quotation marks are used to enclose a speaker's exact words.

EXAMPLES Imogene asked, "What goes in first?"
"The butter," answered Lem, "and then add the milk."

Only the exact words of a speaker are put in quotation marks.

EXAMPLE
DIRECT QUOTATION "I've got the milk in it now," said Imogene.
INDIRECT QUOTATION Imogene said she had the milk in it.

Place a comma in front of the quotation marks at the beginning and end of a quotation.

EXAMPLE Lem exclaimed, "Hold the milk," and he rushed to the stove.

See Commas, pp. 319–320

Hint: A quotation is set off from the rest of the sentence with commas.

14r Single quotation marks are used to enclose a quotation within a quotation.

EXAMPLE "I thought I heard you say, 'it doesn't burn'," said Imogene.

14s Quotation marks are used to enclose titles of chapters, articles, short stories, poems, songs, and other short pieces of writing.

EXAMPLES The audience joined in the singing of "America, the Beautiful."
The next chapter is titled "Crossing the Great Divide."

14t Quotation marks are used to enclose special terms or slang.

EXAMPLES Yesterday's slang terms are usually today's dead language; think, for example, of "twenty-three skidoo" and "oh, you kid."

EXERCISE 8 Number a sheet of paper 1–6 and write the following items. Put in quotation marks where they are needed.

EXAMPLE Thomas Paine wrote a famous article, The Crisis.

Thomas Paine wrote a famous article, "The Crisis."

1. He said, These are the times that try men's souls.
2. Poe's poem The Raven repeats the word *Nevermore.*
3. In Lincoln's time was it common to sing the Battle Hymn of the Republic?
4. Frank R. Stockton's The Lady or the Tiger became the most popular short story of its day.

5. O. Henry's story The Gift of the Magi also was popular.
6. A word he used is the old slang term masher.

14u A period always goes inside the end quotation marks.

EXAMPLE Isobel spoke in a mumble, "I'll make it."

A question mark or exclamation mark goes inside the end quotes if the quotation itself is a question or exclamation. If the introductory expression is the question or exclamation, the mark goes outside the quotation marks.

EXAMPLES "What will you make?" asked Jody.
What makes a person say, "I'll make it"?

EXERCISE 9 Number a sheet of paper 1–8. Then copy the following sentences. Add quotation marks, single quotation marks, and commas wherever they are needed and circle them.

EXAMPLE Emily Webb said George Gibbs, up to a year ago I liked you a lot.

Emily Webb said, "George Gibbs, up to a year ago I liked you a lot."

1. George stammered What do you mean?
2. Up to a year ago I used to like you, but then you changed she went on.
3. I haven't been feeling well George answered.

4. A year is a long time to be sick she added. You should see a doctor.
5. Did you say see a doctor? asked George.
6. Actually, I haven't been eating well lately George said.
7. The kind of food you eat he went on affects your health and your mood.
8. I wonder interrupted Emily whether you should begin taking vitamins.

Parentheses

14v Parentheses are used to enclose extra items added in a sentence.

EXAMPLE The directions are clear (see the bottom of the page) and should be followed carefully.

Often these extra items might go in a following sentence. However, if you want them to be close to the statement of the sentence, include them in parentheses.

EXERCISE 10 Write the following sentences on a sheet of paper. Put in the missing quotation marks, end punctuation, and parentheses.

EXAMPLE Hold it, Harold, yelled Asa she had seen him open the trunk, I've got the chains here

"Hold it, Harold," yelled Asa (she had seen him open the trunk), "I've got the chains here."

1. Where did you find those asked Harold he was astounded at what he saw
2. The truth is, answered Asa she was somewhat embarrassed, I had them in my trunk
3. You mean, exclaimed Harold his voice was near to cracking as he stumbled toward her, you had them all the time
4. Yes, but I didn't know how to tell you, she said.
5. Well, he muttered for he had controlled his emotion, let's get them on and go

REVIEW EXERCISE A **End Punctuation**

Copy the following sentences on a sheet of paper and number them 1–10. Put periods, question marks, or exclamation marks where they belong in the sentences. Circle the marks you add.

EXAMPLE The American red fox is about 36 in long, not including its 17-in tail

The American red fox is about 36 in. long, not including its 17-in. tail.

1. I saw one out on Rte 3, scampering across the road
2. You'll never believe where it hid
3. It ran under a mailbox marked W D Fox
4. I would hate to look under W D Lyon's mailbox
5. Did you know that red foxes have a single mate and usually pair for life
6. The Peoria, Ill, *Times* reported seeing one on Main St not long ago

7. Red foxes eat birds, small mammals, fruit, insects, and carrion
8. The National Zoo, in Washington, D C, has a captive red fox
9. Did you know that the red fox has three color phases
10. Dr Joseph A Davis is an expert on foxes and is curator of the North Carolina Zoological Park in Ashboro, N C

REVIEW EXERCISE B The Comma

Commas are missing in the following sentences. Number a sheet of paper 1–10. Next to each number write the words just before and after each missing comma. Place the comma between the words.

EXAMPLE American folk songs include work songs that were sung by men working on the canals on the railroads on the chain gangs and in the fields.

canals, on
railroads, on
gangs, and

1. Protest songs nonsense songs spirituals and mountain love songs are part of the tradition.
2. Americans especially lovers of Western lore are fond of cattle songs.
3. One favorite *Home on the Range* is known to almost everyone.

4. Black artists have probably contributed more to world music than any other group of Americans however.
5. Their music based on African rhythms vocal devices and musical devices produced new sounds.
6. The weary sad songs of the slaves the "sorrow songs" were one kind of Black music.
7. But gospel songs jazz spirituals and rock-and-roll music are also derived from Black music forms.
8. "I have a lot of Billie Holliday records" Paul said to Yoko "Have you ever heard her singing?"
9. "No but I'd like to" she answered.
10. Billie Holliday one of the great blues singers was the subject of a movie *Lady Sings the Blues*.

REVIEW EXERCISE C The Semicolon and the Colon

Number a sheet of paper 1–11. Next to each number write the words before and after the place where a semicolon or a colon is needed and supply the missing punctuation.

EXAMPLE No two persons have ever been found to have identical fingerprints even identical twins have completely different markings.

fingerprints; even

1. Each person has a different ridge arrangement on each finger this arrangement remains the same throughout life.
2. Sir Francis Galton, a nineteenth-century English scientist, explained, "The ridge arrangement is constant" and his work impressed the British government.
3. A committee headed by Sir Richard Henry was appointed it produced a classification system still used today.
4. Some of the patterns into which all finger impressions are divided are the arch, the tented arch, and the radial loop there are ten in all.
5. The classification system—the Henry system—requires that fingerprints be taken in a certain sequence the thumb should be taken first.
6. At 1000 A.M., when the tour of the FBI starts, we'll be able to see some fingerprinting techniques.
7. I received a letter saying, "Dear Madam You must be fingerprinted before our firm can hire you for a job."
8. Classification of fingerprints by the FBI is a staggering task under the Henry system it is remarkably rapid.
9. One message the FBI has for criminals is this "Don't bother trying to erase your fingerprints!"
10. This is a costly, illegal procedure it has never been successful.
11. Fingerprints are commonly used for the following identification purposes drivers' licenses, check-cashing cards, and certain job applications.

REVIEW EXERCISE D The Dash, the Apostrophe, and Italics

Following is a true-or-false exercise. Number a sheet of paper 1–11. Next to each number, put *T* if the statement given is true, or *F* if it is false.

EXAMPLE This word needs hyphens: *brother-in-law.*

T

1. A dash is used to set off certain interruptions in a sentence.
2. The apostrophe in this statement is placed correctly: people's lives can change suddenly.
3. Never underline the title of a movie.
4. This statement needs a hyphen: the badly overworked horses collapsed.
5. This statement needs a hyphen: twenty two flavors are all this ice cream store offers.
6. A plural noun ending in *s* forms the possessive with an apostrophe only.
7. This statement is written correctly: I wouldnt want to be in Mathildas shoes.
8. A singular noun forms the possessive with a hyphen and an *s*.
9. This statement needs an apostrophe: I think I've got too many *5*s.
10. Titles of books, movies, and periodicals should be underlined.
11. This statement is written correctly: *Star Wars* was one of the most successful films of the 1970's.

REVIEW EXERCISE E **Enclosing Punctuation**

Copy the following sentences on a sheet of paper and number them 1–5. Punctuate each sentence correctly. Circle the punctuation marks you add.

EXAMPLE I've just finished reading *Murder on the Moon,* said Eugene.

"I've just finished reading <u>Murder on the Moon</u>," said Eugene.

1. These space people here in the picture are living on the moon Eugene continued.
2. Crime on the moon seems odd Maria answered.
3. The first chapter is titled Everyday Life Eugene said he was flipping through the pages and it tells about living on a space station.
4. Rooms are called cubes illustrated in this picture on page 79 he continued.
5. Get to the part about the murder Maria said and tell me how it happened.

UNIT FIVE

AIDS AND ENRICHMENT

Speaking and Listening
Spelling
Sources of Information
Using Words

CHAPTER

15

SPEAKING AND LISTENING

Information Conversation, Formal Speaking and Listening, Group Discussion

You relate with almost everyone around you by speaking and listening. Through speaking and listening you give and you get a first impression when meeting a new person. As you become friends with that person, you find out about him or her by speaking and listening.

Of course, no one can tell you exactly what to say or what to listen for in your communication with others. No one knows exactly what you and others will say or hear. However, certain basic guidelines apply in the various communicating situations, both formal and informal, in which you engage. They will help you improve your effectiveness as a speaker and a listener.

INFORMAL CONVERSATION

15a Think before you speak.

Failing to think ahead is the most common mistake people make in conversation. Test yourself to find out how well you plan what you say. Do you talk about topics that interest your listeners? Do you ask about their interests? Do you give others a chance to talk without interruption?

Carrying on a good conversation requires more than just the desire to talk. It calls for thinking and practice. You may be able to improve your conversations if you follow certain basic guidelines.

(1) Start with a topic that will interest your listener.

Not all people have the same interests. In a conversation, make an effort to talk about topics that will interest the person with whom you are talking. If you are a boy talking with a girl, remember that not all girls are interested in all the topics that interest boys. The same is true the other way. Not all boys are interested in everything girls talk about. Yet you do have many things in common with members of the opposite sex. Find one of the topics that are interesting to both of you.

(2) Ask questions that will involve your listener.

In general, asking a question is a good way to involve someone in a conversation. Whether you know the other person or whether you have just met, asking a question usually brings an answer. An answer often leads into further discussion.

Some kinds of "starter" questions are better than others. The general question that needs only a short answer is of little use. Instead of a general question, think of a specific question. Make the specific question apply to the person you are with.

EXAMPLES

GENERAL QUESTION	Do you like sports? [The answer can be a short "yes" or "no." The question doesn't need any more conversation.]
SPECIFIC QUESTION	Which sports do you like the best? [The answer will probably be more than one or two words. Moreover, if the person mentions a sport, you can talk further about it and other sports.]
GENERAL QUESTION	Have you been to (name of a popular vacation spot or gathering place) lately? [Again, the answer can be too short for much conversation.]
SPECIFIC QUESTION	What sorts of things do you like to do on vacation? [This type of question opens up a range of possible answers.]

(3) Listen to and look at the person talking.

People communicate with their faces and their movements as well as with their words. Because of this, successful face-to-face conversation consists of more than just opening your ears. When another person is talking to you, pay close attention to what is being said. Use your eyes as well as your ears. Look into the eyes of the person talking. Often you will be able to hear more clearly because you will see the other ways the speaker is using to communicate with you.

EXERCISE 1 Study the following conversation among three persons. Be prepared to tell which speakers seem to be good conversationalists and which do not. Tell why. What suggestions can you offer to improve any parts of the conversation?

Speaker A: "We lost electricity at our house last night."
Speaker B: "We didn't."
Speaker C (to Speaker A): "What happened?"
Speaker A: "I was watching TV. My mom was in the hallway. Suddenly everything went dark. Our . . ."
Speaker B: "Don't you have an emergency light? We do."
Speaker C (to Speaker A): "What did you do?"
Speaker A: "I got a flashlight and we lit some candles. But, you know, we couldn't remember which lights in the house were on."
Speaker C: "Well, you knew the TV was on."
Speaker B: "You should have all your switches marked for off and on."
Speaker A: "Sure, well, I turned off the TV. But we wondered if the power came on, would some lights turn on in the middle of the night."
Speaker C: "Maybe you could . . ."

Speaker B (breaking in): "Just unscrew the light bulbs."
Speaker A: "Yes. That's what we did. After that the power came right back on."

EXERCISE 2 Take roles with classmates in the following situations.

1. In a downtown office you get in line to take a test for a driver's license. Another student from your school gets in line behind you. You have seen the student at school but have not become acquainted. You begin a conversation.
2. While waiting at a check-out counter at a local market the parent of a student you know lines up with you. The parent does not recognize you, even though you saw each other when you recently visited at the student's home.

15b Speak and listen the way you want others to speak and listen to you.

This is the Golden Rule in conversation. When you practice it, you become more aware of the give-and-take in a conversation. You are alert to what others say because it becomes as important as if you were saying it. You include in what you say the kinds of things you want to hear.

Hint: A conversation needs more than one person to be successful. Make sure you include others in your conversation.

INTRODUCTIONS

Your purpose in introducing people is to help them get to know each other. Introductions are most effective when you follow certain steps. These steps also make introducing or being introduced quite easy. Once people are introduced, they feel free to engage in conversation.

15c Introduce people who do not know each other.

If you are introducing two people who have never met, use a standard expression to make them known to each other. Following are the customary wordings:

"May I introduce (name)."
"Let me introduce (name)."
"I'd like you to meet (name)."
"I don't think you have met (name)."

Be sure you also mention the name of the person to whom you are speaking.

Because these expressions are standard, some people think they are too formal. However, it is better to be thought formal than it is to be thought impolite.

Say the names of the people you are introducing clearly enough so that the other person can hear. Say a person's name in the direction of the person who doesn't know the name. This way, the name of the person being introduced will be heard more clearly.

Examples of introductions:
(You are introducing a young adult to an older adult.)
"Mr. Kendrick, let me introduce Steve Brown. Steve, meet Mr. Kendrick."

(You are introducing a student to a teacher.)
"Mrs. Gilchrist, I'd like you to meet Ollie Bloom. Ollie, this is Mrs. Gilchrist."

15d When introducing a person who deserves special respect, mention that person's name first.

Begin an introduction by saying the name of the person who deserves special respect. Then introduce the other person.

EXAMPLES "Dr. Dorsky, let me introduce Bunny Switzer. Bunny, meet Dr. Dorsky."

"Mrs. Schultz, I'd like you to meet my friend Ramon Perez. Ramon, meet Mrs. Schultz."

EXERCISE 3 Take roles with classmates in the following introduction situations.

1. Introduction of a student friend (Doretta May) to another friend (Jay Switzer).
2. Introduction of a friend (Ed Mahan) to an adult neighbor (Mr. Furth).
3. Introduction of an adult relative (mother, uncle) to a teacher (Mrs. Wolden).

4. Introduction of a friend (José Garcia) to your dentist (Dr. Wert) whom you meet shopping in a store.
5. Introduction of a foreign student visiting your school (Kristi Kover) to the principal (Mr. Ying).

15e When being introduced, pay close attention to the names of people.

A person's name is important to him or her. You will make your new acquaintance feel you want to know her or him if you remember the name.

Pay close attention to the name of each person introduced to you. Then during the following conversation or later you will be able to address the person directly.

If by chance you don't hear a person's name, ask politely that it be repeated.

EXAMPLES "Excuse me, I didn't hear your name. Would you repeat it, please?"
"I'm sorry, but I missed your name. What is it again?"
"Pardon me, but would you tell me your name again?"

A good way to remember someone's name in an introduction is to repeat it as it is said to you. In this way, you can establish it in your mind. You can also make sure that you are pronouncing the name correctly. If you mispronounce it out loud to the person whose name it is, you will most likely get an immediate correction.

EXAMPLE "It's a pleasure to meet you, Dr. Dorsky."

Hint: Avoid embarrassment. Remember the names of others introduced to you.

EXERCISE 4 Repeat the roles you took in Exercise 3 on page 352. This time, as you are introduced, pretend you do not hear the name of the person you are meeting. Find out that person's name.

THE TELEPHONE

Talking on the telephone is such a common occurrence that it hardly needs to be treated here. However, when you are giving or taking a message —perhaps an important message for someone else —a few words of caution may help.

15f Develop an effective telephone technique and manner.

Here are some guidelines for using the telephone:

1. Make sure you have the right number and are dialing it correctly.
2. Have a reason for calling and tell it to the person you call.
3. When the other person answers, state your name immediately and the reason for your call.

4. If the person you are calling is not there, leave your name and phone number. Any message you leave should be short. Taking down a long message is not easy, especially over the phone.

If you take a message over the phone, follow these steps:

1. Ask the caller whether a return call is desired.
2. Write down basic information. Don't trust your memory.
3. Include in the information (a) the name of the caller, (b) the time the call came in, (c) the number to call in return, and (d) other specific information given you.

GIVING DIRECTIONS

From time to time you are called upon to give directions. Directions are mainly of two kinds: (1) how to reach someplace, and (2) how to make or do something.

15g When directing someone to a place, put yourself in that person's place.

In giving directions for getting from one place to another, think of the route as though you were taking it yourself. You can then tell the other person how to travel the same route.

First, find out how much of the way is already known to the person. If the person knows some parts of the way, you can use those as points of familiarity.

In giving directions, think through the answers to these questions:

1. Which way does one go first? Avoid using compass directions in your directions. Instead, use the names or descriptions of landmarks that the person will see.
2. What landmark is just before a turn?
3. Which direction, right or left, is the correct turn?
4. About how far in each direction does one go?
5. What easy-to-see landmarks are on the way?

Sometimes a person following your directions may miss a turn. In giving directions, include landmarks that show a person has missed a turn or gone too far.

If you are not sure of the complete directions, say so. Give someone else the job of giving directions. The safest direction you can give is, "I'm not sure; you'd better ask someone who really knows the way."

EXERCISE 5 Choose a location in your community, for example, a store. Imagine you are a mile or more away on a different street. With you is someone who doesn't know the streets but wants to get to the location. Give directions to that stranger. You may give directions orally or write them.

EXERCISE 6 Listen to directions another student gives for Exercise 5. Tell that student how the directions can be improved.

15h When giving directions for making or doing something, think of the necessary materials and the required steps.

Some directions for making things are quite complicated. Giving complicated directions orally can be confusing. For this reason, write out complicated directions for making something. Following are four steps in giving directions for making something:

1. List the objects necessary to make the item.
2. Explain each small step clearly in the correct order.
3. Describe what the item will look like at each step in the process.
4. Warn about things that might go wrong.

EXERCISE 7 Be prepared to give directions for making one of the following items.

1. Diapers for a baby
2. A fire for the barbecue
3. A neat, inexpensive folder for a term paper
4. Decorations for a party table
5. An object out of papier-mâché
6. An item of your choice

FORMAL SPEAKING AND LISTENING

In school or out of school, you more and more will be expected to know how to speak *formally* before a group. You might be called upon to give a talk in a history or science class about some project.

Perhaps in a club meeting you will have to make an announcement. Other occasions will arise where you have to speak to a group.

Speaking to a group always requires care in choosing what to say and how you say it. The following rules are guides for public speaking.

15i Use clear, exact language when speaking to a group.

The main goal of speaking to a group is to share with *everyone* the information you have. In order for everyone to hear, you must speak "loud and clear." Almost as important, your language should be more exact than what you use in everyday conversation to be sure that your audience has the same understandings of your words that you do.

The basic rules you should follow are listed here and elsewhere in this text.

1. Use easily understood words.

   Avoid rarely used words or slang. Terms that are used in ways not known to the audience should be explained or defined.
2. Use the correct forms of words.

   Avoid too many contractions. Use the acceptable persons and tenses of verbs, case forms of pronouns, plural forms of nouns, and comparative and superlative forms of adjectives and adverbs.
3. Pronounce words correctly.

   If in doubt about the pronunciation of a word, look it up in a dictionary.
4. Make pronouns agree with their antecedents and verbs agree with their subjects.

5. Use complete sentences, not fragments.
6. Avoid stringing sentences together with *and's* or *but's*.

Making an Announcement

When you are to make an announcement to a group, plan ahead to include all parts of the information. Begin by naming those you are addressing. If your information concerns only girls who are trying out for sports, begin by saying, "The following announcement is for all girls trying out for sports." If your announcement is directed at the whole student body in school, say, "This announcement concerns all students" or "Attention, all students."

Speak slowly enough so that listeners can follow the information you are giving. Remember that you may not have the full attention of a group when you begin your announcement. Because of this, be sure you begin slowly and clearly.

Include in your announcement the basic facts. Think of these as answering the questions contained in the words *who, what, when, where,* and *why.*

EXAMPLE "This announcement is for all juniors. (WHO) There will be a meeting (WHAT) of the junior class (WHO) in the auditorium (WHERE) during the first period tomorrow (WHEN) to meet representatives (WHY) from campuses of the state universities and colleges."

If you believe it is necessary, repeat the basics of the announcement.

EXAMPLE "Remember, all juniors meet in the auditorium first period tomorrow."

Hint: The *who, when,* and *where* of an announcement about a meeting are most important. The *what* and *why* can be explained again at the meeting after the people have gathered.

Introducing a Speaker

On some occasions you may be the one to introduce a speaker. You will want to know how best to do this. Assume that not everyone in the audience knows the speaker. Your first obligation is to find out about him or her. The speaker may be someone from out of town. It may be a local person who has done something unusual. It may be a student who is running as a candidate for office.

15j Find out important information about the speaker in advance.

Ask the speaker well before the meeting to give you special information you can use in your introduction. Ask for special accomplishments that will be of interest to the audience. Also, be sure to clarify what it is the speaker plans to talk about.

Keep your introduction brief. After all, the speaker is the one the audience should spend time listening to, not you. Avoid trying to be funny unless you know that the speaker would like you to amuse the group.

Example of an introduction:

It is my privilege to introduce (name of speaker), who will tell us of her experiences as a professional athlete. (Name of speaker) is a nationally ranked tennis player and spent four years playing tennis for the Texas Tornadoes of the National Tennis League. She now gives tennis lessons and conducts clinics in various parts of the United States. She also writes a weekly column about tennis for her local paper. This afternoon after school she will conduct a short tennis clinic on the local courts and will accept a three-game challenge from any tennis player in the school. It's a pleasure for us to have (name of speaker).

EXERCISE 8 Write out one of the following announcements or introductions. Be prepared to give it.

1. Introduction of the coach of a visiting sports team.
2. Introduction of the visiting principal from another school.
3. Announcement for all girls: tryouts for the school volleyball team to be held in the gym Friday after school.
4. Announcement to all students: tryouts for the annual talent show (for benefit of the student body fund) to be held Thursday and Friday at noon and after school in the auditorium.

Giving a Speech

15k Prepare your talk in advance.

When preparing to give a talk, gather as much information about your topic as you possibly can. You may have been assigned a topic. Or you may have chosen a topic. Whichever condition applies, study in advance to put together a complete body of information about your topic.

Here are the basic steps in preparing a talk on a topic of your choice:

1. Choose a topic you know about or can find out about.
2. Choose a topic that will interest most of your listeners.
3. Find out more information than you can use in your report.
4. Select the information that will mean the most to your listeners.
5. Organize your information in three main parts: (1) the introduction, (2) the body, and (3) the conclusion.
6. Write out your report. Then write notes. These may be in short sentences. You may find an outline helpful. Or follow your teacher's directions.
7. Practice giving the report by referring only to your notes.

With your talk written out or with complete notes, you can try out your talk in advance. Memorize at least a short beginning. Perhaps it will be only one or two sentences. Learn them by heart. This way you don't have to refer to your notes at the beginning. You can start your talk by looking directly at your audience.

Outlining

You will find it useful to put your notes in the form of an outline. The outline will help you see which points are the major ones and which are not so important. The major points are those placed at the left next to Roman numerals. The less important points, or subpoints, are indented and placed next to capital letters. Any subpoints under the capitalized subpoints are indented further in, next to Arabic numerals.

STANDARD FORM OF AN OUTLINE

(Title or topic of the talk)

I. (First main point)
    A. (First subpoint)
    B. (Second subpoint)
II. (Second main point)
    A. (First subpoint for second main point)
    B. (Second subpoint for second main point)
        1. (First minor point for subpoint B)
        2. (Second minor point for subpoint B)
        3. (Third minor point for subpoint B)
III. (Third main point)
    A. (First subpoint for third main point)
    B. (Second subpoint for third main point)

Points made in an outline can be written in short form or as complete sentences. Try to make groups of points on one indention line equally important. The outline shows the relative importance of the points you will use in your talk.

On the following page is an example of an outline for a talk telling how to refinish a piece of furniture.

How to Refinish Furniture

I. Materials needed
  A. Cloths
    1. For wiping off paint remover
    2. For protection from spattering
  B. Sandpaper
  C. Paint scraper
  D. Wood filler or putty
  E. Primer or undercoat
  F. Paint or varnish
  G. Paint brush(es)
  H. Wax
II. First steps
  A. Scraping off old finish
  B. Using paint remover, if necessary
  C. Wiping clean
  D. Sanding
    1. Rough
    2. Smooth
III. Final steps
  A. Filling cracks, dents, or holes with putty
  B. Sanding
    1. Rough
    2. Smooth
  C. Priming or undercoating
  D. Painting or varnishing
  E. Waxing and polishing

EXERCISE 9 Choose one of the following topics. Make a list of points you would use as the basis for a talk on your chosen topic. On a sheet of paper write those points in the form of an outline.

1. Wash and wax a car
2. Change a tire on a wheel (car or bike)

3. Bake a cake or pie from scratch
4. Mix, pour, and finish cement
5. Repair a simple machine or appliance
6. Wash, trim, and deflea a shaggy dog

Delivering Your Talk

15l Deliver your talk the way you would want to listen to it.

(1) Speak clearly.

A speaker who mumbles words makes listening difficult. Work to make listening easy for your audience. Enunciate words and phrases so that they will be clear.

Every member of your audience deserves the chance to hear your words. Talk to the person in your audience who is farthest from you. To do this, you not only must enunciate but speak with enough volume.

(2) Speak to your audience.

What you do with your head and your eyes, in fact, with your whole body, makes an impact on your audience. If you keep your eyes down or look off at a corner or the ceiling, your audience will wonder if you know they are there. Moreover, with your head bent, you cut down on the opening of your windpipe and your vocal chords. This can severely restrict the amount of air from your lungs and the "voicing" you put into your talk.

Choose a few people sitting in the back of the room, on each side, and in the front. Glance at these people from time to time during your talk. By looking at them, you will see the majority of your audience. In this way you will not give members of the audience the feeling that you are leaving them out of your talk.

(3) Remain still except to make a point.

Each time you move, you attract the attention of your audience. A good magician uses that fact in creating magical illusions. A wave of one hand will attract the eyes of the audience while the other hand slips a card out of a sleeve.

You don't want to be a magician. Remember that your motions attract attention. For this reason, remain still except to underscore a special point. Extra motions of your arms or your head will distract the attention of your listeners. Keep your body still, too. Even a slight swaying can distract your audience.

Do you find it difficult to decide where to put your hands? If so, press them lightly against your hips or put them behind your back. Hold your hands still. Keep your notes in one hand. Then when you want to refer to your notes, bring them up in front of you, but not in front of your face. After you have checked your notes, put your hands down again.

Hint: Anything you move in front of an audience will attract attention.

---

(4) Appear at your best.

An old saying is, "Look your best and you'll do your best." This applies particularly to speaking before a group. On the day of your talk, dress neatly. Remember to smile at your audience from time to time, especially at the opening and closing of your talk.

(5) Avoid useless words and sounds.

During a talk be careful you don't add extra words or mumblings that get in the way of what you're saying. "Ah," "um," or even "well-a" have little meaning. Any one of these will detract from your talk. If you need a short pause to think of your next point, make it a silent pause.

EXERCISE 10 Prepare a talk on one of the following topics. Deliver your talk as your teacher directs.

1. What this school needs most
2. What this school should get rid of
3. Three simple ways to build strength
4. An easy way to develop self-confidence
5. Three ways to get yourself awake in the morning
6. Tips on eating
7. Tips on not eating
8. Controlling one's temper

(6) Control your nervousness.

It is perfectly natural to feel nervous when speaking in public. Actors for centuries have known of stage fright. If you never felt nervousness, it would be unusual indeed.

To overcome the effects of stage fright, practice the following techniques:

1. Know your material thoroughly in advance.
   (Ignorance of what you are going to say will only make you more nervous.)
2. Organize your material well.
   (Knowing many points but having them out of order will confuse you and your audience.)
3. Practice giving your talk in advance.
   (Practice in front of a friend or member of your family. Ask for advice on ways to improve your talk.)
4. During your talk, pick out people in the audience.
   (Look at them and talk to them as though you were in a smaller group conversation. Talking to fewer people is sometimes easier than talking to more people.)
5. Make no unnecessary moves during your talk.
   (If you control your motions, you are on the way to controlling nervousness.)
6. Smile at your audience from time to time.
   (By smiling from time to time during your talk, you help your audience enjoy your talk.)

THE PURPOSES OF TALKS

In addition to announcements and other brief talks, addressing groups in two other formal situations is common. These talks are the *explanatory talk* and the *persuasive talk*. The purpose of one differs from that of the other. However, sometimes parts of one are mixed with the other. It will help you and your audience if you make it clear early in your talk what purpose you have in giving the talk.

The Explanatory Talk

15m Use an explanatory talk to explain something.

The explanatory talk has as its purpose the explaining of something. You may explain a process. Or you may explain the history of something. You may even explain an idea.

Examples of topics for explanatory talks:
How to change a tire (cycle or automobile)
How the ancient Egyptians used make-up
The meaning of (democracy or capitalism, for example)
Down-home cooking techniques
How (not) to tell a funny story

As you choose a topic for an explanatory talk, be sure you follow these basic steps:

1. Choose a topic you know about or can find out about.
2. Choose a topic that will interest a majority of your audience.
3. If your topic is generally known, find a special aspect of it to talk about.
4. Organize your talk.
5. Demonstrate something to accompany your talk.

An explanatory talk is often more vivid when accompanied by a demonstration. Pictures, charts, or diagrams may be of help. Be sure they are large enough so that people in the back of the room can see clearly what you are demonstrating. Otherwise you will lose the attention of the part of your audience that cannot see what you have to show.

Possibly you will want to bring some objects to show, such as a collection of unusual shells, stamps, or butterflies. These are difficult to see if they are small. Therefore, do not use these small items as a basic part of your talk. Instead, have an enlarged picture of representative items in your collection. This you can point to. Others can then see the details you are explaining.

As for your collection, point to it also. But suggest that persons interested should inspect the collection after your talk. In that way, they can see more clearly what you have been explaining.

EXERCISE 11 Prepare an explanatory talk on one of the following topics. Deliver your talk as your teacher directs.

1. How a bird builds its nest
2. Making super chili
3. Bookbinding
4. How an engine's oil filter works
5. How a TV tube shows a picture
6. How (a holiday) began
7. How your telephone rings
8. The best ways to save money while spending it
9. The best ways to spend money while saving it
10. How to overcome shyness
11. The runner's diet
12. A topic of your choice

The Persuasive Talk

15n Use a persuasive talk to try to persuade someone to think or act in a certain way.

A talk that attempts to persuade an audience requires planning and practice if it is to succeed. The persuasive talk can be more effective, also, if you use a number of techniques and treat your topic skillfully.

Examples of topics for persuasive talks:
Smoking should be banned in public buildings
The farm subsidies for (name) must be increased
Our student council should have more (less) power
Support for school sports (should) (should not) come from the school budget

The persuasive talk may use some techniques of the explanatory talk. For example, you may wish to explain the background of some situation before you try to persuade your listeners to change their minds about it.

Always remember, though, that the purpose of a persuasive talk differs from that of an explanatory talk. The purpose of a persuasive talk is not to explain, but to persuade listeners to change their attitude and their actions. Thus you must spend only a little of your time explaining. You should spend the majority of it persuading.

Members of your audience may or may not hold the same belief you do about your topic when you begin talking. You hope, however, that at the end they will share the same belief you do. Even if your listeners share your belief at the beginning, you will want to strengthen their belief before you finish.

To bring about a change in belief, you need to use one or more persuasive techniques. Learning to be a good persuasive speaker means learning these techniques. Then you can apply them in your talks.

Here are some basic techniques for a persuasive talk:

1. Plan ahead.

   Planning includes choosing a topic or position about which you know something. If you do not know much about it, you must learn enough so that you can talk with knowledge. Planning also includes organizing your points so that they lead sensibly from one to the next.

2. Use facts instead of your own opinions.

   Too often someone may hope to persuade others just through the force of opinion. Holding an opinion is an individual's right, but an opinion alone probably will not persuade others.

   It is best to present facts that support your position. If you wish to persuade others that the student council should have more power, for example, find out about other student body councils in schools the size of yours. Do other schools give more power to their student councils? If so, use that fact to persuade.

   Suppose you wish to persuade your listeners that financial support for some activity should come from a new source. Find out exactly what amounts of money now come from what sources. Then present straightforward arithmetic facts to show what the changes would bring about.

3. Present a few strong favorable arguments rather than many.

   Choose two or three strong arguments or reasons for your position. Deal with those rather than with many. If you pile up too many reasons for your position, you have little time to back up each reason with facts. Besides, most of your audience will be able to remember only two or three strong points. They might not remember much if you load on too many points.

4. Be enthusiastic about your position, but avoid emotional outbursts.

   You surely want your audience to think you believe in your position. Strong belief is often shown through an enthusiastic voice. However, too much enthusiasm can spoil the effect. People begin to think that the idea is too weak to stand without such emotional support. Too much raving on your part may leave some of your audience suspicious of your purpose.

   Be enthusiastic but control that enthusiasm. Your sincerity is less likely to be questioned.

5. State and restate the basic reasons for the position you want your audience to take.

   Repetition can be forceful. Do not hesitate to restate the points you have made. Doing so at the close of your persuasive talk will leave those points in the minds of your audience.

EXERCISE 12 Prepare a persuasive talk on one of the following topics. Deliver your talk as your teacher directs.

1. The age at which a student may quit school should be lowered
2. (A kind of sport) should be added in school

3. There should be more government support of
   a. Solar energy research
   b. Electric-powered automobiles
   c. Space colonies
   d. Control of crime
   e. The handicapped
   f. Mass transit
4. There should be less government control of (choose from *a–f* under 3, above)
5. The importance of lifelong exercise

GROUP DISCUSSION

15o Group discussions allow a number of people to discuss a single topic.

People in every community need to share their ideas about important matters. One of the most popular ways of sharing ideas is through a group discussion. A school is a kind of community. Ideas held by members of the school community can be shared through a group discussion.

A useful group discussion follows a few basic guidelines, whether the group chooses to have a *panel discussion,* a *round-table discussion,* or some form of *town meeting.*

A panel discussion uses a group of up to seven people who present their views on a topic while seated together in front of an audience. Only after each panelist has spoken and has questioned other members of the panel does the chairperson accept questions from the audience.

A round-table discussion is a less formal panel discussion. Participants may speak out any time instead of for a limited time only.

A town meeting is used to permit any member of the audience to speak his or her views. It is often led by a chairperson who accepts and comments on remarks from the audience.

Preparing for a Group Discussion

If you are going to take part in a group discussion, you should be aware of what you need to do. The following guidelines apply to group discussions in general.

1. Learn about the topic.

   Any time you expect to engage in a serious discussion, learn about the topic. Find out in advance as much as you can about the matter to be discussed.

   You may not be directly engaged in the discussion, but as a listener you should be informed.
2. Find out about the people who will conduct the discussion.

   Arguments presented by an articulate person can sound very good. However, if you know about the person's background, you are in a better position to judge the value of the points being made. You will be ready to comment on what is being said.
3. Find out about the physical arrangements of the place of the discussion.

   Learn ahead of time what will be the arrangement of the room. A classroom has certain kinds of restrictions. A larger hall has other kinds. Will there be a stage separating you from the audience? Will you have a table or desk to write on or to put your papers on?

Will there be a microphone? Are you prepared to use a microphone? If you are not, practice ahead of time using the microphone.

Carrying on a Group Discussion

The following guidelines may prove useful to you in a discussion.

1. Learn how to lead a group discussion.

   You may be appointed to lead a group discussion. As chairperson, you have to know the steps that will carry the discussion from beginning to end.

   A. Become familiar with the topic and with the others in the group, called *discussants*.

   B. If possible, bring the discussants together before the discussion. Share with them the plan for the discussion. Warn them about time limitations. Ask if anyone needs anything special, such as a portable chalkboard or a projector and screen, and arrange to have them provided. Be sure the source of electrical power and the length of the power cord are appropriate.

   C. Welcome the audience and offer a brief background on the topic if that seems appropriate. Announce whether questions from the audience will be taken during or after the presentations.

   D. Introduce discussants in the order in which they will speak. Give a short background for each.

E. Call on each discussant to speak in turn.
F. Warn discussants with prearranged silent signals that their time is up.
G. Call on members of the audience (one at a time) if they have questions. A question may be addressed to the whole group. If it is, ask who would like to respond, or direct it to one discussant.
H. Call the discussion to a conclusion. Be prepared to summarize key points of the discussion, if appropriate.

2. Learn how to be a discussant in a group discussion.
   A. Learn about the topic.
   B. Keep your remarks to the point of the topic. Supply specific examples or reasons for your general statements.
   C. Back up your own opinions with references to other sources that may be more expert than you.
   D. Respect the opinions and rights of other discussants and audience members. Avoid getting into a heated argument.
   E. Stay within the area of the topic and the time limits agreed upon.
3. Learn how to be a good listener.

   Listening seems like a simple process. Actually, it demands more work than is apparent. A good listener takes part in the discussion through listening and thinking. Perhaps he or she says nothing during a discussion. Then again, a listener may enter into the discussion with a comment or a question. Being a good listener means following a few guidelines.

A. Know something about the topic.
B. As an audience member, if you don't know anything about the topic, just listen. The discussion and questions may give you the information you are looking for.
C. If you ask a question, make it as specific as you can. Also address it to a specific discussant if you can.
D. Remain quiet while others are speaking. Interrupting when someone else is speaking is a poor way to help the progress of a talk or discussion. The only person who ever should interrupt a speaker is the chairperson, and even then the only cause for interruption is to police a speaker who has exceeded the time limit or broken some other rule. Audience interruptions, such as talking without being recognized by the chairperson or making a disturbance, cannot be permitted.
E. Take notes if you are expected to contribute to the talk or the discussion. It is difficult to keep points in mind during a lively discussion. Your notes will make it possible for you to stay on the points.

Keep in mind that being a good listener is an important part of the speaking and listening process.

EXERCISE 13 Listen to a group discussion in class, on television, or on the radio. Answer as many of the following questions as you can. Take notes so that you can discuss these in class.

1. What was the subject being discussed?
2. Who was the chairperson? Why do you think that person led the discussion?
3. Who were the discussants? What authority or special information did any of them have for the discussion?
4. Was there an audience present?
5. Did the participants stay on the subject or did someone wander from the topic? Give an example.
6. Did the discussants or audience members show by their actions or words that they were listening well or poorly? Give examples.

REVIEW EXERCISE A **Formal Speaking: Announcements and Introductions**

Make an announcement to your class about an upcoming event at school. Make sure you include all relevant information.

Or introduce a speaker to your class. Choose a famous or interesting person whom you would like to hear. Prepare and give the introduction as if the person were really going to speak.

REVIEW EXERCISE B **Preparing a Speech**

On a sheet of paper write an outline for an explanatory or persuasive speech. Choose a topic that you think will interest most of your listeners.

EXAMPLE Why I favor the four-day school week

I. The four-day school week will provide extended leisure time
   A. Students can spend time with family and friends
   B. Students can gain practical experience on a part-time job
   C. Students can pursue their interests

II. It will improve grades
   A. Students will concentrate harder on school days
   B. Students will be refreshed and ready to study when they come to school

REVIEW EXERCISE C Delivering a Talk

Deliver your talk, using your outline from Review Exercise B. Follow the guidelines for giving a good speech on page 365.

CHAPTER

16

SPELLING

No one is a perfect speller. Everyone at one time or another lets the twenty-six letters of the English alphabet confuse him or her. For some people, spelling correctly is a very difficult skill to acquire.

One of the reasons spelling is a problem is that different letters stand for different sounds in different words. As is shown on page 392 in this chapter, different spelling patterns are used for sounds. The sound of *f* in *fate,* for example, is spelled differently in *stuff, tough,* and *phone.*

If you learn the basic ways letters represent sounds, you can improve your spelling a great deal. Knowing the basic rules of spelling as well as the exceptions to those rules also will make spelling easier.

Finally, there is no substitute for keeping your own list of misspelled words and studying them regularly.

RULES FOR GOOD SPELLING

16a Develop basic spelling habits.

Developing the right habits can make spelling easier.

(1) Keep a list of troublesome words.

You should already know the kinds of words that cause you the most spelling trouble. If you have not already made a list of troublesome words, begin now.

Each time you misspell a word in your writing, add it to your list. When you think you have mastered the spelling of a word on your list, check it off. Try to check off all the words on your list.

See Master Spelling List, pp. 398–400

(2) Study the hard parts of words.

Most of the words you misspell have a part that is more difficult than the rest. Focus on the part that causes your trouble. For example, *familiar* is sometimes misspelled because it is confused with the word *similar* in the last few letters. Very few people misspell the *famil-* of *familiar.* Concentrate on the hard parts of words that give you trouble.

(3) See each syllable. Say each syllable. Write each syllable.

Look carefully at the word, especially the hard part. While you are looking, pronounce the word syllable by syllable. Then, while still looking at it, write it out.

Learn how to break a word into its syllables. Recognize the sound of each syllable. Then combine the syllables into the entire word.

EXAMPLES

AD-O-LES-CENT (adolescent)	The four syllables in this word need to be handled separately and then put together. The first and the last syllables you probably recognize as words in themselves. (*Ad* is a short term for *advertisement.*) The other syllables by themselves are easy to spell.
CAL-CU-LA-TOR (calculator)	Taken one at a time, each syllable is clear. Only the last can cause much trouble. Remember that the last syllable is *tor.*

(4) Use a dictionary.

Besides giving the correct spelling of words, a dictionary breaks every word into its syllables. You can find the spelling of almost any word by knowing its beginning letters.

See Sources of Information, pp. 403–410

16b Learn basic spelling rules.

The rules of spelling apply to nearly every word you use. By learning the rules, you can spell easily thousands of words.

Of course, there are exceptions to certain rules. Learn the exceptions as you learn the rules.

See Plural Nouns, p. 6

(1) Regular nouns form their plurals by adding *s* or *es*.

EXAMPLES

Nouns that add **s** dog, dog**s**
book, book**s**

Nouns that add **es** match, match**es**
hiss, hiss**es**
bunch, bunch**es**

Add **es** to nouns that end in **ch, s, sh, x,** or **z.** Add **s** to all other regular nouns.

EXERCISE 1 Number a sheet of paper 1–10. Write the plural of the following nouns.

1. bruise
2. gash
3. bike
4. word
5. latch
6. puff
7. lunch
8. rash
9. clip
10. box

(2) Nouns ending in *y* after a consonant change the *y* to *i* and add *es* to form the plural.

EXAMPLES navy, nav**ies**
dictionary, dictionar**ies**

When a vowel comes before the final **y,** add only **s.**

EXAMPLES alley, alley**s**
key, key**s**

EXERCISE 2 Number a sheet of paper 1–8. Next to each number write the plural of the following nouns.

1. primary
2. baby
3. donkey
4. folly
5. gully
6. trolley
7. county
8. ally

(3) Most nouns ending in *f* add *s* to form the plural.

EXAMPLES staff, staffs
whiff, whiffs

(4) Some nouns ending in *f* or *fe* change the *f* to *v* and add *es* or *s*.

EXAMPLES wife, wives
thief, thieves

(5) Most nouns ending in *o* following a vowel add *s* to form the plural.

EXAMPLES radio, radios
patio, patios

(6) Most nouns ending in *o* following a consonant add *es* to form the plural.

EXAMPLES tomato, tomatoes
hero, heroes

(7) Musical terms ending in *o* add only an *s* to form the plural.

EXAMPLES alto, altos
solo, solos

(8) A few nouns form their plurals without an *s* or *es*. Some change spelling. Some remain the same.

EXAMPLES man, men
woman, women
fish, fish (or fishes)
louse, lice
tooth, teeth
deer, deer

EXERCISE 3 Number a sheet of paper 1–15. Write the plural form of each of the following nouns.

1. birch
2. dolly
3. wolf
4. torpedo
5. ax
6. rodeo
7. sheep
8. soprano
9. knife
10. sixty
11. clutch
12. lash
13. puppy
14. mass
15. toss

EXERCISE 4 Number a sheet of paper 1–10. Write the plural form of each of these nouns.

1. brush
2. country
3. leech
4. buzz
5. army
6. life
7. excess
8. crush
9. kiss
10. piano

(9) Most compound nouns form the plural by adding *s* to the noun part, not to the modifier.

EXAMPLES brother-in-law, brother**s**-in-law
passer-by, passer**s**-by

The plural of compound nouns that end in **ful** is formed by adding **s** to the **ful**.

EXAMPLE handful, handful**s**

(10) Foreign words form their plurals in various ways.

EXAMPLES alumna, alumnae
datum, data

You will find that most foreign words borrowed directly into English form their plurals in unusual ways.

Prefixes

Prefixes are groups of letters added to regular words or roots in English. Often the spelling of the prefix changes to match the beginning of the word it joins. For example, the prefix **in-** means "not." Added to the word *capable,* it makes *incapable,* which means "not capable." In this case the prefix **in-** does not change. However, when **in-** is added to the word *legal,* it does change. The new word is *illegal.*

(11) A word or root that adds a prefix does not change spelling.

A word or root is spelled the same even when a prefix is added. Examples are shown here.

PREFIX	WORD or ROOT	NEW WORD
un-	necessary	unnecessary
	usual	unusual
dis-	taste	distaste
	favor	disfavor
	-turb	disturb
mis-	take	mistake
	spell	misspell

EXERCISE 5 Number a sheet of paper 1–6. Next to each number write the new word formed by adding one of these prefixes to the word or root.

PREFIXES	
ex-	un-
in-	pro-
dis-	re-

EXAMPLE nounce

pronounce, renounce

1. -duce
2. -pel
3. do
4. belief
5. -ject
6. port

Do not change the spelling of a word or root when adding a prefix. Only the spelling of the prefix may change.

(12) Some prefixes change spelling when joined to a word or root.

Several prefixes work this way when added to certain words or roots.

PREFIX	WORD or ROOT	NEW WORD
in-	polite	impolite
	logical	illogical
	regular	irregular
com-	-dense	condense
	-fer	confer

Suffixes

Suffixes are added to words or roots to make new words. The suffixes *-ly* and *-ness* are examples. They make words such as *carefully* and *sickness*.

(13) Most words adding the suffixes *-ly* and *-ness* keep their same spelling.

EXAMPLES rapid, rapid**ly**
quiet, quiet**ness**

(14) Words ending in *y* following a consonant change the *y* to *i* before adding a suffix that does not begin with *i*.

EXAMPLES hasty, hast**ily**
silly, sill**iness**
weary, wear**ied**

(15) Words or roots ending in *ie* usually change the *ie* to *y* when the suffix *-ing* is added.

EXAMPLES tie, t**ying**
lie, l**ying**

(16) Most words ending in *e* following a single consonant omit the *e* when adding a suffix that begins with a vowel.

EXAMPLES rate, rat**ing**
pine, pin**ing**

(17) Most words ending in *ce* or *ge* keep the *e* when adding a suffix that begins with *a* or *o*.

EXAMPLES charge, charge**able**
replace, replace**able**

(18) Most words ending in *e* keep the *e* when adding a suffix that begins with a consonant.

EXAMPLES defense, defense**less**
taste, taste**less**

(19) One-syllable words ending in a single consonant following a single vowel double the consonant when adding the suffixes *-ed, -ing,* or *-er*.

EXAMPLES pin, pin**ned**, pin**ning**
hit, hit**ting**, hit**ter**

(20) Double the final consonant when adding *-ed, -er,* or *-ing* to words with two or more syllables ending in a single consonant following a single vowel, if the accent is on the last syllable.

EXAMPLES refer, refer**red**
occur, occur**ring**

EXERCISE 6 Following are words and suffixes. Number a sheet of paper 1–20. Next to each number write the new word you make by joining the word and its suffix.

EXAMPLE move + ing
moving

1. place + ing
2. like + able
3. juice + less
4. try + ing
5. trot + ing
6. grace + fully
7. force + ing
8. trace + able
9. die + ing
10. top + ing
11. occur + ed
12. hop + ed
13. employ + ment
14. boy + ish
15. happy + ness
16. drop + ing
17. drape + ing
18. begin + er
19. frame + ing
20. bore + ing

SOUNDS OF LETTERS

As you know, a single sound in English can be spelled in different ways. For example, the words *ship* and *sure* both begin with the same sound. In one, the **sh** stands for the sound that **s** stands for in the other. The same sound is spelled **ti** in words like *nation* and *patient*.

16c Learn the different ways of spelling sounds.

Following is a list of common sounds in English and their various spellings. Study the ways these sounds are spelled.

SOUND	EXAMPLES OF SPELLING PATTERNS
ch as in *chop*	**ch**op, wit**ch**, den**tu**res
f as in *five*	five, cli**ff**, tou**gh**, tele**ph**one
g as in *gear*	gear, **gh**ost
j as in *jump*	jump, ca**g**e, mid**g**et, sol**d**ier
k as in *kettle*	**k**ettle, **c**arnival, a**ch**e, lo**ck**
m as in *math*	**m**ath, co**mb**, swi**mm**er, pal**m**
n as in *noon*	**n**oon, **kn**ack, wi**nn**er, **gn**u, **pn**eumonia
sh as in *shell*	**sh**ell, mi**ss**ion, **s**ure, lo**ti**on, ma**ch**ine
t as in *tone*	**t**one, look**ed**
z as in *zebra*	**z**ebra, i**s**, de**ss**ert
a as in *fake*	f**a**k**e**, r**ai**d, w**ay**, st**ea**k, **ei**ght
e as in *be*	b**e**, s**ee**d, v**ea**l, p**eo**ple, gr**ie**f, l**ei**sure, quarant**i**ne, cloud**y**
i as in *pipe*	p**i**p**e**, l**ie**, b**uy**, sk**y**, **eye**
i as in *quick*	qu**i**ck, b**ee**n, b**u**sy, b**ui**lding
o as in *home*	h**o**m**e**, t**oa**d, w**oe**, sh**ow**, s**ew**
u as in *fume*	f**u**m**e**, b**eau**tiful, **you**
u as in *dune*	d**u**n**e**, s**ui**t, st**oo**l, gh**ou**l, m**o**v**e**, can**oe**

Homonyms

Words that sound the same are called *homonyms*. Examples of homonyms are *there, they're,* and *their*.

Because homonyms sound the same, they can confuse your spelling.

16d Learn which spelling of a homonym belongs with the meaning you want.

HOMONYM	MEANING
affect	to influence or to change
effect	the result of a cause
already	earlier, before
all ready	(two words) prepared, completed
capital	city, seat of government
capitol	government building
cents	pennies
scents	odors
sense	intelligence
cite	to quote, or to name as example
sight	vision, to see
site	place
cereal	grain; breakfast food
serial	something done in parts, or in a series
flare	flame
flair	judgment, taste

miner	worker in a mine
minor	small
pair	couple
pare	to peel
pear	a kind of fruit
peace	opposite of war
piece	one part of something
raise	lift up
raze	cut down, level to the ground
rain	water falling from sky
reign	rule of a king or queen
rein	strap for guiding a horse
rapped	hit
rapt	fascinated
wrapped	covered
way	path
weigh	to be a certain number of pounds
whey	thin, sweet watery party of milk

EXERCISE 7 On a sheet of paper write the answers to the following questions by writing one word that best answers each question. Select words from the list of homonyms above.

1. What do you do to take the skin off an apple?
2. What do you do to lift up a lid?
3. On what is a building built?

4. What's another word for good thinking?
5. What kind of an accident is not large?
6. What does royalty do?
7. If you enclosed a package in something, what did you do to it?
8. What burns and gives light?

REVIEW EXERCISE A **Noun Plurals**

Number a sheet of paper 1–15. Next to each number write the plural of the noun given.

EXAMPLE watch

watches

1. hash
2. play
3. library
4. woman
5. soprano
6. hoof
7. video
8. potato
9. country
10. whiff
11. fox
12. life
13. hutch
14. hiss
15. half

REVIEW EXERCISE B **Prefixes**

Following are ten roots or words and a list of prefixes. Number a sheet of paper 1–10. Next to each number write the word formed by adding a prefix to the word or root. Some of the prefixes can be added to more than one root, so there is more than one right answer.

LIST OF PREFIXES

re-	de-
im-	un-
pre-	con-
mis-	in-

EXAMPLE -ject

reject

1. -clude
2. possible
3. lay
4. tie
5. -fide
6. treat
7. -sume
8. arrange
9. -rive
10. -pend

REVIEW EXERCISE C **Suffixes**

Following is a list of roots or words and suffixes. Number a sheet of paper 1–12. Next to each number, write the new word formed by combining the root or word and the suffix.

EXAMPLE slow + ly

slowly

1. hearty + ly
2. die + ing
3. dreary + ness
4. change + able
5. concur + ed
6. run + ing
7. ram + ed
8. try + ing
9. happy + ness
10. bite + ing
11. live + ly
12. trace + able

REVIEW EXERCISE D **Spelling Sounds**

Following is a list of words. Number a sheet of paper 1–10. Next to each number write a word that rhymes with the one given but is spelled in a different way.

EXAMPLE through
blew

1. sleigh
2. their
3. high
4. bough
5. heed
6. peace
7. toe
8. glue
9. receive
10. plain

REVIEW EXERCISE E **Homonyms**

Following is a list of words that have homonyms. Number a sheet of paper 1–10. Next to each number write at least one homonym for the word given.

EXAMPLE bear
bare

1. two
2. piece
3. pain
4. strait
5. serial
6. cents
7. hare
8. four
9. slay
10. plane

MASTER SPELLING LIST

The following list includes words frequently misspelled. Study this list by groups of words. Practice spelling ten or twenty at a time. Be sure you also know the meaning of each word. Where necessary, look up words in a dictionary.

From time to time, review words you have misspelled at an earlier time. By doing this you help to keep their spellings clear in your mind.

The hard parts of words are printed in darker letters. The darkness of the letters will help you pay close attention to the parts often misspelled.

absence
absolutely
academic
acceptance
accidentally
accommodate
accompany
accuracy
achieve
acquaintance
acquire
actually
administration
admittance
adolescent
advertisement
affectionate
agriculture
aisle
allotment
altar/alter
amateur
analyze
annually
anticipate
apology
apparatus
apparent
appearance
appreciate
approach
approval
argument
arrangement
athletic
attendance
authority
available

beginning
behavior
benefited
boundary
breath (e)

calendar
campaign
capital/capitol
certificate
character
choose/chose
Christian
clothes
column
commercial
committee
communist
competitor
conceivable
concentrate
confidential
conscience
conscious
consistency
continuous
controlled
controversial
cooperate
correspondence
courageous
criticism
criticize
cruelly
curiosity
curious
cylinder

de**bto**r
de**cei**ve
de**c**i**s**ion
depend**e**nt
de**s**cribe
de**s**pair
desp**e**rate
di**ff**er**e**nce
di**n**ing
di**s**a**pp**ear**a**nce
di**s**a**pp**oint
dis**ci**pline
duplic**a**te

effect
efficient
eighth
eli**gi**ble
emb**arrass**
emph**a**size
enc**ou**ragement
entir**e**ly
envir**on**ment
equi**pp**ed
espe**ciall**y
e**ss**en**tia**l
e**xagger**ate
e**x**ce**ll**ent
e**x**er**c**ise
e**x**ist**ence**
exper**i**ment
extr**e**mely

fant**as**y
fa**sc**inate
fa**sh**ion**a**ble
fat**a**l
fav**orit**e
finan**cia**l
f**o**r**eig**n
fortunat**e**ly
for**t**y

f**ou**rth

gen**ius**
gov**ern**ment
gra**cious**
guarant**ee**
guid**a**nce
gymnasium

h**ea**vily
height
her**oi**ne
hum**orous**
hypo**crisy**

ignor**ance**
ima**gi**ne
i**mm**ediat**e**ly
incident**ally**
indefin**i**te
indiv**idually**
infl**uence**
ingred**ie**nt
i**nnocence**
insur**ance**
inte**ll**ig**ence**
interf**erence**
inte**rr**upt

jeal**ous**
ju**dg**ment

lab**o**r**ato**ry
lab**o**r**er**
laid
l**ei**sure
li**c**en**s**e
lon**e**liness
l**oo**se/lose/l**oss**
lu**xur**y

maga**zine**
magnifi**cen**t
mainte**nance**

man**eu**ver
manufact**urer**
ma**rriag**e
marv**e**l**ous**
m**ea**nt
me**ch**anic
medic**al**
med**ic**ine
mel**ancho**ly
merch**a**ndi**s**e
mini**atu**re
mi**nim**um
min**ute**
mis**chie**f
misch**ievous**
mor**a**l/mor**ale**
mu**scle**
m**y**steri**ous**

na**rra**tive
natur**ally**
n**iece**
nin**e**ty
noti**cea**ble

obst**a**cle
o**cc**a**s**ionally
o**ccurre**nce
o**ff**ensive
o**ffic**ial
o**miss**ion
o**pp**onent
o**pp**ortunity
opt**i**mist
or**ch**estra
organi**z**ation
origin**ally**

pa**id**
par**allel**
paral**yze**
partic**u**l**ar**

passed/past
peaceful
peculiar
performance
permanent
personality
perspiration
persuade
physical
picnicking
pleasant
politician
possession
practically
practice
preferred
prejudice
preparation
pressure
privilege
procedure
proceed
professor
propaganda
psychology
pursuit

realize
receipt
recognize
recommend
referred
religious
repetition
resistance
resource
responsibility
restaurant
rhythm
ridiculous
roommate

sacrifice
satisfied
scarcity
scene
schedule
scholar
scissors
seize
separate
similar
sincerely
skiing
sophomore
source
specifically
sponsor
straight
strength
stretch
strictly
stubborn
substitute
subtle
succeed
successful
sufficient
summary
surprise
suspense
synonym

temperamental
tendency
therefore
thorough
thoughtful
tragedy
transferred
tremendous
truly

unanimous
unnecessary
useful
useless
usually

vacuum
valuable
various

weather/whether
weird
whole/hole

yield

CHAPTER

17

SOURCES OF INFORMATION

People have been collecting information for thousands of years. This information is stored in a number of places. Most of it is available to you. To use it, however, you need to know how to find it, where it is stored, and how it is arranged.

This chapter deals with the basic sources of information. You already know some of them. The library is one. However, a library can be a puzzling place. Not all libraries are the same. And other sources besides the library have special information you may find valuable.

Get to know more about the many different sources of information available to you. As you know more, you can save much time and learn a good deal as well.

TEXTBOOKS

Books written especially to teach people about something have been published on virtually every subject people are curious about. These books are called *textbooks.* Nearly all textbooks are divided into sections that make them easy to use. Here are the sections in a textbook like *Using English.*

The front cover usually lists the book's title, the author, and the publisher. Often some of the same information is repeated on the *spine,* or back edge, of the book. The publisher is also listed here. The information on the spine makes it possible to identify books when they are stacked together on the shelves.

Many textbooks include space on the *inside cover* to identify whose property the book is and to whom it has been issued. Some textbooks include additional information on the inside cover.

The *title page* lists the title and the names of the author and publisher. The *copyright page* is the back of the title page. This tells you who owns the rights to the book and when it was most recently published. The *introduction* or *preface* lists special features of the book as well as its purposes. The *table of contents* includes the headings of each chapter and subsection, along with page numbers.

The *text* is the main part of the book. This is where the information is actually written. The *glossary* lists the important topics and terms contained in the text. Sometimes examples as well as definitions are given. The *index* lists alphabetically every important topic in the book. Page numbers are given for each entry. Some books combine the glossary with the index.

See Glossary, pp. 438–462; Index, pp. 463–478

THE DICTIONARY

A dictionary is an alphabetical list of all the words in a language and what they mean. The writers of dictionaries study the way people talk. They also study printed material. They look at all the different ways every word has been used, over time as well as in different places. From this study, they write the history of words, their spellings, meanings, pronunciations, and various other features about them.

A dictionary is, therefore, a record of language usage. It is not a lawbook of words. You do not have to say a word or use a word exactly as the dictionary says. However, how you pronounce and use a word is based on the dictionary version. Otherwise, no one would understand what you are trying to communicate.

17a Learn to use the dictionary.

Large dictionaries usually have several separate sections. Each section contains special information that may be of use to you. Finding the information you need means knowing in which section to look.

The main section of any dictionary contains words listed alphabetically with their meanings. Many dictionaries also have sections in the front that tell facts about language. For example, in an introduction you might find an explanation of the way the dictionary was put together. There might also be a section showing how to use that particular dictionary.

Many large dictionaries have other sections as well. Often there is one listing special signs and symbols relating to the sciences, mathematics, and medicine. Another section might list weights and measures in both the English and the metric systems. The names of geographical locations, with facts about them, are often available as well. In sum, a good dictionary offers a great deal of information.

(1) Words are listed alphabetically.

The words listed in a dictionary are called *entry words.* To make good use of them, you first need to know how to find the one you want.

All entries are in alphabetical order, as you know. If a word shares the same first letters with other words, it will be grouped with those words. The order is determined by the first letter that is different. For example, the words *conceit, conceive, conception,* and *concussion* are grouped together because they all begin with the letters **conc.** The fifth letter makes the difference alphabetically. And it is by the fifth letter that they are arranged.

(2) Guide words at the top of each page show which words are on that page.

Every dictionary page of entries is headed by two words. These are usually printed in dark type and separated from the entries. For example, one dictionary has the words *hesitant* and *hieroglyphic* at the top of a page. This means that the words on that page will fall alphabetically between *hesitant* and *hieroglyphic*. Such words as *hew, hibernate,* and *hiccup* will appear on that page. But the word *herd* will not be there. Nor will the word *history* be on the page. They come before or after that page.

hesitant 343 **hieroglyphic**

H

hes·i·tant [hez′ə·tənt] *adj.* Lacking certainty; hesitating; doubtful: He appeared *hesitant* in asking for the raise. **— hes′i·tant·ly** *adv.*

hes·i·tate [hez′ə·tāt] *v.* **hes·i·tat·ed, hes·i·tat·ing** **1** To be slow or doubtful in acting, making a decision, etc.; pause or falter: He *hesitated* before giving the order; Don't *hesitate* to call me. **2** To be unwilling or reluctant: I *hesitate* to say what's really on my mind. **3** To stammer in speech.

hes·i·ta·tion [hez′ə·tā′shən] *n.* **1** The act of hesitating; wavering or doubt: She said "I do" without the slightest *hesitation*. **2** A pause or faltering in speech.

Hes·per·i·des [hes·per′ə·dēz] *n.pl.* In Greek myths, the nymphs who together with a dragon guarded the golden apples of Hera.

Hes·pe·rus [hes′pər·əs] *n.* The evening star.

Hes·sian [hesh′ən] *n.* One of the German soldiers hired to fight for the British in the American Revolution.

het·er·o·dox [het′ə·rə·doks′] *adj.* **1** Different from an accepted view or standard. **2** Rejecting accepted views or standards.

het·er·o·ge·ne·ous [het′ər·ə·jē′nē·əs] *adj.* Consisting of parts or units that are not alike: a *heterogeneous* collection of rubbish; Ours is a *heterogeneous* society.

hew [hyōō] *v.* **hewed, hewed** or **hewn** [hyōōn], **hew·ing** **1** To cut or strike with an ax, sword, etc.: to *hew* branches. **2** To make or shape with blows of a knife, ax, etc.: to *hew* railings. **— hew′er** *n.*

hex [heks] *U.S. informal* **1** *n.* An evil spell. **2** *v.* To bewitch. ◆ *Hex* comes from the German word for *witch*.

hex·a·gon [hek′sə·gon] *n.* A closed plane figure having six sides and six angles.

hex·ag·o·nal [hek·sag′ə·nəl] *adj.* Having the form of a hexagon: a *hexagonal* building.

Hexagons (the red one is regular)

hex·a·he·dron [hek′sə·hē′·drən] *n., pl.* **hex·a·he·dra** [hek′sə·hē′drə] or **hex·a·he·drons** A solid figure bounded by six plane faces.

hex·am·e·ter [hek·sam′ə·tər] *n.* A line of
having six rhythmic feet, as "Thĕn
pássed bȳ | thĕir vōi |

Hi·a·wath·a [hī′ə·woth′ə *or* hī′ə·wô′thə] *n.* In Longfellow's poem *The Song of Hiawatha*, the hero, a young Indian brave.

hi·ber·nate [hī′bər·nāt] *v.* **hi·ber·nat·ed, hi·ber·nat·ing** To spend the winter sleeping or dormant, as bears and certain other animals do. **— hi′ber·na′tion** *n.*

hi·bis·cus [hī·bis′kəs] *n.* A plant having large showy flowers of various colors.

hic·cough [hik′əp] *n., v.* Another spelling of HICCUP.

hic·cup [hik′əp] *n., v.* **hic·cuped** or **hic·cupped, hic·cup·ing** or **hic·cup·ping** **1** *n.* A sudden, involuntary gasp of breath which is immediately cut off by a spasm in the throat. **2** *v.* To undergo these spasms; have the hiccups.

hick·o·ry [hik′ə·rē] *n., pl.* **hick·o·ries** **1** Any of several North American trees related to the walnut and having a hard wood and edible nuts. **2** The wood of this tree. ◆ *Hickory* comes from an Algonquian Indian word.

hide[1] [hīd] *v.* **hid** [hid], **hid·den** [hid′(ə)n] or **hid, hid·ing** **1** To put or keep out of sight; conceal: to *hide* a key; Smoke *hid* the building. **2** To go or remain out of sight. **3** To keep secret: to *hide* one's fears. **4** *adj. use:* *hidden* treasure.

hide[2] [hīd] *n.* **1** The skin of an animal, especially when stripped from its carcass. **2** *informal* The human skin: I'll tan your *hide!*

hide-and-seek [hīd′(ə)n·sēk′] *n.* A game in which a person who is "it" has to find others who have hid and touch home base before they do.

hide·bound [hīd′bound′] *adj.* Narrow-minded, obstinate, and with little imagination.

hid·e·ous [hid′ē·əs] *adj.* Very ugly; horrible. **— hid′e·ous·ly** *adv.* **— hid′e·ous·ness** *n.*

hide-out [hīd′out′] *n. informal* A hiding place, especially for criminals.

hid·ing[1] [hī′ding] *n.* **1** The act of a person or thing that hides. **2** A place out of sight.

hid·ing[2] [hī′ding] *n. informal* A whipping or flogging.

hie [hī] *v.* **hied**,
ing To
myself

EXERCISE 1 On a sheet of paper write the following words in alphabetical order. Draw a line under each word that would appear on a dictionary page with the words *dean* and *decade* at the top.

debunk deceit debate
deadbeat deacon deathless
debris debark debut
death dearly dearth

See Syllable, p. 460

(3) Words are spelled out by syllables.

A syllable is the part of a written word that stands for at least one vowel sound. A syllable as it is written may have more than one vowel, but it must have at least one vowel sound. It usually contains one or two consonant sounds as well.

In the word *incident,* the syllables are *in-ci-dent.* When you look up that word in a dictionary, you will find it separated by syllables. The same is true for every other entry word. When you wish to know how to divide a word at the end of a written line, the dictionary will show you.

EXERCISE 2 The following pairs of words contain one word spelled correctly and one word spelled incorrectly. The first syllable of every word is correct. Number a sheet of paper 1–10. Write the correct spellings on your paper. When in doubt, check a dictionary.

EXAMPLE in-vi-si-ble
in-vi-sa-ble
invisible

1. ap-pe-tite
   ap-et-ite
2. hos-pi-tle
   hos-pi-tal
3. sin-ser-ity
   sin-cer-ity
4. im-ag-i-nar-y
   im-ag-i-nery
5. re-sis-tence
   re-sist-ance
6. ac-quain-tance
   ac-quain-tence
7. ther-mom-e-tor
   ther-mom-e-ter
8. phy-si-cian
   phy-si-sian
9. per-for-mence
   per-for-mance
10. por-tray-al
    por-tray-el

(4) Capitalized words are shown.

Every proper noun and every proper adjective is shown with its capital letters. *England* and *English,* for example, are capitalized in the dictionary.

See Capitalization, p. 295

(5) The pronunciation of every word is given.

To show you how to pronounce an entry word, a dictionary uses special symbols that go with sounds. The symbols are called *diacritical marks.*

Not all dictionaries use the same diacritical marks. However, each dictionary lists the diacritical marks it uses at the bottom of every second page. This listing makes it easy for you to check the pronunciation for any word you find in a dictionary.

If a word has two pronunciations, both are given. The first pronunciation is usually the one more widely used.

> **hide**[1] [hīd] *v.* **hid** [hid], **hid·den** [hid′(ə)n] or **hid, hid·ing** **1** To put or keep out of sight; conceal: to *hide* a key; Smoke *hid* the building. **2** To go or remain out of sight. **3** To keep secret: to *hide* one's fears. **4** *adj. use:* *hidden* treasure.

EXERCISE 3 Number a sheet of paper 1–6. Next to each number write the word listed. Next to each word write the way it is pronounced. Show its preferred pronunciation by using the diacritical marks and phonetic spelling (if any) of a good dictionary.

1. genuine
2. tomato
3. futile
4. mischievous
5. economic
6. turbine

(6) The part of speech is given for each entry word.

The pronunciation of each word is followed by an abbreviation that shows its part of speech.

Some words are used as more than one part of speech. This fact will also be shown.

(7) Unusual plural spellings are given.

See Spelling, pp. 384–387

For those nouns that have unusual plurals, the spellings will be included. The abbreviation *pl.* tells you that the spelling is plural.

EXAMPLES *ox* (pl. *oxen*)
index (pl. *indexes* or *indices*)

EXERCISE 4 Number a sheet of paper 1–6. Next to the numbers write the plural forms of the following words. Check a dictionary if necessary.

1. deer
2. attorney general
3. handful
4. bureau
5. father-in-law
6. grandchild

See Verbs, pp. 39–40

(8) Irregular verb forms are given.

Each irregular verb listed in the dictionary will have its past and past participle forms shown. For example, the dictionary will show you that the verb *break* has *broke* as its past and *broken* as its past participle.

(9) Comparative and superlative forms are given for many adjectives and some adverbs.

See Adjectives, pp. 21–24; Adverbs, pp. 48–49

Certain adjectives and a number of adverbs in the dictionary have their comparative and superlative forms listed. The adjective *fat* has *fatter* and *fattest* with it. The adverb *well* has the forms *better* and *best* included.

(10) The background of a word may be given.

Words change and develop over long periods of time as people change the original sounds to suit their purposes. Many dictionaries trace this process for you. The word *narcotic,* for example, has come to the English language by way of Middle English and Old French from ancient Greece thousands of years ago. The Greek word *narkoun* meant "to make numb."

(11) Various meanings of words are given.

Many words have different meanings. The dictionary lists those different meanings. Look for the meaning that best suits your purpose.

See Using Words, p. 426

EXAMPLE **rise** (verb intransitive)

1. to get up
2. to return to life after dying
3. to rebel
4. to go up
5. to swim to the surface of the water in order to take bait
6. to increase in some way
7. to come up to a higher level of accomplishment

Rise has the several meanings listed here, and more. You can choose the one that is most appropriate for your meaning by looking at its *context,* the way it is used in relation to the other words in the sentence.

EXAMPLE If you cast your line over by that pool near the bank, the fish should *rise.*

Anyone who knows about fresh water fishing will know that the word *rise* in this context means the fish will come to the surface to take the bait.

Quite another meaning comes from this next context:

This is a challenge. Will Marsha *rise* to it?

Here the meaning of *rise* is different. It means "come up to a higher level of accomplishment."

Still another meaning is found in the phrase "get a rise out of." This is a slang expression meaning "make angry." Many dictionaries will include this meaning, as they do other slang terms.

EXERCISE 5 The following words have three or more different meanings. Write each word on a sheet of paper. Next to each word write at least three meanings people give it.

EXAMPLE spring

spring: a source of water;
a season of the year;
a metal coil of wire

1. reel
2. pole
3. net
4. rail
5. margin
6. heart

THE LIBRARY

17b Learn how to use the sources of information in a library.

(1) The librarian.

The librarian is the most immediate source of information in the library. He or she knows where all the materials in the library are stored. Maybe your library doesn't have the special piece of information you are looking for. Your librarian can either order it for you, get it on loan from another library, or direct you where to find it.

As helpful as the librarian is, you should learn to use the sources of information in the library on your own. You'll be able to find what you are looking for much more quickly that way.

(2) Books of fiction.

Most libraries keep books of fiction on open shelves. This means you can walk along beside the shelves reading the titles and authors.

Books of fiction are arranged alphabetically by the last names of the authors. Authors whose last names begin with *A, B,* or *C* have their fiction works at the beginning of the first shelf near the top. Authors whose names begin with *Y* or *Z* have their fiction works at the far end of the shelves at the bottom.

An author who has several different fiction works on the shelves will have books arranged alphabetically by titles.

(3) Books of nonfiction.

True stories and books of fact or opinion are called nonfiction books. These are arranged on shelves by subjects rather than by authors or titles. However, index cards for them in the card catalog in the library are arranged by subjects, by authors, and by titles.

The ten major subject areas for nonfiction follow the *Dewey decimal system.* For every subject area there is a number. This number appears in the spine of the cover of a book and on the related cards in the card catalog. The number given a nonfiction book is its *call number.* An individual call number is given to every book that is published.

Using the call numbers of the Dewey decimal system is the best way for you to find a book on any subject.

THE DEWEY DECIMAL SYSTEM

BOOK NUMBERS	SUBJECTS
000–999	General information (encyclopedias and other reference sources)

100–199	Philosophy (people's thoughts and beliefs about values and the meaning of life, including psychology and ethics)
200–299	Religion (mythology, religious faiths)
300–399	Social Sciences (economics, history, government, and more)
400–499	Language (language histories, word backgrounds, word meanings)
500–599	Science (astronomy, biology, chemistry, and other sciences)
600–699	Technology (engineering, inventions, agriculture, and more)
700–799	The Arts (painting, music, sports, dance, and others)
800–899	Literature (poetry, plays, television scripts, and books about literature)
900–999	History (biographies, information about the past, and travel books)

If you want to find a book about raising hamsters, look in the 600 range. This number range includes books about farming and related applied sciences. Sports books have a call number in the 700 range.

EXERCISE 6 Find in a library a nonfiction book for each subject listed here. For each book write its title, author(s), copyright date, and call number.

EXAMPLE Hawaii

Hawaii's Enchanted Islands, Czolowski and Sharp, 1968, 996.9

1. Caterpillars
2. Water conservation
3. Cosmetics
4. Automobile maintenance
5. The Civil War
6. Space vehicles
7. Moslem religion
8. Slang
9. Dancing
10. Television production

(4) The card catalog.

The cards in the card catalog are kept in narrow drawers organized alphabetically. The cards make up an index to all the books in the library. Every card gives the following information:

1. The book's call number.
2. The publisher and the date of publication.
3. The title and a brief description of the book's contents.
4. The author or editor.
5. The number of pages and the headings where the book is listed in the card catalog.

Fiction books have *title cards* and *author cards* but not *subject cards*. Nonfiction books have separate cards for title, author, and subject. Here are examples of all three kinds of cards.

(5) Reference works.

Encyclopedias are like dictionaries of knowledge. In them, you can find general information about most subjects.

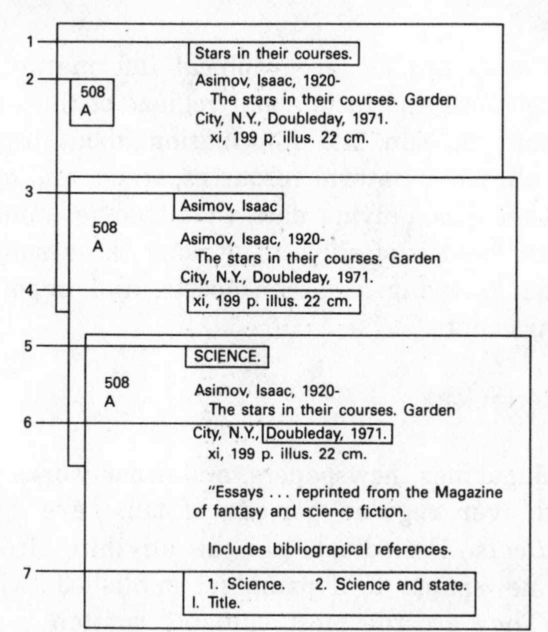

1. Title heading
2. Call number
3. Author
4. Book's physical description
5. Subject heading
6. Publisher, publication date
7. Other headings under which the book is listed.

Like those of a dictionary, an encyclopedia's entries are arranged alphabetically. However, instead of being words, an encyclopedia's entries are articles sometimes several pages long on broad topics. Guide words help you to locate an entry quickly.

Encyclopedias usually contain several volumes. They are arranged alphabetically, according to the beginning letters of their entries. Guide letters on their spines help you decide which volume you need.

Sometimes encyclopedias contain articles on general subjects in the sciences and humanities. Sometimes they give information on more detailed subjects in only one field of interest. In the *Encyclopedia of Science and Technology,* for example, articles are restricted to scientific and technical topics.

Atlases provide geographical information, including maps and facts about regions of the world. In them you can find information about populations, climates, natural resources, trade, and more.

Almanacs provide data that change annually about a variety of subjects. Among those subjects are the following: weather, sports, and important annual events.

(6) Periodicals.

Magazines, newspapers, and other works published over regular periods of time are called *periodicals*. Periodicals can be anything from a daily newspaper to a pamphlet published twice a year. They are the most valuable written sources for current information. Most libraries subscribe to a select number of periodicals. However, so many periodicals come out that it is almost impossible for any library to receive and keep all of them.

Magazines contain a great deal of information in their articles and features. How can you get at it without reading the table of contents of every magazine that comes out? Look in the *Readers' Guide to Periodical Literature*. Published twenty-two times a year, the *Readers' Guide* is an index of articles and stories appearing in approximately one hundred different magazines.

Here is part of a page from the *Readers' Guide*.

ART, Abstract
Concoran Biennial: a generational split. B. F. Forgey. il Art N 76:106+ My '77
See also
Abstract Expressionism
ART, Amateur
Armenian Grandma Moses. P. J. Thomajan. il por Ret Liv 17:50 My '77
ART, American
Gallery (cont) il Ms 5:33-5 F; 43+ My '77

(7) Audiovisual materials.

Some libraries keep a collection of records or cassettes. Others may also have filmstrips and even motion pictures. Some libraries have large collections of art prints available.

Ask your librarian if any or all of these materials are available. You might find items of particular interest to you and others.

A BASIC LIST OF CONTENTS OF THE LIBRARY

Almanacs: Books and pamphlets usually published annually, containing facts about all kinds of subjects.

Atlases: Maps of regions of the world are contained in atlases. Additional printed information relating to these regions is usually included.

Audiovisual materials: Audio recordings on discs, tapes, or cassettes; filmstrips; motion picture films; prints; microfilm; video recordings.

Bibliographies: Lists of books, usually arranged alphabetically by titles, authors, or subjects, including information about publishers. In an annotated bibliography, there are also brief comments about the contents of each book.

Books

Fiction: Stories made up by writers, including short stories and novels.

Nonfiction: Books of fact and opinion, covering a wide range of topics, including biographies and instructional materials.

Collected works: Plays, television scripts, poems, songs, musical pieces, photographs, and art reproductions.

Dictionaries: Alphabetical listing of words giving their meanings, pronunciations, uses, and other practical information.

Encyclopedias: Dictionaries of knowledge containing an alphabetical arrangement of factual articles.

Indexes: Subject matter such as topics and names listed alphabetically, with page numbers.

Pamphlets: Loosely-bound, paper-covered booklets containing nonfictional information.

Periodicals: Newsletters, newspapers, and magazines that are published over regular intervals.

EXERCISE 7 Number a sheet of paper 1–10. Next to each number write the source or sources you would go to in order to find answers to each question.

EXAMPLE What day of the week will Christmas fall on next year?

almanac

1. Who received the Nobel Peace prize last year?
2. What does the opening of Beethoven's *Fifth Symphony* sound like?
3. Where and when was Elvis Presley born?
4. What is the meaning of the term *entre nous?*
5. What are several titles of poems by Emily Dickinson?
6. What is the size and shape of Iceland?
7. Who won the World Soccer Cup in 1974?
8. What fuel is used in race cars at Indianapolis?
9. What plays did Thornton Wilder write?
10. How high is San Francisco Mountain in New Mexico?

OTHER SOURCES OF INFORMATION

17c Make use of other sources of information.

The first place people turn when they are looking for information is to printed matter in the library. This is a good place to start, but they sometimes forget that books and periodicals are written by people. These people often have studied their subjects for a long time. But they are not the only authorities.

Lots of people know a great deal about a variety of subjects, although they may not have written books about them. Some of them live in your community. Community leaders, firefighters, scientists, tradespeople, and elected officials are only a few examples of people who could be excellent sources of information.

Federal and state governments publish thousands of printed booklets each year. In them you can find up-to-date information on many subjects. The list of federal publications can be obtained through the Superintendent of Documents, Washington, D.C. State governments publish their material from their state capitals.

Large corporations also produce and distribute information related to their activities. Thus a major oil company may publish information about the known oil reserves in a region of the earth. Another may have a booklet on the million-year-old process by which oil and coal have been made.

Learn to search out information you need from the many sources open to you. As you continue your education and one day leave school, using sources of information wisely will benefit you.

REVIEW EXERCISE A The Dictionary

Following is a true-or-false exercise. Number a sheet of paper 1–10. Next to each number write *T* if the statement given is true and *F* if the statement is false.

EXAMPLE The two words printed in heavy type at the top of a dictionary page show that the words on that page will be alphabetically arranged between them.

T

1. A dictionary shows how to divide every word in it into syllables.
2. Proper nouns are not included in dictionaries.
3. Diacritical marks show how to pronounce a word.
4. Dictionaries do not tell what part of speech a word is.
5. Unusual plural spellings are given in the dictionary.
6. Irregular verb forms are given in the dictionary.
7. Certain adjectives and adverbs have their comparative and superlative forms listed in the dictionary.
8. The dictionary does not provide background information about a given word.
9. Each word in the dictionary has one meaning and one meaning alone.
10. These words are alphabetized correctly: *destroy, destruction, destitute.*

REVIEW EXERCISE B **Sources of Information**

Following is a matching exercise. Number a sheet of paper 1–10. Next to each number write the letter of the source of information from the list that matches the description.

WORD LIST

a. almanac
b. bibliography
c. atlas
d. index
e. audiovisual materials
f. collected works
g. pamphlets
h. fiction
i. encyclopedia
j. periodical
k. Superintendent of Documents

EXAMPLE Gives annual facts about a variety of subjects, including the weather.

a

1. Covers nearly every subject that people have thought about
2. Provides geographical information, including maps
3. List of books
4. Loosely bound paper-covered booklets containing nonfictional information
5. Newsletter, newspaper, or magazine that is published regularly
6. Alphabetically lists topics and names; gives page numbers
7. Filmstrips, records, tapes, cassettes, and the like

8. Stories made up by writers, for example, novels
9. The plays, poems, or songs of a single author
10. Provides a list of government publications

CHAPTER

18

USING WORDS

A single word can have as many meanings as its user wants to give it. The word *human* has so many meanings that it is almost impossible to list them all. *Human* applies to every one of the billions of people now living. It also applies to the billions who are no longer living.

Your understanding of the meaning of the word *human* is based on your experience with human beings. Someone else's understanding may be different because his or her experiences are different.

Meanings for words grow with an individual's experiences. The meanings of words differ depending upon the way people use them. How you use words can make a great difference in how you communicate your thoughts to other people.

Problems in communication occur from time to time. Many of them can be traced to the fact that different people have different experiences. They use the same words to stand for those different experiences. Even in the dictionary, however, one word may have several meanings. And often the same object or idea can be called several different names.

This chapter presents a few basic facts about the way people use words. It is a guide for making words work better for you.

THE MEANING OF WORDS

18a The meaning of a word is in the minds of the people who use it.

The only meaning attached to a word comes from the minds of the people who use it. They know what meaning they want to attach to that word.

You can prove to yourself that a word has no meaning in itself. Simply leaf through the pages of a dictionary. Every few pages there will be one or more words new to you. The word *exiguous* is an example. It is a word in English, but what meaning do you attach to it? If you are like most other people, you attach no meaning to it at all. The relatively few people who know the word attach the meaning "small" or "scanty" to it.

Another word is *nyet.* This may not be known to you. Yet hundreds of millions of people use it to mean "no." It is a Russian word.

Millions of foreign words mean nothing to you and others who speak only English. When you hear them, you hear only the sound, without calling to mind an object or an idea. Yet some people get a meaning from the sound as immediately as you think of your best friend when you hear his or her name.

EXERCISE 1 Look through newspapers, magazines, and books to find five words new to you. Copy the sentences in which the words appear. Underline the words. First, write what you think the word means from its use in the sentence. Then, look up in a dictionary the meanings the writers meant to attach to these words. Write the writers' meanings next to what you have written.

18b Expand your vocabulary by expanding your experience with words.

You learn new words by experiencing them. One kind of experience is using the word in connection with an object or an activity. If, for example, you do not know what a *mango* is and even if you have not heard the word, you will learn the meaning when you eat your first mango. A mango is a tropical fruit that you can touch, smell, and taste.

Other kinds of experiences come through words only. You can hear others describe a mango, or you can read about the mango.

First-hand experiences usually convey meanings most strongly. But it takes many experiences to learn all the words you will use this way. Learning words through listening and reading is quicker. You can expand your vocabulary more efficiently through listening and reading.

EXERCISE 2 Look over the Master Spelling List, pages 398–400. Choose five words for which you have leraned meanings through your first-hand experiences. Then choose five other words whose meanings you have learned through listening or reading. Be prepared to explain how you learned the meanings of the words.

See Dictionary, pp. 403–410

18c A word may have more than one meaning.

The word *play* is an example of this rule. In the sentence *Let's play a game, play* has one meaning. In the sentence *They put on a play in the theater, play* has another meaning.

The word *bank* in the following sentences has three different meanings:

1. The *bank* opens for business at 9:30.
2. The tractor pulled the old wreck up the *bank*.
3. Try to *bank* the billiard ball into the pocket.

The word *bank* in the first sentence names a place where money is kept. In the second sentence *bank* names the side of a hill. In the last sentence it is a verb telling of the action of bouncing a ball off a billiard cushion.

Game and *bank* are two examples of words that stand for more than one meaning. While you are expanding your vocabulary, look for words that stand for more than one meaning.

EXERCISE 3 Write the following ten words in a column at the left of a sheet of paper. Skip a line between each word. Next to each word on the same line write one meaning for which the word stands. On the next line write a second meaning.

EXAMPLE call

call - a yell or shout
to telephone

bear	game
check	hang
die	hook
duck	land
fine	mark

18d More than one word may be used to stand for a single meaning.

You know what courage is. The word *courage* means boldness, audacity, intrepidity, daring, bravery, and more. All these different words stand for the same or nearly the same meaning. When two or more words have the same meaning, they are called *synonyms*.

EXAMPLES deity—god
break—fracture
hungry—starved
lovely—charming

EXERCISE 4 The following two columns contain synonyms. Number a sheet of paper 1–10. After each number write the word from column A. Next to each word write a synonym from column B.

EXAMPLE pleasant

pleasant - agreeable

	COLUMN A	COLUMN B
1.	active	arrogant
2.	begin	spontaneous
3.	proud	restless
4.	scholarly	authority
5.	automatic	ludicrous
6.	power	corrupt
7.	laughable	commodity
8.	financial	studious
9.	product	monetary
10.	wicked	commence

18e The meaning of a word is often shown by its context.

When you see or hear a word that has several meanings, you have to figure out which meaning applies in that case by seeing it in *context.* That means by seeing how it is used with the words around it.

What does the word *fault* mean, for example? The word *fault* might mean "a mistake or error." However, if the subject is earthquakes, the word *fault* has an entirely different meaning. It means "a break in the earth."

Words with several definitions are given clear meaning by their *context.*

EXAMPLES Erica couldn't bring herself to do the *deed.*
[Erica couldn't act.]

The lawyer presented the *deed* for the land.
[The lawyer gave the paper showing ownership.]

Be sure as you speak and write that you put your words into the context you want. Otherwise, the meaning you intend may be misunderstood.

Listen carefully to the context used by others. Notice in your reading, too, how the context determines the meanings of words.

EXERCISE 5 Write each of the following words in a context of your own making to give it meaning. After each context write the definition of the word.

EXAMPLE pine

Rover seems to pine for his lost master.—grieve

1. deep
2. conviction
3. eye
4. instrument
5. stamp
6. defect
7. bright
8. faint
9. glass
10. resort

EXERCISE 6 Choose one of the meanings for each underlined word. On a sheet of paper write the word and its meaning next to each number.

EXAMPLE Franco Gomez was a mediocre soccer player; he needed to improve.
mixed-up average brilliant

mediocre—average

1. Shelley thought the lovers' meeting in the second act was touching and poignant.
   panting painful to the feelings poorly done

2. When the letter came back undelivered, Kate found she had been given a fictitious address.
   false distorted foreign
3. The coyote, whose hunting is feared by farmers, is widely considered a predator of sheep.
   eater herder robber
4. The enemy, unwilling to surrender, will try to retaliate after the attack.
   pay back in kind run away and hide
   be brave

EXERCISE 7 Choose five words from the Master Spelling List on pages 398–400. On a sheet of paper write five sentences of your own construction. Use a different word correctly in each sentence.

18f Words change in many ways.

Every language that people use changes. Most of the changes are slow, but some of them happen rapidly. New words are added to the language. Old words are not used and therefore die. Expressions change as well. Some disappear while new ones take their places.

(1) Words change in their meanings.

Most of the words in English have a history. During their history they have changed in meaning. On the following page are listed several examples of the ways word meanings have changed over a period of time.

WORD	PRESENT MEANING	OLDER MEANING
poach	cook an egg in water	put in a bag
candidate	office-seeker	person dressed in white
basin	bowl	soldier's helmet
alimony	payment after divorce	money for eating

(2) Words vary in their forms and pronunciations.

Words vary in their appearance and in the way they are pronounced. The name *Heathcote* looks as though it should be pronounced to rhyme with "teeth-coat." However, the people who know the word pronounce it "heth-cut." The city of Worcester in Massachusetts is not said as three syllables, as its spelling shows. Instead people call it "wooster," with only two syllables. This is not at all as the spelling would indicate. Strangers seeing these words for the first time would naturally "mis-pronounce" them or not associate them with the sounds they had heard spoken.

Differences and changes occur throughout the English language, just as they do in other living languages.

When an English word is used in different ways, it can change its pronunciation. This happens when a word is used as different parts of speech. The word *object* is an example.

ob′ject	The *object* lying in the street is a pumpkin. (noun)
object′	Do you *object* if I pick it up? (verb)

The accent shifts from the first to the second syllable when the word *object* is used differently in a sentence. Certain other words follow this same kind of shift.

Another difference in both pronunciation and form comes about when endings are added to words. The word *pronounce* is an example. It becomes *pronunciation.* Notice the changes either in form or pronunciation in the following examples:

electric—electrician
elegant—elegance
brilliant—brilliance
nation—national—nationality

18g Different groups of people who speak the same language may use a number of different words, word forms, or pronunciations to mean the same things.

Every language has several forms, known as *dialects,* which are variations of the standard form in either meaning or pronunciation. You may be astonished to learn that you speak a dialect. A dialect is a particular form of any language.

Different words may be used in different dialects.

EXAMPLES pigsty—pigpen
comforter—quilt
blinds—shades

Different forms of the same words may be used.

EXAMPLES six *miles* down the road, six *mile* down the road
two *feet* high, two *foot* high

Different pronunciations of words may be used.

EXAMPLES creek (rhymes with "sleek")
creek (rhymes with "slick")
root (rhymes with "boot")
root (rhymes with "put")

These variations in American English occur in different regions throughout the United States.

18h One dialect is neither better nor worse than others; it is only different.

A person brought up in Georgia speaks a dialect that is different from the dialect spoken by a person brought up in Oregon. Neither dialect is better than the other. They are only different.

The test of whether a dialect works is whether a speaker's neighbors can understand what the speaker intends. Language, and any dialect within a language, is a means of communicating. The value and usefulness of both must be judged on how well they convey thoughts and emotions.

People communicate most easily in their own dialects. Because of this, if you use one dialect, you may be at a disadvantage in communicating with people of another dialect. This is the reason why it is valuable for you to learn about different dialects of English. When you see that a dialect works better than yours among a group of people with whom you need to communicate, you might find it useful to acquire some features of their dialect. It may be that you will have to learn only a few special words or different forms and pronunciations of words you already use.

Once you learn a new dialect, you will be able to switch between your old language and your new one. In a sense, you are becoming bilingual.

Many settlers who helped build our country spoke a different dialect at first and then learned a new one. In fact, many spoke an entirely different language from English. Today, a great number of Americans with Spanish-speaking backgrounds use English with a Spanish dialect. Their cultural heritage carries with it some of the regular features of the Spanish language. Black Americans speak several dialects with regular features, as do some Native Americans and Asian Americans. All play their part in the great language arena of American life.

Standard English—so-called because it is used by those who speak or write material to be widely understood—serves as a dialect useful for the broadest number of people. Radio and television announcers; editors of newspapers, magazines, and books; officials in agencies dealing with the public—these people usually make standard English their dialect. It has become, as its name states, the standard for English dialects in the United States.

REVIEW EXERCISE A Using New Words

Look up in a dictionary the meaning of five of the following words. Number a sheet of paper 1–5. Next to each number write a sentence using each word and showing its meaning.

EXAMPLE harbinger

The first yellow leaf appeared, a harbinger of fall.

exfoliate
divagate
ditty
lamella
lancet
prevalent
puissant
pumice
luminary

REVIEW EXERCISE B Words with More than One Meaning

Following is a matching exercise. Number a sheet of paper 1–10. Next to each number write the letter of the correct word from the list that matches the meaning.

WORD LIST

a. lace
b. figure
c. low
d. grid
e. feature
f. legend
g. leisure
h. company
i. intelligence
j. grill
k. item

EXAMPLE a written symbol representing a number

b

1. secret information
2. of less than usual depth
3. an explanatory caption on a map, chart, or illustration
4. unhurried state
5. to thread a cord through eyelets or around hooks
6. an entry in an account
7. a football field

8. to question relentlessly
9. the main presentation in a motion picture theater
10. a guest or guests

REVIEW EXERCISE C Synonyms

Number a sheet of paper 1–10. Next to each number write the correct word from the ones in parentheses that is a synonym for the underlined word in the sentence. If you have any doubts, check a dictionary.

EXAMPLE The judge handed down a disinterested decision. (impartial/uncaring)
impartial

1. Hector always thinks of himself first; he's very egocentric. (selfish/modest)
2. I can't believe the perfidy he showed me when he told the principal about me! (honesty/faithlessness)
3. Granted, the way I acted was unwarranted. (unnoticed/unauthorized)
4. I suppose I shouldn't have prevaricated about it. (delayed/lied)
5. I guess it did show a certain lack of probity on my part. (pride/honesty)
6. Still, I don't feel very amicable towards Hector. (friendly/hateful)
7. I feel full of ire. (humor/anger)
8. My life is a shambles. (chaos/litheness)

9. I'll never be able to make restitution for the mess I made. (repayment/profusion)
10. I guess the saffron dye will just have to wear off Hector's face. (green/yellow)

REVIEW EXERCISE D Meaning Shown by Context

Following is a list of words. Number a sheet of paper 1–10. Next to each number, write a sentence of your own that puts each word in a context that gives it meaning.

EXAMPLE game

Jeremy cooked the deer he shot and the whole family enjoyed the taste of the game.

1. gap
2. front
3. force
4. dip
5. commission
6. cabinet
7. light
8. particular
9. position
10. sign

GLOSSARY

In this glossary you will find special terms used in the text. The meaning of every term is given with it or in a cross reference. Many examples also are included.

Certain terms are referenced to sections of the text, where treatment is more complete.

adjective A word that describes a noun or a pronoun. (See also **article.**) See **1g.**

The *tall* building had a *yellow* roof.

They are *long* and *skinny.*

An adjective helps *compare things.* Most adjectives change form to show comparison.

An *old* board is on the ground.

Some *older* boards are in the shed.

The *oldest* boards are rotting.

adverb A word that describes sentence actions. An adverb tells *where, when,* or *how* something happens. It usually does this by describing the verb in the sentence. An adverb can also describe some other part of speech. See **2h.**

The following adverbs tell *where* action occurs.

She put the hammer *down.*

She turned the anvil *over.*

These adverbs tell *when* action occurs.

Abel can go *today.*

He told us *yesterday.*

These adverbs tell *how* or *how often* action occurs.

The pump runs *frequently.*

It pumps *vigorously.*

agreement The forms of words that show the same number. See **10a.**

A pronoun agrees with its antecedent in gender and number.

Maria gave *her* ring to Tony.

A verb agrees with its subject in number.

She *makes* more money than I.

antecedent The word or group of words referred to by a following pronoun.

A broken fishing line is useless. *It* won't help catch fish.

antonym A word that means the opposite of another word.

back/forth in/out

apostrophe A mark that looks like a comma above the line to show possession, missing letters, or the plural of numbers. See **14l (1)–(3), 14m, 14n.**

Matt's paper, won't, A's

appositive A word or group of words placed next to another to identify someone or something or to explain a meaning or idea.

Len watched the bird, *a mere speck in the sky.*
People near the sea must watch for a *tsunami, a kind of tidal wave.*

article The words *a, an,* and *the.* An article is a kind of adjective.

auxiliary verb Words that are used with main verbs. The most common auxiliary verbs are listed here. See **2a (5).**

be: am, are, is, was, were, being, been
do: do, does, did, done
have: have, has, had

Here are some other common auxiliary verbs:

can, could, may, shall
will, would, might

Auxiliary verbs help the verbs express their actions.

Maureen *was* changing a tire.
She *had* patched an old one.

Auxiliary verbs also help show time.

Her plan *will* work out.
It *had been* formed in earlier weeks.

case The form of a pronoun that shows its relation to other parts of the sentence. See **1f.**

SUBJECTIVE CASE usually serves as the subject of a sentence.

They passed a hospital.

OBJECTIVE CASE usually serves as the object of the sentence or the object of a preposition.

The sight quieted *them.*

POSSESSIVE CASE shows ownership.

Their headlights lit a sign.

clause A group of words with both a subject and a predicate. A clause can be a sentence or part of a sentence. See **4a, 4b, 4c.**

INDEPENDENT CLAUSE A clause that can stand alone as a complete thought.

A computer looks like a machine, but *it can sometimes think like a human.*
A computer looks like a machine.
It can sometimes think like a human.

DEPENDENT CLAUSE A clause that depends upon an independent clause to complete its thought.

While a computer looks like a machine, it can sometimes think like a human.

colloquial Acceptable words or forms in informal conversation, but usually not acceptable in formal speech or writing.

Get along with you.
Hold it.

comparison The forms of an adjective or adverb that show more or less about the words they describe. (See also **modifiers**.) See **1h, 2i.**

POSITIVE quick, late

COMPARATIVE quicker, later

SUPERLATIVE quickest, latest

completer A word or words that complete a statement about the subject of a sentence. A completer comes after the verb. It is part of the predicate. (See also **predicate**.) See **5k, 5l.**

Completers are words or phrases that can fit in sentence blanks like these:

Ariel ate ______.
She was ______.

NOUNS AND NOUN WORD GROUP COMPLETERS
Ariel ate *dried beans*.

ADJECTIVE COMPLETER
She was *hungry*.

ADVERB COMPLETER
She stayed *there*.

complex sentence A sentence with an independent clause and a dependent clause. (See also **clause**.) See **5e.**

Ramon lifted the heavy rock when Ping yelled down.

compound A word or group of words made up of two or more parts that could stand alone.

COMPOUND WORD *football, brother-in-law*

COMPOUND SUBJECT *Roses* and *petunias* bloomed in the garden.

COMPOUND OBJECT She planted *beans* and *corn.*

COMPOUND PREDICATE Waiters *serve the customers* or *clean the tables.*

compound sentence A sentence made up of two or more independent clauses. See **5d.**

May emptied the wastebasket; then she went back upstairs.

compound-complex sentence A sentence made up of two or more independent clauses and at least one dependent clause. See **5f.**

If you expect to sell your motorcycle, you ought to clean its engine, and you should polish the metal parts.

compound verb Two or more verbs in a clause or sentence. See **5b (4).**

Tomás *stepped* on the gas pedal and *turned* the wheel sharply.

conjunction A word that connects words, phrases, or clauses. Two kinds of conjunctions are *coordinating conjunctions* and *subordinating conjunctions.* See **21.**

COORDINATING CONJUNCTIONS connect words, phrases, or clauses. The most common coordinating conjunctions are *and, but,* and *or.*

dogs *and* cats.
Give a bone to the dog *and* fish to the cat.

Other coordinating conjunctions are *either . . . or/neither . . . nor/not only . . . but also.* These are called *correlative conjunctions.*

Either you jump in and swim *or* I'm going to leave.

SUBORDINATING CONJUNCTIONS connect ideas not equal to each other. Some examples are *after, although, as, because, before, like, since, though, unless, until, when, where, while.*

While you may have trouble winning, you surely do keep the ball in play.

connector Word used to connect other words or groups of words. Some examples are conjunctions, such as *and, but, after;* and connecting adverbs, such as *then, therefore,* and *afterward.*

consonants All alphabet letters that are not vowels (*B, C, D,* for example). Consonant sounds are made in speaking by closing or bringing together parts of the throat, mouth, teeth, tongue, or lips.

context The words surrounding a word that help define it. See **18e.**

contractions A word form using an apostrophe to show missing letters.

can't, don't, could've

correlative conjunctions (See **conjunction.**)

dangling modifier A modifying word or word group without a subject to modify. See **6c.**

Swinging daringly on vines from the trees, we watched in amazement during the filming of the jungle scene.
[This sentence seems to say that we were swinging on vines, when it should say that Jane—or some acrobat—was doing the swinging.]

CORRECTED Swinging daringly on vines from the trees, *the acrobat* amazed us during the filming of the jungle scene.

dash A line like a long hyphen used to show a continuation of related ideas in a sentence. See **14k.**

dependent clause (See **clause.**)

determiner (See also **article.**) Determiners are words like *a, an, the, one, some, their.* A determiner is a kind of adjective that always is followed by a noun.

a jet, *the* board

Determiners help tell whether a noun is singular or plural.

one light, *some* lights

diacritical marks Marks used with letters to show how they are pronounced.

Examples are ā [as in say], ĕ [as in set], ä [as in father].

diagraming A way of showing how parts of a sentence relate to one another. Two main types of diagraming are sometimes used. One type is a traditional diagram. The other is a tree diagram.

Any diagram of a sentence is only one way of showing the relationship among its parts.

TRADITIONAL DIAGRAMING Six sentences are diagramed below. Each diagram shows how added parts of a sentence fit together.

(1) The waiter poured the water.

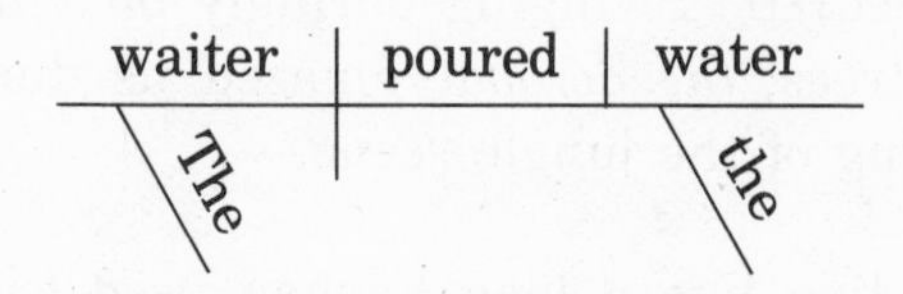

[The simple subject belongs first on the horizontal line. Under it on a slanted line belongs its modifier. The verb follows the simple subject, separated by a vertical line through the horizontal line. The direct object follows the verb, separated by a vertical line resting on the horizontal line.]

(2) The old waiter poured the water.

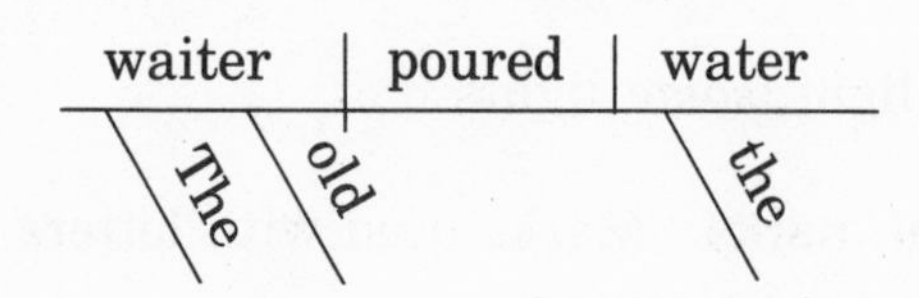

[Additional modifiers of the subject belong on additional slanted lines.]

(3) The old waiter in the restaurant poured the water.

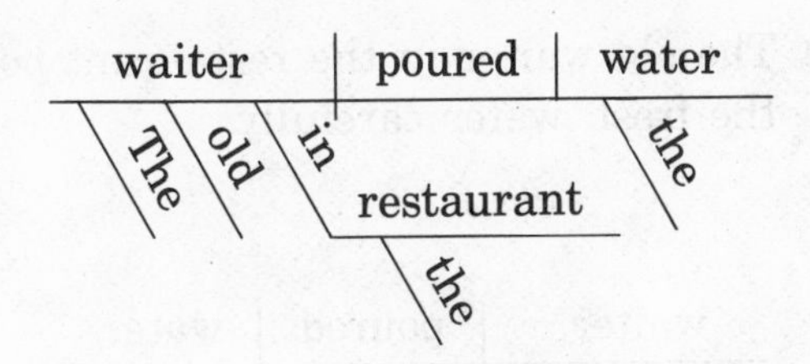

[A prepositional phrase modifying the subject belongs on slanted and horizontal lines as shown in (3) above.]

(4) The waiter had poured the water.

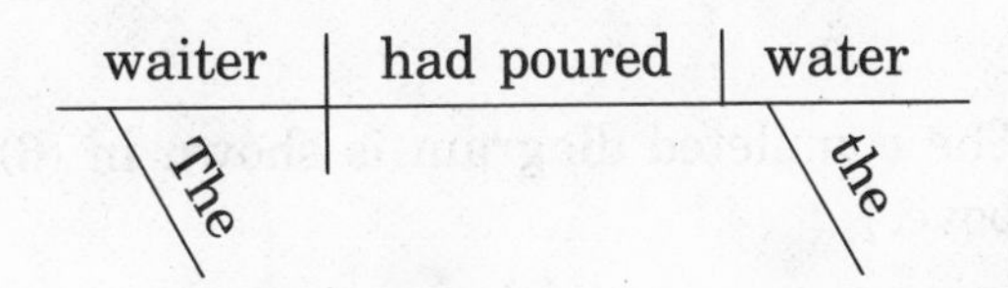

[Auxiliary verbs belong with the main verb on the horizontal line.]

(5) The waiter poured the water carefully.

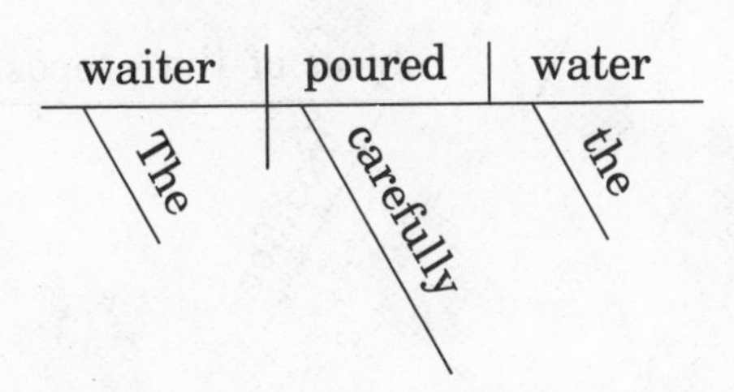

[An adverb belongs on a slanted line under the verb it modifies.]

(6) The old waiter in the restaurant poured the fresh water carefully.

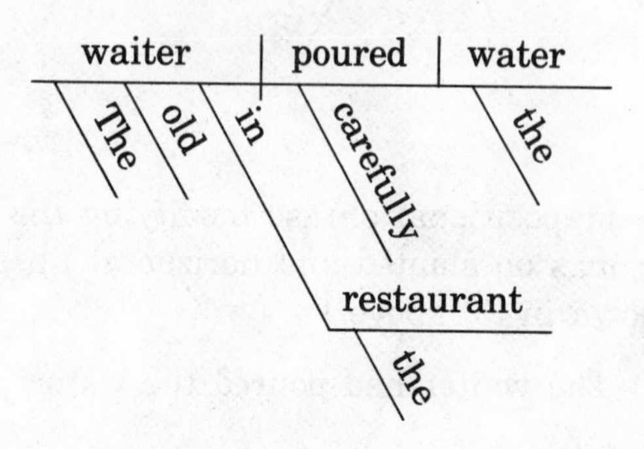

[The completed diagram is shown in (6) above.]

(7)

subject | verb | object

modifier
modifier
preposition
modifier
modifier
object of the preposition
modifier

[All parts of the sentence are shown in (7) above.]

TREE DIAGRAMING

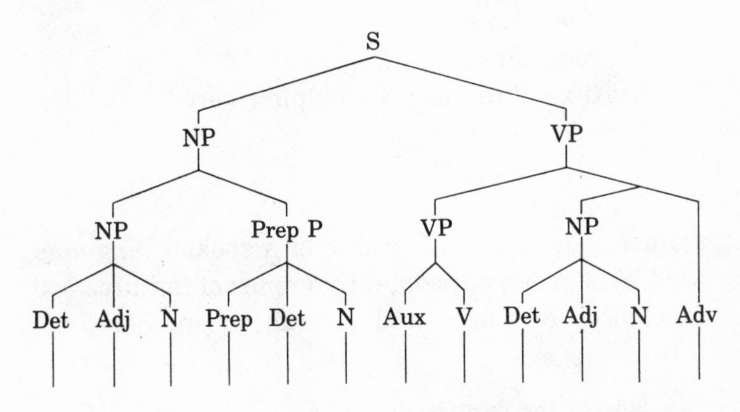

The old waiter in the restaurant had poured the cold water carefully.

A tree diagram gets its name from its shape. Turn it upside down and it looks a little like a tree. The abbreviations used in the tree diagram have the following meanings. These meanings are not all the same as those in traditional grammar. Follow your teacher's direction in using these meanings.

S: Sentence

NP: Noun phrase   A noun phrase is often the complete subject or the object of a sentence. It may have another, smaller phrase in it.

VP: Verb phrase   A verb phrase can be the complete predicate of a sentence. It can have a verb phrase and a noun phrase in it.

Prep P: Prepositional phrase

Det: Determiner

Adj: Adjective
N: Noun
Prep: Preposition
Aux: Auxiliary [a helping verb]
V: Verb
Adv: Adverb

dialect The special features of a spoken language used by a group of people. Examples of features are in choices of words and pronunciation. See **18g, 18h.**

sweets for *candy*
"idear" for "idea"

direct object The primary receiver of sentence action. (See **object**.) See **5k.**

The band played a *march*.
[What did the band play? Answer: *march.*]

double negative The incorrect use of two words that mean "no" in the same sentence. The most common negatives are *no* and *not*. Other negatives are *none (no + one), nothing (no + thing) never (not + ever),* and *neither (not + either)*. See **10r.**

Here are examples of double negatives:

1. You don't see nothing.
2. We can't hardly move.

CORRECTIONS

1. We don't see anything.
   We see nothing.
2. We can hardly move.
   We can't move.

expletive A word without meaning used as the subject of a sentence.

That is the first time you have missed.
It is foggy.

Also, an expletive is an interjection that expresses strong feeling.

What *in blazes* went wrong?

exposition Writing that expresses, explains, or "exposes" one's ideas, for example, a newspaper editorial, an essay, or a research paper.

fragment An incomplete sentence, one without either the necessary subject or predicate. See **6a.**

The boat cruising down the river. (What is the boat doing or like while cruising?)

CORRECTED The boat cruising down the river has a full load of passengers.

gender Male or female or neuter (neither male nor female).

MALE *He* wept.

FEMALE *She* laughed.

NEUTER *It* broke.

gerund A verb form used as a noun, usually ending in *d, ed,* or *ing*. See **2e.**

The *hunted* never sleep calmly.
Canoeing is fun.

helping verb (See **auxiliary verb**.)

idiom A word or phrase used in a special way.

> She *wrapped up* the business arrangement.
> (She completed it.)

independent clause A group of words having a subject and predicate able to stand by itself without need of other words to finish its meaning. [See also **clause**.] See 4b.

indirect object The secondary receiver of sentence action. (See **object**.)

> Fay gave *him* a letter.
> (To whom did Fay give a letter?
> Answer: *him*.)

infinitive The standard or base form of a verb, often with *to*.

> to hold, to free

The infinitive is sometimes used as a noun. See 2g.

> *To climb* the apple trees takes agility.

inflection The change in the form of a word to show a change in meaning or grammatical use.

> *mouse* (singular), *mice* (plural), *mouse's* (singular possessive)
> *run* (present), *ran* (past), *run* (past participle)

interjection A part of speech showing strong feeling. An interjection is not grammatically related to the sentence. See 2m.

Pshaw! You've nothing to lose!

irregular verb A verb that does not add **ed** to form the past tense. (See also **verb**.) See **2d.**

italics Slanted letters printed to draw special attention. See **14o, 14p.**

linking verb A verb that links the subject to the subject completer. See **2a (4).**

appear, become, fell, look, and forms of the verb *be.*

main clause An independent clause.

metaphor A figure of speech in which one item is compared to another.

The tree was dressed in a *wedding gown* of pure white.

misplaced modifier A modifying word or phrase too far from its subject to be clear in meaning. See **6c.**

Working frantically, the store was opened by the clerks on time to let in the crowd.
(This seems to say that the store was working frantically.)

CORRECTED *Working frantically,* the clerks readied the store on time to let in the crowd.

modal auxiliary A verb used as a verb helper that does not change form.

can, could, might, ought

modifiers Words used to describe someone, something, or some action. (See also **adjective** and **adverb.**)

nominative The subjective case. (See also **case.**)

nonrestrictive clause or **phrase** A group of words that tells something more about someone or something in the same sentence. A nonrestrictive clause or phrase is not necessary to make the sentence complete, but it adds to its meaning.

> The flower sellers, *finished for the day,* closed their stalls and left. (phrase)
>
> The flower sellers, *who were finished for the day,* closed their stalls and left. (clause)

noun A word or group of words used to name a person, place, thing, or idea. See 1a.

> Names of persons: George Price, Miyeko Akuda [proper nouns]
> Names of places: Point Lobos, Atlanta [proper nouns]
> Names of things: plastic, water [common nouns]
> Names of ideas: democracy, loyalty [common nouns]

number One or more than one person or thing. In English, singular or plural number is shown in most nouns by the addition of *s* or *es.*

> horse/horses, match/matches

A few nouns change their spelling in special ways.

> mouse/mice, woman/women

Number is shown in most pronouns by a change in form.

these/those, this/that
he, she/they, her, him/them
hers, his/theirs

object The result of action or the receiver of the action in a sentence. See **5k.**

DIRECT OBJECT Ellie watched *him.*

INDIRECT OBJECT The timekeeper told *her* the time.

The object of a preposition is a noun or pronoun which is related to another word by the preposition.

The timekeeper told the time to *her.*

objective case Pronouns show the objective case when they serve as the objects of a sentence or of a preposition. (See also **case**.) See **10n.**

The boys and their climbing gear completely disappeared. Rescuers found *them* and *it* in a small cave.

paragraph A paragraph is a group of sentences beginning with an indention. All the sentences in a paragraph treat one topic or idea. The topic may be a description of something or it may be an event or an idea. See **7a.**

A topic sentence in the paragraph states the topic clearly. The other sentences develop that topic. In the following paragraph the first sentence is the topic sentence.

Dental detection—the study of teeth and bite marks connected with crimes—is an important new tool for law enforcement. No two sets of teeth wear down in exactly the same way. For this reason, a person's bite marks are as individual as fingerprints. Teeth can help to identify murder or accident victims. And evidence from bite marks has already helped to convict several criminals. In one case a man was convicted of starting a fire because he took a bite out of an apple. He left the apple at the scene of the fire. Police proved that the bite marks in the apple matched the man's teeth exactly.

participle The **ing** or the **ed** form of a verb that can be used as an adjective. A few irregular verbs form their participles in irregular ways. (See also **phrase**.) See 2f.

walking, sewing [present participles]
walked, sewn [past participle]
broken [past participle of irregular verb *break*]

parts of speech English sentences can have eight main kinds of words in them. These eight kinds of words are called parts of speech. These words do the work of the sentence. They help show meaning.

The eight parts of speech are *noun, pronoun, verb, adjective, adverb, preposition, conjunction,* and *interjection.* (See separate listings.)

persuasive speaking or **writing** Speaking or writing that attempts to convince someone to hold a certain opinion or carry out a certain action. See **15n**.

phrase A group of words belonging together, but not making a complete statement. See **3a.**

PREPOSITIONAL PHRASE over the lamp

VERB PHRASE has slept

NOUN PHRASE the low bridge

PARTICIPIAL PHRASE falling behind

plural More than one. The plural is shown by words that mean more than one *(some, twenty)*. It is also shown in the forms of nouns *(wallet, wallets)*, pronouns *(I, we)*, and verbs *(it moves, they move)*.

possessive A form of a noun or pronoun showing that someone owns something or that things belong close together. See **1c, 1f.**

the *cat's* tail (possessive noun)
her lunch (possessive pronoun)

predicate The part of a sentence that tells about the subject. See **5b.**

The rocket *tumbled toward the sea.*
It *landed with a tremendous splash.*

PREDICATE ADJECTIVE (See **completer**.)

PREDICATE NOUN (See **completer**.)

prefix A prefix is one or more syllables added to the front of a word or root to affect its meaning. See **16b (11)–(12).**

misread, **un**aware, **in**tend

preposition A part of speech used to show the relationship between its object (usually a noun or pronoun) and some other word in a sentence. Prepositions can show time, position, or another relationship. See **2j.**

Rick met Joan *after* school.
They sat *in* her car.

prepositional phrases (See **phrase**.)

pronoun A word that can stand for a noun or pronoun. Usually, a pronoun stands for a group of words in which the noun is the main word. See **1d.**

People from the ballgame crowded the road. *They* seemed happy. [*They* stands for *people from the ballgame.*]

There are three cases of pronouns. The first is the *subjective case.* It usually shows the doer of the action in a sentence.

They were patient.
She smiled.

The second case of the pronoun is the *objective case.*

A patrolman directed *them* on the roadway.

The third case of a pronoun is the *possessive case.*

He made *their* travel easier.

The common kinds of pronouns are *personal, demonstrative, indefinite, interrogative, reflexive,* and *relative.* See **1f.**

punctuation The marks used with words to show how they relate and how they are to be read. See Chapters 13–14.

root The basic part of a word. Parts are added to it to change its meaning. (See also **prefix** and **suffix**.)

un**welcome**, re**turn**able

run-on sentence Two or more sentences run together without correct punctuation or connecting words. See **6b.**

Superstition causes people to do strange things they overlook the reality of the world.

CORRECTED Superstition causes people to do strange things. They overlook the reality of the world.

sentence A group of related words needing no other words to complete its thought. A sentence has a subject and a predicate. See **5a.**

SENTENCE Kipling, who wrote novels and poetry, spent time in India.

FRAGMENT Kipling who wrote novels and poetry.
(See also **fragment**.)

sentence combining A method of joining two or more sentences into one. (See **clause**.) See **5o.**

simile A comparison of two things or qualities using *like* or *as* to show the relationship.

As sad as a soaked puppy.

singular Only one of anything. (See plural for comparison.)

slang A word or phrase not accepted for general use by most educated people.

Let's *rap.* (Let's talk.)

subject A noun (or its equal) that the rest of its sentence says or asks something about. The subject of a sentence is the *who* or *what* that belongs with the predicate. See **5b.**

Clouds covered the sky.
They looked dark.

subject completer (See **completer**.)

subordinate clause A dependent clause. (See also **clause**.)

subordinating conjunction (See **conjunction**.)

suffix One or more syllables that add meaning to a word or root. A suffix is added to the end of a word or a root. See **16a (13–19).**

quiet**ly**, break**able**, fool**ish**

syllable A letter or group of letters containing a vowel that is pronounced as one unit. A syllable may be a single vowel.

un-war-y, il-lum-in-ate

Most syllables contain a vowel sound plus a consonant sound or sounds.

in-tend (2 syllables)
in-ten-tion (3 syllables)
in-ten-tion-al (4 syllables)

synonym A word that means the same as another. See 18d.

attraction/appeal, damp/wet, heavy/weighty

syntax The arrangement of words and parts of a sentence.

A store mailed Kim a brochure.
A store mailed a brochure to Kim.
Kim was mailed a brochure by a store.
[All three sentences mean the same. However, the syntax, or order of words, is different in each.]

tense Time as shown by the form of a verb. See 2b.

PRESENT she *washes,* they *wash*

PAST she *washed,* they *washed*

FUTURE she *will wash,* they *are going to wash*

PRESENT PERFECT she *has washed,* they *have washed*

PAST PERFECT she *had washed,* they *had washed*

FUTURE PERFECT she *will have washed,* they *will have washed*

topic sentence (See **paragraph**.) See 7b.

transformation The changes in form that can be made in sentences and word groups.

unity In composition, making sentences refer to the same topic or subject.

verb A part of speech that shows action *(bake)*, states something *(is)*, or shows condition *(appears)*. Most verbs change their form to show time *(bake–baked)*. (See **tense**.) Other changes show number. See 2a.

One cake *is* finished. The others *are* not ready.

A verb tells the action in a sentence. Or it tells that something exists. Exists means "is" or "to be."

ACTION runs, drops, picks

EXISTENCE is, am, were, seems

verbal A form of a verb used as another part of speech. (See **gerund, infinitive** and **participle**.)

vocabulary The words and their meanings used in a language.

voice The form of a verb that shows who or what is doing something.

ACTIVE VOICE Ali *crowned* Timbu.

PASSIVE VOICE Timbu *was crowned* by Ali.

vowel The letters *A, E, I, O, U,* and sometimes the letters *Y* and *W*.

INDEX

D

L

M

N

O

P

Q

R

S

TAB KEY INDEX

CORRECTION SYMBOL	DEFINITION	CHAPTER
ad	adjectives and adverbs	10
adj	adjective	1
adv	adverb	2
agr	agreement of subjects and verbs	10
ap	apostrophe	14
cap	capital letter	12
cl	clause	4
comp	incomplete or false comparison	
conj	conjunction	2
cxt	context	18
dm	dangling or misplaced modifier	6
dn	double negative	10
frag	fragment	6
g	good use	
glos	glossary	
info	sources of information	17
inj	interjection	2
ital	italics	14
k	awkward sentence	
let	letter writing	9
n	noun	1
nc	not clear	
p	error in punctuation	
paral	parallelism	6
phr	phrase	3

TAB KEY INDEX
(Continued)

CORRECTION SYMBOL	DEFINITION	CHAPTER
plan	planning and writing a composition	8
prep	preposition	2
pro	pronoun	1, 10
ref	reference of pronouns	10
ro	run-on sentence	6
sp	spelling	16
spk	speaking and listening	15
ss	sentence structure	5
verb	verb	2
ww	wrong word	11
¶	paragraph	7
./	period	13
?	question mark	13
!	exclamation mark	13
,/	comma	13
;/	semicolon	14
:/	colon	14
-/	hyphen	14
”/	quotation marks	14
( )	parentheses	14
[ ]	brackets	
—	dash	14

9 0 C 1 D 2 E 3 F 4 G 5 H 6 I 7 J 8